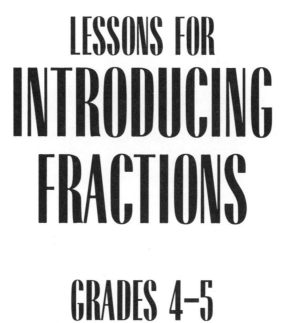

LESSONS FOR
INTRODUCING
FRACTIONS

GRADES 4–5

PUBLISHED TEACHING ARITHMETIC TITLES

Lessons for First Grade
Lessons for Addition and Subtraction, Grades 2–3
Lessons for Introducing Multiplication, Grade 3
Lessons for Extending Multiplication, Grades 4–5
Lessons for Introducing Fractions, Grades 4–5

FORTHCOMING TEACHING ARITHMETIC TITLES

Lessons for Place Value, Grades 1–2
Lessons for Extending Division, Grade 3
Lessons for Extending Division, Grades 4–5
Lessons for Extending Fractions, Grades 5–6
Lessons for Decimals and Percents, Grades 5–6

LESSONS FOR
INTRODUCING
FRACTIONS

▲▲▲▲▲

GRADES 4–5

MARILYN BURNS

MATH SOLUTIONS PUBLICATIONS
SAUSALITO, CA

Math Solutions Publications
A division of
Marilyn Burns Education Associates
150 Gate 5 Road, Suite 101
Sausalito, CA 94965
www.mathsolutions.com

Copyright © 2001 by Math Solutions Publications

Library of Congress Cataloging-in-Publication Data

Burns, Marilyn, 1941–
    Lessons for introducing fractions : grades 4–5 / Marilyn Burns.
      p. cm. -- (Teaching arithmetic)
Includes index.
    ISBN 0-941355-33-0 (alk. paper)
  1. Fractions--Study and teaching (Primary) I. Title. II. Series.
  QA117 .B87 2001
    372.7'2—dc21

                                             2001002161

Editor: Toby Gordon
Production: Melissa L. Inglis
Cover & interior design: Leslie Bauman
Composition: Argosy Publishing

Printed in the United States of America on acid-free paper
05 04 03 02 01 ML 1 2 3 4 5

A Message from Marilyn Burns

We at Marilyn Burns Education Associates believe that teaching mathematics well calls for continually reflecting on and improving one's instructional practice. Our Math Solutions Publications include a wide range of choices, from books in our new Teaching Arithmetic series—which address beginning number concepts, place value, addition, subtraction, multiplication, division, fractions, decimals, and percents—to resources that help link math with writing and literature; from books that help teachers more deeply understand the mathematics behind the math they teach to children's books that help students develop an appreciation for math while learning basic concepts.

Along with our large collection of teacher resource books, we have a more general collection of books, videotapes, and audiotapes that can help teachers and parents bridge the gap between home and school. All of our materials are available at education stores, from distributors, and through major teacher catalogs.

In addition, Math Solutions Inservice offers five-day courses and one-day workshops throughout the country. We also work in partnership with school districts to help implement and sustain long-term improvement in mathematics instruction in all classrooms.

To find a complete listing of our publications and workshops, please visit our Web site at *www.mathsolutions.com*. Or contact us by calling (800) 868-9092 or sending an e-mail to *info@mathsolutions.com*.

We're eager for your feedback and interested in learning about your particular needs. We look forward to hearing from you.

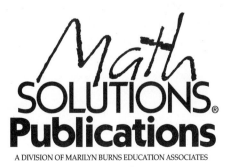

A DIVISION OF MARILYN BURNS EDUCATION ASSOCIATES

CONTENTS

BLACKLINE MASTERS

INDEX

INTRODUCTION

Learning about fractions in the upper elementary grades is hard. Really hard. Fractions are hard not only for children to learn but for teachers to teach.

I've been concentrating on teaching fractions to fourth- and fifth-grade classes for the past six years, and I'm very excited about what I've learned and the progress that the students I've taught have made. For each of the lessons I taught, I kept a detailed record of what I did and how the students responded. I saved all of the student work and pored over it to analyze, in depth, the teaching and learning that occurred. I revised lessons and retaught them in other classes. I now feel better prepared than ever before to build students' understanding of fractions, support their ability to compute and solve problems with fractions, develop their number sense about fractions, and help them see how fractions connect to other areas of mathematics.

I realize that teaching, recording, and revising lessons in this way is unrealistic for most full-time classroom teachers, so I'm pleased to be able to offer here what I've learned from my experiences. Included in this book are the most successful of the lessons I have taught, those that are now a mainstay of my teaching repertoire. Each chapter provides all of the information necessary to be successful presenting the lesson to your classes.

My goal here is to help all students see the sense in fractions. To accomplish this, I teach fractions through a think-and-reason approach, not through a memorize-and-practice approach. When learning and practicing procedures becomes the focus, the main goal of instruction—making sense of mathematics—too often takes a backseat. All of the lessons included in this book address building students' understanding as well as their skills.

When teaching the lessons in this book, I was often amazed and delighted by what I learned from students. For example, Claudia, a fifth grader, came to class one day in November and announced to me, "I know that one-fourth plus one-sixteenth plus one-forty-eighth equals one-third."

"What made you think about that?" I asked.

"The fraction kit game," she said. We had made fraction kits in class and used them for a variety of activities. (You can read about fraction kits in Chapter 2. It's the single most useful experience I've provided to introduce fractions to students, and in this book I've included the most recent revisions and improvements I've made to the lesson.)

Claudia continued in a burst, "I was trying to see which pieces I could use to cover a third of the whole strip. It looked like one-fourth and one-sixteenth would work, so I put them down three times, but there was a piece at the end still uncovered. Then I saw that the missing piece was one-sixteenth, so I figured out that if I cut one-sixteenth into three skinny pieces, I could add each piece to the one-fourth and one-sixteenth. I tried it and it worked. So then I thought about what to call the skinny pieces and I figured out they were one-forty-eighths."

Claudia's way of using the fraction kit to think about one-third was new to me. I had trouble following her reasoning, but I was interested in understanding her idea. "Could you get your thinking down on paper so I can understand it better?" I asked.

"Sure," Claudia said. She both drew illustrations and wrote about her ideas (see Figure 1). Not only did Claudia's discovery push me to think differently about one-third, it also reminded me that learning activities should have the potential to open children's mathematical imaginations.

I learned something very different from seeing what Robert, a classmate of Claudia's, had done on one of the fraction kit assignments. The assignment was to decide if fractions were closest to zero, one-half, or one, and explain their reasoning. It seemed simple for Robert; at least he had ordered all of the fractions correctly. But his explanation for correctly identifying one-sixteenth as the smallest fraction in one of the sets troubled me. Included in what he had written was $\frac{1}{16}$ *is the lowest number in fractions* (see Figure 2). I wasn't sure if Robert was referring only to the fractions in the kit or to all fractions. I asked, and Robert was surprised to hear that I knew of smaller fractions. (I gave Robert the set of sixteenths I had cut for another kit and asked him to cut them each in half and figure out what fraction to use to label them.) Without the information Robert revealed in his writing, I might have missed this gap in his understanding. This experience reminded me of the importance of having students communicate about their thinking and reasoning.

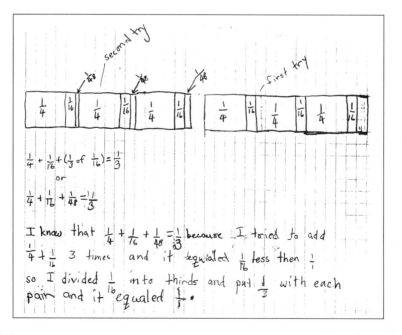

▲▲▲▲▲▲Figure 1 *Claudia explains how she figured out that $\frac{1}{4} + \frac{1}{16} + \frac{1}{48} = \frac{1}{3}$.*

In another situation, I learned how important it is to listen carefully to children's ideas rather than to listen for a particular response that I am expecting. Davey, another of the fifth graders, added three-fourths and seven-eighths correctly and got the answer of one and five-eighths. (I gave this assignment after students had experienced the *Only One* activities described in Chapter 15 and were building their facility with combining fractions.) He wrote: *What I did is I converted* $\frac{3}{4}$ *into* $\frac{6}{8}$ *and added* $\frac{6}{8}$ *and* $\frac{7}{8}$ *and got* $1\frac{5}{8}$. When he brought his paper to me, I asked him to explain more about how he combined six-eighths and seven-eighths, assuming that he had first arrived at thirteen-eighths and then changed the improper fraction to one and five-eighths. Davey returned to his desk and wrote: $\frac{8}{8}$ *is* $\frac{1}{1}$ *and I needed to take* $\frac{2}{8}$ *from* $\frac{7}{8}$ *so the* $\frac{6}{8}$ *turned into* $\frac{1}{1}$ *and the* $\frac{7}{8}$ *turned into* $\frac{5}{8}$ *so if you add* $\frac{1}{1}$ *and* $\frac{5}{8}$ *you get* $1\frac{5}{8}$. Instead of what I had expected, Davey had an entirely different approach to combining six-eighths and seven-eighths, using a "make a whole" strategy (see Figure 3). This reminded me of the importance of supporting students to make sense of ideas in *their* ways rather than imposing or insisting on *my* way.

These classroom experiences, along with others that I've had, have reinforced for me that asking students to reason and explain their reasoning builds their understanding, introduces them to different ideas, encourages flexibility in their thinking, and supports the idea that making sense is key to learning math. My classroom experiences also reminded me that it's extremely important for teachers to have an in-depth

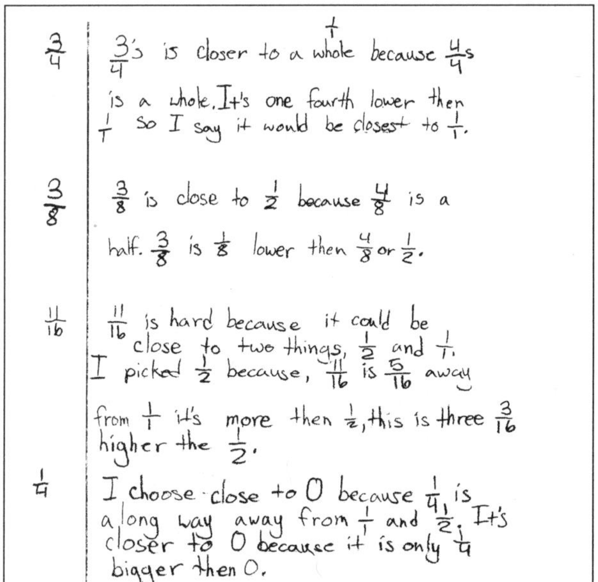

$\frac{3}{4}$ — $\frac{3}{4}$'s is closer to a whole because $\frac{4}{4}$'s is a whole. It's one fourth lower then $\frac{1}{1}$ so I say it would be closest to $\frac{1}{1}$.

$\frac{3}{8}$ — $\frac{3}{8}$ is close to $\frac{1}{2}$ because $\frac{4}{8}$ is a half. $\frac{3}{8}$ is $\frac{1}{8}$ lower then $\frac{4}{8}$ or $\frac{1}{2}$.

$\frac{11}{16}$ — $\frac{11}{16}$ is hard because it could be close to two things, $\frac{1}{2}$ and $\frac{1}{1}$. I picked $\frac{1}{2}$ because, $\frac{11}{16}$ is $\frac{5}{16}$ away from $\frac{1}{1}$ it's more then $\frac{1}{2}$, this is three $\frac{3}{16}$ higher the $\frac{1}{2}$.

$\frac{1}{4}$ — I choose close to 0 because $\frac{1}{4}$ is a long way away from $\frac{1}{1}$ and $\frac{1}{2}$. It's closer to 0 because it is only $\frac{1}{4}$ bigger then 0.

$\frac{1}{16}$ — $\frac{1}{16}$ is very easy it is close to 0. $\frac{1}{16}$ is the lowest number in fractions. It is practically 0.

Figure 2 ***The errors on Robert's paper indicates his need for a good deal more experience and instruction.***

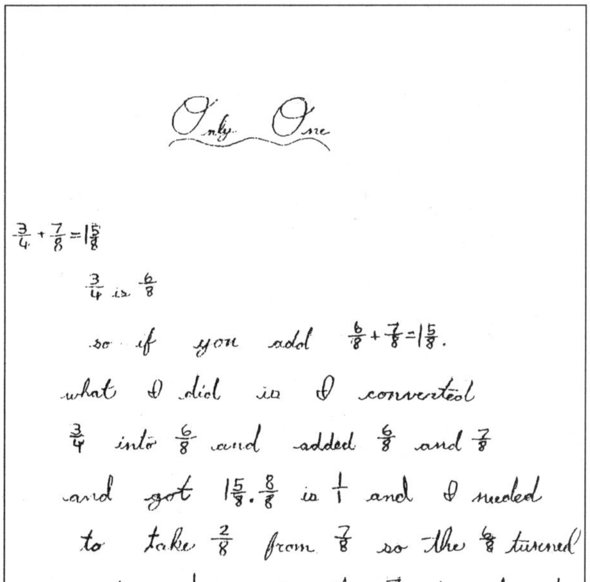

Only One

$\frac{3}{4} + \frac{7}{8} = 1\frac{5}{8}$

$\frac{3}{4}$ is $\frac{6}{8}$

so if you add $\frac{6}{8} + \frac{7}{8} = 1\frac{5}{8}$.

what I did is I converted $\frac{3}{4}$ into $\frac{6}{8}$ and added $\frac{6}{8}$ and $\frac{7}{8}$ and got $1\frac{5}{8}$. $\frac{8}{8}$ is $\frac{1}{1}$ and I needed to take $\frac{2}{8}$ from $\frac{7}{8}$ so the $\frac{6}{8}$ turned into $\frac{1}{1}$ and the $\frac{7}{8}$ turned into $\frac{5}{8}$ so if you add $\frac{1}{1}$ and $\frac{5}{8}$ you get $1\frac{5}{8}$.

Figure 3 ***Davey explains how he added*** $\frac{3}{4}$ ***and*** $\frac{7}{8}$.

and thorough understanding of the mathematics we are teaching. While the discussions that will occur in your class won't be identical to those in mine, your students' ideas will lead to other discussions about the mathematics involved. Without a strong knowledge base, following students' reasoning and responding appropriately simply isn't possible.

This book doesn't contain all the lessons I taught or all the lessons needed for teaching fractions. Rather, it's a collection of lessons that I found most effective for introducing fractions to students; building a foundation of understanding about equivalence; and helping students learn to compare, order, and combine fractions. A companion to this book, *Extending Fractions, Grades 5–6*, reinforces the learning in this book and extends it to include multiplying and dividing fractions. The lessons in this book can help you become more comfortable with ideas about fractions as you help your students build their understanding.

Goals for Fraction Instruction

Our goal in teaching fractions is to give all students the chance to learn how to

- ▲ name fractional parts of wholes and sets;
- ▲ represent fractional parts using the standard notation, including proper fractions, improper fractions, and mixed numbers, and also with concrete and/or pictorial representations;
- ▲ understand equivalence;
- ▲ compare and order fractions;
- ▲ make reasonable estimates with fractions;
- ▲ compute with fractions;
- ▲ apply fractions to a variety of problem-solving situations from all areas of the mathematics curriculum.

I've found that it's important when talking with students about fractions to focus them on what the whole is and also to emphasize that the same-size fractional parts are equal-size parts of the whole. Although it's colloquial to say that "your half is bigger than my half," this is not mathematically correct. But while two halves of the same whole have to be the same size, if you have half of an orange and half of a grape, the two halves won't be the same. It's important to be clear at all times about what the whole is. Also, it's important in fraction instruction not to present a particular procedure as the only or correct way to solve a problem. When comparing fractions, for example, I was taught to convert fractions to fractions with common denominators, then the fraction with the largest numerator was the largest. However, as the students' methods described previously indicate, there are several ways to compare fractions correctly and efficiently. The lessons in this book help children develop a variety of strategies, including using benchmarks of one-half and one and comparing denominators of fractions that have common numerators. When combining fractions, Davey's approach described earlier also illustrates the result of teaching that aims at helping children use their number sense to reason with fractions.

The Structure of the Lessons

The lessons in the book vary in several ways. Some span one class period, others take longer, and some are suitable to repeat over and over throughout the year, giving students a chance to revisit ideas and extend their learning. Some use manipulative materials, others ask students to draw pictures, and others ask students to rely on mental reasoning. And while some lessons seem to be more suited for beginning experiences, at times it's beneficial for more experienced students to engage in them as well. An activity that seems simple can reinforce students' understanding or give them a fresh way to look at a familiar concept. Also, a lesson that initially seems too difficult or advanced can be ideal for introducing students to thinking in a new way.

To help you use the lessons in this book, each is organized into the following sections:

Overview   To help you decide if the lesson is appropriate for your students, this is a nutshell description of the mathematical goal of the lesson and what the students will be doing.

Materials   This section lists the special materials needed along with quantities. Not included in the list are regular classroom supplies such as pencils and paper. Worksheets that need to be duplicated are included in the Blackline Masters section at the back of the book.

Time   Generally, the number of class periods is provided, sometimes with a range allowing for different length periods. It is also indicated for some activities that they are meant to be repeated from time to time.

Teaching Directions   The directions are presented in a step-by-step lesson plan.

Teaching Notes   This section addresses the mathematics underlying the lesson and at times provides information about the prior experiences or knowledge students need.

The Lesson   This is a vignette that describes what actually occurred when I taught the lesson to one or more classes. While the vignette mirrors the plan described in the teaching directions, it elaborates with details that are valuable for preparing and teaching the lesson. Samples of student work are included.

Extensions   This section is included for some of the lessons and offers follow-up suggestions.

Questions and Discussion   Presented in a question-and-answer format, this section addresses issues that came up during the lesson and/or questions that have been posed by other teachers.

How to Use This Book

To teach the lessons as described in the fifteen chapters requires at least twenty-five days of instruction, not including time for repeat experiences, as is recommended for some lessons, or for the ten individual assignments suggested. While it is possible to spend a continuous stretch of five or six weeks on these lessons, I don't think that is the best decision. In my experience, time is required for children to absorb fraction concepts, and I would rather spend a three-week period and then wait two months or so before returning for another three-week period, or arrange for three chunks of time, each two weeks or so, spaced throughout the year. When students return to ideas after a break, they bring not only the learning they've done in other areas but also a fresh look that some distance can provide. Also, spending time in between on whole number multiplication and division, on learning about decimals and percents, and on experiences with measurement, geometry, and probability will strengthen children's learning of fractions.

The five introductory lessons in the book are suitable for students who have or have not had prior formal instruction in fractions. My advice is not to skip these lessons. As beginning experiences, they build the foundation for developing understanding. As a review for students who already have begun to study fractions, they give both you and your students the chance to find out what they know and also to approach ideas in different ways. Chapter 2, "The Fraction Kit," calls for the greatest commitment of instruction time—five class periods—and the most preparation time in terms of cutting construction paper strips and preparing dice. This may dissuade you from using this lesson, but I advise you not to skip it. I make this point several times in the lesson. It is the single most effective activity for building students' understanding, especially with regard to naming fractions and equivalence. After the introductory lessons, choose those that you think will best meet your students' needs.

Most fifth graders will benefit from repeat experiences with the lessons if they were introduced to them in the previous year. Also, you may choose to use these lessons along with other instructional materials or learning activities. It's important, however, to be consistent so that in all lessons you encourage students to make sense of ideas, communicate about their reasoning both orally and in writing, and apply their learning to problem-solving situations.

CHAPTER ONE
FRACTIONS AS PARTS OF SETS

Overview

Children need experience thinking about fractions both as parts of wholes and as parts of groups, and this lesson focuses on using fractional notation to represent parts of groups. Starting by defining groups within the class according to different attributes, the lesson moves to examining collections of objects. Children also have experience comparing fractions to one-half. The lesson is useful for assessing children's understanding and also offers the class a beginning experience thinking about equivalent fractions.

Materials

Sets of objects, such as the following:

▲ a collection of pennies, nickels, and dimes, about ten of each
▲ interlocking cubes, at least ten in two colors
▲ colored pencils, at least twelve in three colors
▲ index cards, at least twelve in two or three colors

Time

▲ at least one class period

Teaching Directions

1. Determine with the class the number of students present. Then determine the number of girls and boys.

2. Write on the board a statement that describes what fractional part of the students are girls. For example, $\frac{11}{26}$ *of the students are girls.* Ask a student to read the sentence and have classmates indicate whether they agree with, disagree with, or don't understand the statement. One way to do this is to ask them to show a thumb up, a thumb down, or a thumb sideways. Ask a student to explain why the sentence makes sense. Also ask: "Are more or less than half the students girls?" This question gives children experience relating different fractions to one fraction that is familiar to them. Be sure to have students explain their reasoning.

3. Ask: "What fraction of the students are boys? Are more or less than half the students boys?" Again, be sure to have students explain their reasoning when answering.

4. Continue with other questions that relate to the class:

What fraction of the students at these two tables are girls?

What fraction of the students at these two tables are boys?

What fraction of the students are wearing long sleeves?

What fraction of the students wear glasses? What fraction of the students are wearing shoes with laces?

What fraction of the students are fourth graders? (This introduces the idea of writing a fraction to indicate the whole group, such as $\frac{26}{26}$.)

What fraction of the students have a birthday today? (This can introduce the idea of a fraction with zero for the numerator.)

For each question, also ask if the fraction is more or less than half.

5. Using groups of objects, ask the students to identify fractional parts. Begin with a train of ten interlocking cubes made with four blue and six yellow cubes. Ask: "What fraction of the train is blue? Is this more or less than half?" Have one or more students answer and explain their reasoning. Then ask: "What fraction is yellow? Is this more or less than half?" Again, have children explain their reasoning.

6. Continue with other groups of objects, such as a handful of colored pencils in three colors; a collection of pennies, nickels, and dimes; and index cards in two or more colors.

7. To introduce the idea of equivalent fractions, give a cube to each of six students, giving two students yellow cubes and the others blue cubes. (The colors don't particularly matter, but the numbers of each color work well for this activity.) Ask: "What fraction of the students with cubes have yellow cubes?" It should be obvious that $\frac{2}{6}$ represents the number of students with yellow cubes.

8. Write on the board: $\frac{1}{3}$ *of the students with cubes have yellow cubes.* Ask students if they agree, disagree, or don't know, and discuss.

9. If you feel that offering an explanation would be useful for helping students realize that both $\frac{2}{6}$ and $\frac{1}{3}$ can be used to describe the same part of a group, show the class three index cards, one yellow and two blue. After the students agree that one-third of your cards are yellow, cut each card in half to show that two-sixths of the cards are yellow. Cut them in half again to show yellow as four-twelfths of the cards. Also, draw a pizza, divide it into thirds, and shade one-third. Then draw lines to divide each slice in half and discuss how the shaded part is still one-third of the pizza but can also be thought of as two-sixths.

10. For a last experience, distribute index cards, giving yellow cards to two students and blue cards to six students. Ask: "What fraction of the students with cards have yellow cards?" Once they agree that the answer is two-eighths, write on the board: $\frac{1}{3}$ *of the students at the two tables have yellow cards.* Ask the class if it's true or false, and discuss.

Teaching Notes

While learning to use fractional notation for parts of groups is the primary goal of this lesson, experience with comparing fractions to one-half is also provided. One-half is a familiar fraction to the students, and learning to use one-half as a reference is extremely helpful. Several other lessons in the book also provide students experience relating fractions to one-half, including *Fractions in Contexts* (pages 30–38) and *Introducing One-Half as a Benchmark* (pages 54–58).

Making real-world connections with mathematics supports understanding and motivates students' interest. In that light, using the class and describing different groups of students within it is useful for engaging children in the activity. Using concrete materials and then drawings helps extend children's experiences and offers them options for connecting the abstract symbolism of fractions to various situations and models.

Keep in mind that this introductory experience probably will not be sufficient to help all children become comfortable with using fractional notation. Children need more than one opportunity to learn something new.

The Lesson

▲▲▲

This was the first time I had met this class of fourth graders. I was interested in finding out what they knew about fractions, and I planned to talk with the students about fractional notation and help them begin to think about equivalent fractions. To do this, I would identify different groups within the class and use fractions to represent them.

"How many students are in class today?" I asked to begin the lesson. Some of the students offered answers and a few stood up to count. After a few moments, we agreed that there were twenty-six in the class.

"How many are girls?" I then asked. Cara suggested that the girls raise their hands so we could count. This made it easy to verify that eleven of the students were girls and, therefore, that fifteen were boys. I then wrote on the board:

$\frac{11}{26}$ *of the students are girls.*

"Who can read what I wrote on the board?" I asked. Several hands went up and I called on Drew. He read the sentence correctly.

I next gave a direction that was familiar to the children. "If you agree with what I wrote on the board, show me with a thumb up. If you disagree, hold your thumb down. And if you're not sure or don't understand, then hold your thumb sideways," I said. About half a dozen students showed sideways thumbs; the rest showed thumbs up.

"A few of you aren't sure about what I wrote, so we need an explanation. Who would like to try to explain?" Several volunteered and I called on Diego.

"There are twenty-six of us, and that's the number on the bottom," he said. The eleven is on top because there are eleven girls and that's what we have in our class." Diego's explanation was clear, but I've learned from experience that students can give this explanation without necessarily understanding about fractions, merely by assigning whole numbers to the situation. I've found that relating fractions to one-half is useful for building understanding because one-half is a concept that they have had experience with and, in general, understand.

"Are more or less than half of the students girls?" I then asked. Conversation broke out at the tables. I called the class back to attention and asked, "Who would like to answer and explain?" I called on Marlo.

"It's less because eleven and eleven is twenty-two, and there are twenty-six of us," she said.

"Does anyone have a different way to explain?" I asked.

Margaret raised a hand and then pulled it down. "My way is really kind of the same," she said.

"Tell us anyway," I said.

She said, "Eleven times two is twenty-two, and that's not enough."

Jonathan had another way to explain. "There are fifteen boys and only eleven girls. So eleven girls is less than half."

"What fraction of the class are boys?" I then asked. I called on Kevin, one of the students who hadn't been sure before.

"You write fifteen over twenty-six," he said. I wrote this on the board.

"Is this more or less than half?" I asked.

"It has to be more than half if the girls are less," Marlo said.

"It's more than half because fifteen and fifteen is thirty, and we only have twenty-six," George said.

I then focused the class on the two tables of students at the front of the room. Four students were seated at one and five at the other. "What fraction of the students at these two tables are boys?" I asked. I called on Cindy.

"Five-ninths," she said.

"Show with your thumbs whether you agree with Cindy, disagree, or aren't sure," I said to the class. I checked thumbs and all were up.

"What fraction of the students at these two tables are girls?" I then asked. I called on Drew.

"Four-ninths," he answered. Again, I checked thumbs.

"Five-ninths is more than half," Nickie offered before I could ask. "Half of nine is four and a half, and five is bigger."

I continued with other questions that related to the students. "What fraction of the students are wearing long sleeves?" "What fraction wear glasses?" "What fraction of the students are wearing shoes with laces?" For each, I also asked if the fraction were more or less than half.

When I was sure that these were all easy for the students, I asked, "What fraction of the students are fourth graders?" Giggles broke out.

"What's funny?" I asked.

"You can't do that!" Lawrence said. "It's not a fraction."

"Yes, you can, " Trent replied. "It's twenty-six over twenty-six." I wrote on the board:

$$\frac{26}{26}$$

"Oh yeah," Lawrence said.

"It means all of us," Cindy added with confidence.

"So is that more than half?" I asked.

"I guess so," Cindy answered, all of a sudden not as confident.

"Does anyone else have an idea about this?" I asked.

"It has to be more than half if it's all of us," Jonathan said.

"What fraction of students have a birthday today?" I then asked. We established that no one did. (I already knew that and it was why I asked the question.)

"It's zero twenty-sixths," George said. I nodded and wrote on the board:

$$\frac{0}{26}$$

SETS OF OBJECTS

I then switched the focus from the students to several sets of objects that I had collected before class. I showed them a train of ten interlocking cubes made with four blue and six yellow cubes. "What fraction of the train is blue?" I asked, followed by, "Is this more or less than half?" Then I asked, "What fraction is yellow?" "Is this more or less than half?" For each question, I had the student who answered explain his or her reasoning. I recorded on the board:

$\frac{4}{10}$ blue

$\frac{6}{10}$ yellow

I showed them a handful of colored pencils, some green, some blue, and some brown. "What fraction of this handful of pencils is green?" I asked.

"We need to count them," Sally said. We counted and found that there were six green, four blue, and four brown.

"How many pencils am I holding altogether?" I asked. I waited a moment and asked them to say the answer softly together.

"So what fraction is green?" I asked again.

"Six-fourteenths," Beth answered.

"There are four-fourteenths brown," Ramon said.

"The same for blue," Cara said.

I listed the fractions on the board:

$\frac{6}{14}$ green

$\frac{4}{14}$ blue

$\frac{4}{14}$ brown

We talked about these fractions all being less than one-half. "You'd have to have seven of one color to make half," Margaret said.

"What fraction would that be?" I asked.

"Seven-fourteenths," Margaret answered. I wrote on the board:

$\frac{7}{14} = \frac{1}{2}$

I emptied on one of the tables the coins I had put in a small purse. "There are pennies, nickels, and dimes," I said. The chil-

dren at the table quickly sorted and counted the coins and I wrote on the board:

7 pennies
5 nickels
4 dimes

I asked what fraction of the coins were pennies, then nickels, then dimes. I wrote on the board:

$\frac{7}{16}$ are pennies

$\frac{5}{16}$ are nickels

$\frac{4}{16}$ are dimes

"What does the number sixteen mean in each of these fractions?" I asked.

Ramon answered, "That's how many coins you have."

"Yes," I said. "Are more or less than half of the coins pennies?"

"It's less, because seven isn't half of sixteen," Frank said.

"How many pennies would make one-half?" I asked.

Cara answered, "Eight, because eight is half of sixteen."

"So eight-sixteenths is half," Drew answered. I wrote on the board:

$\frac{8}{16} = \frac{1}{2}$

I felt that most of the students were able to represent fractional parts of different sets and they seemed to be able to compare the fractions to one-half. I decided to push further and see what more I could learn about their thinking.

INTRODUCING EQUIVALENT FRACTIONS

I gave a cube to each of the six students seated at one table. I gave the two Trents, who were sitting next to each other, each a yellow cube and Cara, who was sitting next to them, a blue cube. The class watched as I did this.

"I know!" Celia said. "You're giving yellow to the boys and blue to the girls."

I grinned at Celia as I gave the three students on the other side of the table—Diego,

Maria, and Kevin—each a blue cube. Celia grinned back and shrugged her shoulders.

"Look, she gave yellow only to Trents!" Cindy conjectured.

I turned to the class and said, "What fraction of the students on the window side of the table have yellow cubes?" I was referring to the two Trents and Cara. Hands shot up and I called on Nickie.

"Two-thirds," she answered, and I wrote $\frac{2}{3}$ on the board.

I then said, "What fraction of all the students at the table have yellow cubes?" The class agreed that two-sixths of the students at the table had yellow cubes. I wrote $\frac{2}{6}$ on the board.

I then said to the class, "Watch as I write a statement on the board. Show with a thumb if you agree, disagree, or aren't sure." I wrote on the board:

$\frac{1}{3}$ *of the students at the table have yellow cubes.*

There was a pretty equal split of all three reactions and I asked who was willing to offer an idea. One of the Trents volunteered. "It can't be one-third because there are six of us at this table. That's more than three people, so what you say has to be about sixths."

Jonathan, however, had a different idea. "I think it can be one-third. If you put the two Trents in a group, there are two of them. Then Cara and Maria can be in a group of girls. And Kevin and Diego can be in another group. So you have three groups and the Trents are one of them. I think they're one-third." I drew six stick figures on the board, labeled them *Y* and *B* for the color cubes I had distributed, and drew circles to group them into three groups.

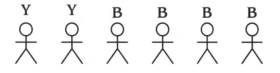

There was still disagreement, and discussion broke out among some of the other chil-

dren. Some students were convinced that it was okay to use one-third, some thought we had to use sixths, and some weren't sure.

"You can't call the same thing one-third and two-sixths," Marlo said. "That doesn't make sense."

"But they both work," Philip said.

"I don't get that," Marlo answered.

"Look at the drawings on the board," Jonathan said. "They prove it."

I interrupted them and asked Jonathan, "So you think that one-third and two-sixths are the same, that both work to describe how many students have yellow cubes?" Jonathan nodded in agreement.

"Do you think that one-third and two-sixths are always the same, no matter the situation?" I asked him.

Jonathan thought for a moment and then said, "I think one-third and two-sixths are the same in this particular situation, but not always." Jonathan's comment reminded me that fragile and partial understanding are part of learning. Also, it reminded me to be sure to probe students' thinking, even when they're correct, so I don't make erroneous assumptions about what they know.

Trent still defended his original idea. "They're not the same. Thirds and sixths aren't the same."

I asked for the students' attention and showed them three 3-by-5-inch index cards, one yellow and two blue. "What fraction of my cards are yellow?" I asked.

"One-third," several students answered together.

I took a pair of scissors, held the three cards together, and cut them each in half. "I still have the same cards, so one-third of what I have is still yellow," I said. "But now I have more pieces." I showed the class the two yellow halves and the four blue halves.

"Yes!" Annie said excitedly. "You have six pieces and two of them are yellow. You changed one-third into two-sixths."

"I still have the same cards, just cut into pieces," I repeated. Then I reached for the scissors and cut the cards in half again.

"How many pieces do you think I have now?" I asked. Some students guessed twelve, a few said nine, some didn't offer an opinion. We counted the pieces to verify that I now had twelve.

"What fraction of my cards are yellow?" I asked.

"Four-twelfths," they answered. I wrote on the board:

$$\frac{1}{3} \quad \frac{2}{6} \quad \frac{4}{12}$$

"But remember I still have the same cards I started with," I explained. "I could say that four-twelfths of my cards are yellow, but I could also say that two-sixths are yellow or one-third are yellow."

Several students felt they understood. "I get it now," Cindy said.

"That's cool," Lawrence said.

"That's pretty good," George added.

"If you cut them again, you'd have eight-twenty-fourths," Diego chimed in.

Not everyone was following the conversation. "This is hard," Annie said.

"I'm confused," the other Trent said.

"Let me try an explanation with pizza," I said. "Pizzas are awfully good for helping us make sense of fractions." I drew a circle on the board and said, "I've made this pizza and invited two friends to share it. So I'll cut the pizza into three parts—three equal parts so we each have the same share. We each get one-third to eat." I shaded in one of the pieces.

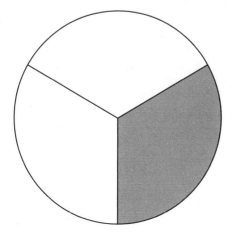

I then turned to the class and said, "One important idea about fractions is that when we divide something up, you have to have equal parts. It's hard to draw thirds. It helps me to think about the letter Y." I turned back to what I had drawn on the board.

"But I don't think that one slice of pizza on a plate will look very interesting," I said. "I know what I'll do—I'll cut each slice in half. Then we'll each have two slices to eat. I know the two smaller slices are the same amount as one larger slice, but I think it will look much better on the plate." As I said this, I divided each slice in half.

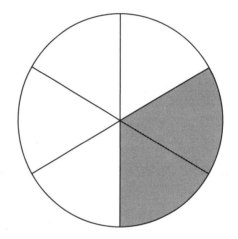

"Now you each get to eat two-sixths," Cara said.

"Two-sixths of what?" I asked her.

"Of the pizza," she said.

"Yes, two-sixths of the pizza is shaded. A second important idea about fractions is that you have to be sure that you keep track of the whole. In this case, the whole is one whole pizza. In our class, the whole is all twenty-six students. Before, it was the three index cards I showed you."

I pointed to where I had written $\frac{1}{3}$ and $\frac{2}{6}$ on the board. "The pizza helps me see that these two different fractions represent the same amount," I said.

I turned back to the board and said, "If two pieces look better on the plate, then maybe more will look even better. I think I'll cut the pieces in half again." The class giggled.

"The pieces are getting smaller," Philip said.

"They're practically only a mouthful," Frank said.

"You'll have twelve pieces now," Margaret said.

"So how much pizza will each person eat now?" I asked.

"Four-twelfths," several answered together.

"Yes, I could say we each get four-twelfths of the pizza, and that's equal to two-sixths of the pizza, and they're both equal to one-third of the pizza."

"Suppose you cut it into a hundred pieces," Jonathan said.

"They'd be *really* small then," Trent said.

"They'd be so small you'd have pizza vapor," Frank said.

"You wouldn't have to chew," Drew said.

Before the class got too silly, I asked, "Suppose I did cut a pizza into one hundred equal slivers. If three of us shared it, how many slices would we each get?" The students were quiet for a moment and then Philip made a guess.

"Twenty-five?" he said.

"That would only make seventy-five," Cindy said.

"I think thirty," Jonathan said. "Thirty and thirty makes sixty and thirty more makes ninety. Oops, that's not enough."

"I think thirty-five," Ramon said. "Thirty-five and thirty-five makes seventy. Uh oh, that's too much."

"How are you sure?" I asked, since Ramon had rejected his idea very quickly.

"Seventy and thirty makes one hundred, so there are five too many," he said.

"I know!" the first Trent said. "Thirty-three and you have a remainder. Three thirty-threes make ninety-nine and there's one extra slice."

"So you each get thirty-three-hundredths of the pizza?" I asked him. He nodded. I wrote on the board:

$$\frac{33}{100}$$

"You could share the last piece," Annie said. "Then you'll have a third of a piece more."

"That's right," I said, and changed the fraction on the board:

$$\frac{33\frac{1}{3}}{100}$$

"You could cut it into a thousand pieces," Jonathan said. "Then each person would get, I think, three hundred thirty-three and a third." I wrote on the board:

$$\frac{333\frac{1}{3}}{1000}$$

Only a few moments remained in the period. I told the class I had one last question to ask them. I focused them on two tables with four students at each. I distributed some of the cut-up index cards, giving yellow pieces to two of the students and blue to the other six.

"What fraction of these students have yellow cards?" I asked. "Let's say the fraction together."

"Two-eighths," the students answered. I then wrote on the board:

$\frac{1}{3}$ of the students at the two tables have yellow cards.

"Thumbs up if you think what I wrote is true, thumbs down if you think it's false, thumbs sideways if you're not sure," I said. There were mostly thumbs down, several thumbs sideways, and two thumbs up. Margaret raised her hand to tell what she thought.

"I disagree, because it has to be broken into groups of two, which will make fourths," she said.

"It should be one-fourth," George added.

I drew eight stick figures on the board, labeled two *Y* for yellow and six *B* for blue, and drew circles around groups of two.

"That's it," Margaret said.

Before I ended the class, I asked the students to look at the chalkboard. I asked, "If someone came into our room now and looked at the board, what would they think you were learning?"

"Fractions!" several answered.

"It looks like hard math," Drew said.

"We could show them how to write fractions," Margaret added.

After a class like this, I know that some students are clear about what we've done and others will need more experience.

Questions and Discussion

▲▲

▲ *Why did you think it was important to introduce the birthday question that resulted in a fraction with zero as the numerator?*

I'm always looking for ways to help children become as flexible as possible in their math thinking. We don't typically see fractions with zero as the numerator, but it's possible to understand such a fraction when children understand the context in which it's being used. It's not essential to include this example, but it helps stretch children's thinking.

▲ *At the end of the lesson, why did you choose to write a false statement on the board, using $\frac{1}{3}$ instead of the correct $\frac{1}{4}$?*

Children sometimes just expect that what a teacher says or writes is correct. Rather than think about a statement, they accept it as true. I'm interested in promoting children's intellectual autonomy and encouraging them at all times to think for themselves. I think that putting up a false statement can help in this regard.

CHAPTER TWO
THE FRACTION KIT

Overview

Students make their own fraction kits by cutting different-colored strips of construction paper into halves, fourths, eighths, and sixteenths. Having students cut and label each of the pieces is an effective way to introduce them to fractions as parts of a whole and to the meaning of standard fractional notation. Students learn, for example, that eight eighths make one whole and that it makes sense to label each of the eight pieces as $\frac{1}{8}$ because each is one of the eight equal-sized pieces they cut. After making their fraction kits, students learn several games to play with them and then are engaged in activities that connect their experience to representing and comparing fractions. Later, students use the kits for additional activities and also extend them by cutting additional strips into thirds, sixths, and twelfths.

Materials

▲ 5 colors of 12-by-18-inch construction paper cut into 3-by-18-inch strips, 3 sets of strips per student, 1 set for you, and several extra sets for possible mishaps (A suggestion: Arrange pieces of 12-by-18-inch construction paper in alternating colors before cutting. Cut 5 sheets at the same time on the paper cutter and you'll have strips in sets of 5 colors.)

▲ fraction dice made from labeling the faces of cubes $\frac{1}{2}$, $\frac{1}{4}$, $\frac{1}{8}$, $\frac{1}{8}$, $\frac{1}{16}$, and $\frac{1}{16}$, 1 per pair of students plus 1 per student to take home

▲ 1-gallon zip-top plastic bags, 2 per student

▲ rules for the game of *Cover Up* (see Blackline Masters)

▲ rules for the game of *Uncover, Version 1* (see Blackline Masters)

▲ rules for the game of *Uncover, Version 2* (see Blackline Masters)

▲ *Comparing Pairs* worksheet, 1 per student (see Blackline Masters)

▲ *What's Missing?* worksheet, 1 per student (see Blackline Masters)

▲ to extend the activity: 3 additional colors of 12-by-18-inch construction paper cut into 3-by-18-inch strips, 1 set of strips per student, 1 set for you, and several extra sets for possible mishaps. Instead of giving students dice to play *Cover Up* and *Uncover,* write fractions on 1-inch square tiles, put the tiles in small bags, and have students draw one at a time for a move, replacing the tile after each move. Use a different color tile and a different bag for each of the three sets.

Set 1: $\frac{1}{2}$, $\frac{1}{3}$, $\frac{1}{6}$, $\frac{1}{6}$, $\frac{1}{12}$, $\frac{1}{12}$

Set 2: $\frac{1}{2}$, $\frac{1}{3}$, $\frac{1}{4}$, $\frac{1}{6}$, $\frac{1}{6}$, $\frac{1}{12}$, $\frac{1}{12}$

Set 3: $\frac{1}{2}$, $\frac{1}{3}$, $\frac{1}{4}$, $\frac{1}{6}$, $\frac{1}{6}$, $\frac{1}{8}$, $\frac{1}{8}$, $\frac{1}{12}$, $\frac{1}{12}$, $\frac{1}{16}$, $\frac{1}{16}$

Time

▲ at least five class periods

Teaching Directions

1. Distribute five 3-by-18-inch strips of construction paper in different colors to each student. Ask students to take a strip of a particular color (that you choose), fold it in half, and cut it into two pieces. Have them label each piece $\frac{1}{2}$, explaining that because the pieces are the same size, each is one of the two pieces, which we represent as $\frac{1}{2}$. Then choose a color for a second strip and have the students fold and cut it into four equal pieces. Instruct students to label each piece $\frac{1}{4}$. Then have them fold, cut, and label a third strip in eighths and a fourth strip in sixteenths. Students leave the fifth strip whole, and label it *1* or $\frac{1}{1}$.

2. Teach the students how to use their fraction kits to play *Cover Up.* (See Blackline Masters for the rules.) Model the game with two students, then distribute a fraction die to each pair of students and have them play the game. Leave time at the end of class for students each to make another fraction kit to take home with a fraction die. Distribute zip-top bags for students to store their fraction kits and an additional set of uncut strips. Give them the homework assignment of cutting the additional set of strips with someone at home and playing the game.

3. On Day 2, have children report their experiences playing the game at home. Then teach the class how to play *Uncover, Version 1,* and have them play during class. (See Blackline Masters for the rules.) Give them the homework assignment of playing the game at home.

4. On Day 3, after children again report their experiences at home, discuss their strategies for exchanging pieces when playing *Uncover.* List their strategies on the board as they report them. Then teach *Version 2* of the game. (See Blackline Masters for the rules.) Give students time to play the game for the rest of class.

5. On Day 4, after children report their experiences at home, introduce *Cover the Whole.* Cover a whole strip with a train of fraction pieces, using three one-fourth pieces and two one-eighth pieces. Then model how to record a sentence that describes the train. Finally, show students how to shorten the sentence by combining fractions with like denominators.

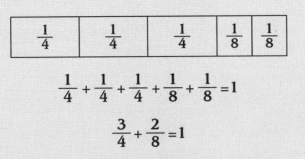

$$\frac{1}{4} + \frac{1}{4} + \frac{1}{4} + \frac{1}{8} + \frac{1}{8} = 1$$

$$\frac{3}{4} + \frac{2}{8} = 1$$

6. On Day 5, introduce *Comparing Pairs* and *What's Missing?* (see Blackline Masters). Model examples for students, including how to explain their reasoning. Tell them: "You have to solve the problems and explain your reasoning for three of them. Then you make up two of your own problems and explain your reasoning for one of them."

7. On subsequent days, take a few minutes and pose one of the challenge problems for a class discussion:

> How many eighths are there in one half?
>
> How many eighths are there in one whole?
>
> How many eighths are there in three fourths?
>
> How many sixteenths are there in one half?
>
> How many sixteenths are there in three eighths?
>
> How many eighths would be needed to cover two wholes?
>
> How many fourths are in one half?

8. As an extension a few weeks later, return to the fraction kits and have students cut three additional strips of different colors into thirds, sixths, and twelfths. Provide time for them to play *Cover Up* and *Uncover* with the sets of tiles described in the "Materials" section on page 11. Also, see Chapter 15, "Only One," for activities that use the kits to introduce combining fractions.

Teaching Notes

The fraction kit has been a long-standing favorite of mine as a jumping-off platform for introducing fractions to students and providing a concrete reference for them to use as they study fractions. The kit initially introduces children to halves, fourths, eighths, and sixteenths and helps them see how these fractions relate to one another. They learn, for example, that halves are larger than fourths, eighths, and sixteenths and that one-eighth of a whole is less than one-fourth of the same whole. They also learn that three-fourths of a whole can be represented by three of the one-fourth pieces or by one one-fourth piece and one one-half piece, that two of the one-eighth pieces takes up the same amount of space as does one of the one-fourth pieces, and that there are sixteen sixteenths in a whole and eight sixteenths in a half. These ideas emerge naturally as students use the kits.

After they cut the kits and learn to play the games, students experience follow-up activities that help them understand equivalence and learn to represent and compare fractions. Eventually, of course, students have to deal with fractions without referring to pieces of paper or any other concrete materials, and these follow-up activities help move students in that direction while still allowing them the support of their kits. Additional activities with the kits are also useful for introducing students to combining fractions (see Chapter 15, "Only One").

For students just beginning to learn about fractions, the fraction kit is the most effective introduction that I've found, even though it initially focuses only on a small set of fractions—halves, fourths, eighths, and sixteenths. Later, extending the kit to include thirds, sixths, and twelfths gives students the opportunity to investigate how these fractions relate to halves, fourths, eighths, and sixteenths and further builds a foundation of understanding that can then be extended to other fractions. My advice is not to skip this chapter under any circumstances and to teach it in its entirety, even if you think that students already understand these ideas. For more advanced students, the experience will cement their understanding and also extend it. Trust me on this one.

The Lesson

▲▲▲

To prepare, I cut 12-by-18-inch construction paper lengthwise into four 3-by-18-inch strips. I used five colors and cut enough strips so that every student would have two of each color, allowing them to make a kit to take home. I also made extra strips for me to use to demonstrate and for extras in case of cutting mishaps. So that I could distribute the strips more efficiently, I organized them into sets of five that included one of each color. I made sure that there were enough scissors available for each student. Also, I made fraction dice from cubes, one for every two students, labeling the faces $\frac{1}{2}$, $\frac{1}{4}$, $\frac{1}{8}$, $\frac{1}{8}$, $\frac{1}{16}$, and $\frac{1}{16}$.

DAY 1

I distributed the sets of five colored strips I had prepared and said to the students, "You'll each make a fraction kit, following along with me so that we all wind up with the same fraction pieces. Then we'll use the kit for games and activities that will help you learn about fractions. First, put the dark blue strip aside. We won't cut that one at all. Let's start with the red strip."

I've learned from experience that it's most successful to lead the students step-by-step through cutting their kits and to have all students use the same color for each fraction. This avoids the kinds of mistakes that students make when they work on their own. I have the students cut and label one color strip before I give instructions for the next one.

I modeled for the class how to fold the red strip and cut it into two halves. Most of the students were familiar with the notation for one-half, but I explained anyway. "After you cut your strip into halves, label each piece. I label them like this." I wrote $\frac{1}{2}$ on one of the strips and explained, "There are two red pieces that make the whole, and this is one of them, so I write one-half on each to show that it's one of two pieces of the whole. Cut and label your two red strips as I did mine."

$\frac{1}{2}$	$\frac{1}{2}$

I waited for all of the students to do this, going over to make sure Tom understood the directions and then prodding Josh not to dawdle.

I then explained to the students what they were to do next. "Watch as I fold, cut, and label my grey strip into fourths." I folded it in half and then in half again and opened the strip to show it divided into four parts. Before cutting, I labeled each part $\frac{1}{4}$.

$\frac{1}{4}$	$\frac{1}{4}$	$\frac{1}{4}$	$\frac{1}{4}$

"Who can explain why it makes sense to label each part as I did?" I asked. I called on Maggie.

"You have four parts, and each part is one of them," she said.

I nodded and asked, "Does anyone have a different way to explain?" No one volunteered. I then gave the students time to fold, cut, and label their grey strips into fourths.

Next I picked up a purple strip. "Watch as I fold it," I said. I folded it in half, half again, and then half again.

"How many sections do you think there will be when I unfold it?" I asked. Some thought six and some thought eight. I unfolded the strip and we counted to verify that there were eight sections.

"Raise your hand if you think you know how I should label each of the parts," I said. I waited until practically everyone had raised a hand. I called on Shannon.

"They're one-eighth because there are eight parts," she said.

"So what do I write?" I asked.

"A one over an eight," she said. I wrote $\frac{1}{8}$ in the first section and asked, as I had done with the fourths, "Who can explain why it makes sense to label this part one-eighth?" Hands shot up and I called on Davey.

"There are eight parts altogether and that's just one of them," he said. I wrote $\frac{1}{8}$ in each section.

$\frac{1}{8}$	$\frac{1}{8}$	$\frac{1}{8}$	$\frac{1}{8}$	$\frac{1}{8}$	$\frac{1}{8}$	$\frac{1}{8}$	$\frac{1}{8}$

Then, before having the students fold, cut, and label their purple strips into eighths, I introduced some vocabulary. "The top number in the fraction is called the numerator," I said.

"Oooh, I know," Claudia said. "The bottom number is the denominator."

"Yes," I said, writing those words on the board.

"What's the line called?" Libby wanted to know.

I stopped for a moment. "I'm not sure it has a fancy name like *numerator* or *denominator*," I said. "I've always heard it referred to as the fraction bar."

"Well, how come they use it to write fractions?" Libby continued. These are the sorts of questions that Libby asked, and I had come to understand that she really wanted to know.

"Sometimes they use a slanty line," Dan said.

"Yes," I said. "You'll see fractions written like this as well." I wrote $\frac{1}{8}$ on the board.

I took a stab at explaining about the fraction bar. "You know about the symbol for division," I said to the class and wrote ÷ on the board. They nodded.

"One way we can think about fractions is by thinking about dividing. When we make eighths for our fraction kit, we're dividing a whole into eight equal parts. That's like dividing one by eight." I wrote on the board: $1 \div 8$. "You can think about writing one divided by eight in the form of a fraction by replacing the dots in the division sign with the numbers one and eight."

It's important for students to understand how fractions relate to division and this was a chance to introduce the idea. I intended to return to it at a later time.

"Any other questions?" I asked. Sean raised his hand.

"Should we write the fractions before we cut the pieces or cut them first?" he asked. In contrast to Libby's questions, Sean's questions more often focus on what he needs to do than on ideas he's considering.

"Either way is fine," I said. "Just be sure when you're done that you have eight pieces."

When they had all finished, I asked them to count their purple eighths to make sure they had eight of them. Then I modeled for them how to cut their light blue strips into sixteenths. The paper gets awfully bulky when the students try to fold the strip four times, so I suggested that they first fold and cut eighths and then fold each eighth in half to make sixteenths. This makes sense to students and helps reinforce that one-eighth is equivalent to two-sixteenths. Some students groaned as they labeled the sixteenths because there are so many of them. The experience of labeling is good, I think, because it helps children understand why sixteenths are smaller pieces even though the fraction has a larger denominator.

After they had cut their pieces, I held up a dark blue uncut strip. "How should we label this one?" I asked. "We're not going to cut it."

"How about one whole?" Robert suggested.

Janie said, "I think one over one, like this." She traced $\frac{1}{1}$ in the air.

"Maybe just plain one," Jennifer said.

"Any and all of those are okay," I said. "After you label your whole, put your initials on the back of every one of your pieces so that we can identify pieces that may get lost."

1							
$\frac{1}{2}$				$\frac{1}{2}$			
$\frac{1}{4}$		$\frac{1}{4}$		$\frac{1}{4}$		$\frac{1}{4}$	
$\frac{1}{8}$	$\frac{1}{8}$	$\frac{1}{8}$	$\frac{1}{8}$	$\frac{1}{8}$	$\frac{1}{8}$	$\frac{1}{8}$	$\frac{1}{8}$
$\frac{1}{16}$ $\frac{1}{16}$	$\frac{1}{16}$ $\frac{1}{16}$	$\frac{1}{16}$ $\frac{1}{16}$	$\frac{1}{16}$ $\frac{1}{16}$	$\frac{1}{16}$ $\frac{1}{16}$	$\frac{1}{16}$ $\frac{1}{16}$	$\frac{1}{16}$ $\frac{1}{16}$	$\frac{1}{16}$ $\frac{1}{16}$

"There's a lot of pieces," Josh complained.

"How many?" I asked, to shift the energy from complaining to thinking mathematically. (There are thirty-one pieces in all.) "If you're interested, try figuring that out in your head first and then count to check." Some of the students were interested while others just got to the task of writing their initials.

Teaching the Rules for *Cover Up*

After the students had written their initials on each of their pieces, I taught them how to play *Cover Up*. I had them gather around one table to watch as I taught Sam and Andrew how to play. (See page 145 for rules.)

"You each start with your dark blue whole in front of you," I said. "The idea is to be the first to cover your whole completely and exactly, with nothing extra hanging over."

I showed them one of the fraction dice I had made. "The die has one-half and one-fourth each written once and one-eighth and one-sixteenth each written twice," I said. "On your turn, you roll the die, see what fraction comes up, and put a piece that matches that fraction on your whole strip."

I then had Sam and Andrew play. "Who will go first?" I asked. They boys shrugged. Then Andrew said that he would and he rolled the die. It came up $\frac{1}{8}$, and Andrew took one of his purple pieces and put it on his dark blue whole strip. While he was doing this, Sam reached for the die. I stopped him, however. "It's important that you watch each other. Sam, you need to watch to be sure you agree with what Andrew does. Andrew, when you've played, say 'Done' to signal Sam that he can roll. Until Andrew says 'Done,' Sam shouldn't even reach for the die." Sam nodded and waited.

"Say 'Done,'" Davey said to Andrew.

"Oh yeah," Andrew said. "Done."

Sam reached for the die and rolled. He got $\frac{1}{2}$. "Way to go!" he said, and put a red half on his whole. Then he said, "Done."

Andrew rolled next and got $\frac{1}{16}$. "Yuk," he said. "This is getting me nowhere." Sam waited a moment and then prompted Andrew to say "Done." Andrew did so and Sam reached for the die. This time he rolled $\frac{1}{4}$, put a grey piece on the whole, and said, "Done."

Dan said, "Sam only needs another fourth, but Andrew needs more."

"Lots more!" Andrew added, reaching for the die.

"Before you roll, can you tell how much more you need to cover the whole?" I asked.

"Even a half isn't enough," Claudia commented.

"I think I need a half and a fourth and something more," Andrew said, studying his board.

"He needs a half, a fourth, another sixteenth, and then another fourth," Jennifer said. Jennifer wasn't correct, since a half and two fourths would cover the entire whole, but I didn't correct her or take the time to have her check her prediction with her pieces. Most of the students were more interested in the game than my question, so I kept the focus on the rules for play and didn't further interrupt the game. I decided that it was enough to plant the idea that they might think about how much there was left to cover.

Andrew rolled $\frac{1}{4}$. "Now that's better," he said, putting a grey one-fourth piece on his whole. "Done," he said, passing the die to Sam.

Sam rolled $\frac{1}{2}$. Some of the students let out a cheer.

"Not so fast," I said. "Remember what I said about covering the whole completely but exactly. The one-half piece is too big."

"So what happens?" Lily asked.

"Sam can't put anything on. He has to say 'Done' and pass the die to Andrew."

"Things are looking up," Andrew said, getting ready to roll the die. I let the boys play out the game. Then I had the students return to their seats to play with partners.

Observing the Students

All of the students were interested in the game and stayed engaged for the rest of the period. I circulated as they played, watching to make sure they were following the rules and listening to hear what they were saying.

I noticed that Joey and Robert were racing through a game, rolling and putting pieces on their whole strips but not paying attention to what each other was doing. Also, they weren't following the rule of saying "Done." I stopped the boys and talked with them. "Not only is it good to check on what your partner does, but I'm trying to slow the game down enough so you also have time to think about the mathematics involved," I explained.

"What do you mean?" Robert asked.

"You can be thinking about what you hope you'll roll next, or how many more rolls you think you'll need to cover your whole, or how much ahead one of you is than the other. Remember the game is to help you learn about fractions. I want you to enjoy playing, but I also want you to do some thinking." The boys nodded. I made one last comment.

"So, remember, no grabbing for the die. Also, be sure to say 'Done' after you play, and pay attention to each other's pieces." Again the boys nodded. I stayed for a bit while they resumed play to make sure they were following my directions. I had to talk with several other pairs in the same way.

I then noticed that Carol and Sarah had stopped playing and Carol was trimming slivers from her fraction pieces. I've seen other students do this and I talked to Carol about why I thought it wasn't necessary. "Measurement is never exact, so it's likely that your pieces aren't exactly the right sizes. Trimming can't really solve that problem. What's important is that you think about the fractional sizes the pieces are supposed to be, rather than just relying on the paper pieces you've cut."

"I want them to be even," Carol countered. I wasn't able to convince her of the futility of trimming. Her sense of order seemed somehow violated by the inconsistencies. After a few more snips, she gave it up and she and Sarah returned to the game.

When the class time was nearly over, I called the students to attention and asked them what they thought about the game. Many of the students raised their hands. I called on Tom first and got a typical answer.

"It's fun," he said.

"What makes it fun?" I asked.

"Rolling the dice. Moving the pieces. Watching your partner get stuck." The others laughed.

I called on Sarah. "I rolled one-half twice in a row once and won," she said.

"Me, too," Lily chimed in.

"So you like winning," I said. They nodded.

"Did anyone else roll one-half twice in a row?" I asked. No one else had.

"I rolled one-sixteenth a lot," Martin said.

"Yeah, me too," Josh added.

"It's hard to get one-half," Joey said. "There's only one of them on the cube and there are two eighths and two sixteenths."

Some nodded, indicating that they had noticed the same thing. Claire, however, carefully inspected one of the fraction cubes. She looked at the fraction on each face.

"Oh yeah," she said. "That explains it."

"That explains what?" I asked.

"Why I didn't get one-half at all," she said.

I then collected the fraction dice and gave each student a plastic 1-gallon zip-top baggie for their pieces. By folding the whole in half, all of the pieces fit in nicely.

For homework that night, I had the students each take home another set of strips to cut into a fraction kit and to teach someone at home to play *Cover Up*. I wanted them to have kits at home, but I didn't want to risk having them take home their class sets and not remember to bring them back. I duplicated and distributed the rules and also gave each student a cube to make a fraction die. I knew that some students would forget to return their cubes, but I had extras and it wouldn't be disastrous if I lost a few.

I planned to start the next day's class by having the students report what happened when they played the game at home. Then I would have them play again at the beginning of the next day's class. While they played, I would circulate and have conversations with as many of them as possible, asking how much more someone needed to cover the board, or how much farther ahead was the person who was winning so far. This would be valuable assessment time, but I also wanted to be sure that I didn't interfere with their enjoyment of the game. I planned to use the second half of the next day's lesson for a brief class discussion about *Cover Up* and then teach them how to play *Uncover*, another game with the fraction kit.

DAY 2

I began class as I had planned, asking the students about their experiences playing *Cover Up* at home. They seemed to have enjoyed the experience.

"I beat my dad three times," Tom said.

"My mom said the game was fun," Delia said.

"I was really lucky. I kept rolling one-half," Sarah said.

I then told the students that I'd like them to play for just a short while. "I want to be sure everyone knows how to play the game. Then I'll teach you another game to play with the same pieces." The students were happy to return to the game.

As I observed them play, I tried to assess their understanding as much as possible. But I waited to interrupt until I was sure that they were clear about how to play the game. I tried to be sensitive not to interfere with their enjoyment of the activity.

Jeremy had two fourths and one sixteenth on his whole strip. I asked him how much more he needed to cover the strip. He shrugged, completely disinterested in my question and eager to take his turn and roll the die. I didn't push it at that time.

But when I interrupted Jennifer and Delia, they were more interested in my question than the game. "The game is just luck," Jennifer said. She likes to think about problems, and I saw Delia benefit from Jennifer's interest. The girls each had five pieces on their whole strips. Delia had two fourths, two eighths, and one sixteenth on hers; Jennifer had one sixteenth, one half, then three more sixteenths on hers.

Delia

$\frac{1}{4}$	$\frac{1}{4}$	$\frac{1}{8}$	$\frac{1}{8}$	$\frac{1}{16}$	

Jennifer

$\frac{1}{16}$	$\frac{1}{2}$	$\frac{1}{16}$	$\frac{1}{16}$	$\frac{1}{16}$	

Instead of asking them how much more they needed to cover their whole strips, I asked, "Who's ahead?"

"I think I am," Delia said. They pushed their whole strips side by side. "See, I have one-sixteenth more on mine."

"How much more do you need to cover your whole?" I asked them.

"I need one fourth," Jennifer said.

"I need three more sixteenths," Delia said.

"So I have a better chance of winning," Jennifer announced.

"No, you don't," Delia said. "I'm ahead."

"Yes, I do," Jennifer answered. "I can win in one turn if I'm lucky, but you have to take three turns." She turned to me and asked, "If I don't like what I roll, can I skip my turn?"

I thought for a moment. "I don't see why not," I said.

"Why would you skip your turn?" Delia asked.

"Well, I wouldn't really skip it. I'd roll first and then decide. Because if I roll one-sixteenth, then I'll need three more. But if I roll one-fourth, I'm through in one roll, and if I roll one-eighth, I could be through in one more roll with another eighth."

"Well, roll then," Delia said. She didn't seem to grasp Jennifer's strategy and was more interested in continuing with the play.

But I was still curious about Jeremy. I returned to him when he and Josh had just finished a game. "Say, Jeremy, if you had put just one red one-half piece on your whole strip, do you know how much more you would need to cover it entirely?" I had the strips there and put a red on the dark blue.

"Easy," he said. "Another half."

"What if you had one half and one fourth on it?" I asked, putting down a grey fourth.

Jeremy looked for a moment. "You need another grey one," he said, adding a one-fourth piece to the strip. I didn't insist that Jeremy identify the grey piece with its fractional name. Instead I posed another question.

"Suppose you had this on your strip," I said. I removed both grey pieces, left the red one-half piece on, and placed a purple one-eighth piece next to it.

"That's hard," he said. "Can I use the pieces?"

"Yes, but tell me what you're thinking," I said.

"A grey one fits," he said, putting on a one-fourth piece. "And there's still room, maybe for a light blue or a purple. I'm not sure." He started to fit pieces on, relying only on what he could do with the pieces, not thinking about the fractions.

"Thanks, Jeremy," I said. "I think this might be a good problem to talk about with the whole class."

One or two encounters with a student don't give me conclusive information about what he or she understands. But over time, with more conversations, I build deeper pictures of how students think, what they know well, and where the soft spots are in their understanding.

Teaching the Rules for *Uncover*

About fifteen minutes into the class period, I called the class to attention. I said, "I'd like to teach you the rules for playing another game. It's called *Uncover*." This time I wrote the rules on the board so that students could refer to them as I introduced the game and when they played. This game is a little more complicated than *Cover Up*. I had also duplicated copies of the rules for their reference. (See page 145 for rules.)

I had the class gather around Martin and Lily to watch them play a game. I read the rules on the board and had Martin and Lily follow them. I had to remind both of them to watch what each other did to be sure they agreed. "You can't take the die to roll it until the other player says 'Done,'" I said several times. "It's important that you watch each other's moves to make sure you agree with the exchanges or what's being removed."

After a few turns, Martin and Lily got into the swing of saying "Done." The others watching chimed in as well, so they all got into the habit of saying it. After this demonstration game, the students returned to their seats to play in pairs.

Observing the Students

From playing *Cover Up*, some students were familiar enough with the pieces so that they could make exchanges easily. Joey, for example, couldn't remove a piece after rolling $\frac{1}{8}$ on his first roll. "I'll exchange," he said to his partner, Josh, removing one of the one-half pieces. "I'll put down four eighths." Joey reached for the eighths and laid them in the vacant space.

Sarah had the same experience, rolling $\frac{1}{8}$ on her first roll. She deftly exchanged one of the one-half pieces for two one-eighth pieces and four one-sixteenth pieces.

At another table a bit later in a game, Mariah was left with two one-fourth pieces. She rolled $\frac{1}{8}$. "Not again!" she said. "I'll get ready for that." She removed one of the one-fourth pieces and efficiently reached for a one-eighth piece and two one-sixteenth pieces. "Now I'm ready," she said.

Other students, however, needed to compare pieces in order to be sure how to make a fair exchange. Claire, for example, rolled $\frac{1}{16}$

on her first roll. Her partner, Sarah, had gone first and made her exchange. Claire, however, seemed unsure how to exchange. She removed one of the one-half pieces and mused aloud, "I think I'll take three of these and three of these." She took three of the one-eighth pieces and three of the one-sixteenth pieces. She began placing them carefully on the vacant half of her whole strip. I watched to see what would happen. Sarah was waiting patiently but not paying close attention.

"Uh oh," Claire said. "I think that's too many. Is it, Sarah?"

Sarah had been watching Joey and Josh but turned back to look at Claire's pieces. "Take off one of the sixteenths," she said. "Then it works."

Claire did that and announced, "Done."

I didn't intervene. At this point, Claire was focusing on the pieces and not thinking about their fractional names and the relationships between them. I decided to allow Claire time to play and see what she would notice for herself with additional experience.

Jeremy was also unsure about how the fractional pieces related to one another or whether they did at all. His partner, Claudia, watched him closely. "You can't do that," she said when Jeremy tried to exchange a one-fourth piece for a one-eighth piece and a one-sixteenth piece. "They don't match up."

"What do you mean?" Jeremy said.

"Look," Claudia said. "There's a space left over. You have to put on another sixteenth." Claudia did this for Jeremy.

"Oh, I get it," he said.

No matter how clear I think my directions are, there's typically someone for whom they don't make sense.

The spirit in the class was high during the game, with the sound of animated involvement.

A Class Discussion

About fifteen minutes before the end of class, I told the children that I would interrupt them in one minute for a class discussion. I've found that when I give the children a warning first, it's easier for them to stop their activity when I ask them to give me their attention.

I began the discussion by asking, "How does this game compare to *Cover Up?*"

There was an outburst of comments.

"Cool."

"It's better."

"I won twice."

"I like this one."

"Wait, wait," I said. "Raise your hand if you want to tell how you think the games compare." I called on Andrew.

"I think it's better," he said. "You get to decide what to do, and I like that."

I called on Delia next. "You can play a different way each time."

"Explain more about that," I said.

"Well, the first time I just exchanged a one-half piece for two fourths, but then I kept rolling eighths and sixteenths," she said. "So the next game I did a different exchange."

Other students were also interested in explaining the exchanges they made and I kept the discussion going until the end of class. For homework, the students were to take home the rules and play *Uncover* with someone in their families.

DAY 3

At the beginning of class I had the students report what happened when they played *Uncover* at home. Many were eager to report who won and how many times. Some had developed theories about rolling the cube to get the desired outcome, by dropping it from on high to keeping it close to the tabletop. Most agreed that *Uncover* was a better game than *Cover Up.*

"There isn't much strategy with *Cover Up,*" Maggie said.

"There isn't *any* strategy with *Cover Up,*" Andrew countered.

"It's just luck," Lily added.

"What strategies did you use for your first roll when playing *Uncover?*" I asked. Conversation burst out. Students were eager to report their ideas. I quieted them and asked them to raise their hands if they wanted to tell their ideas. Robert went first.

"If I don't roll one-half, then I exchange one of the one-half pieces so I have one fourth, one eighth, one sixteenth, and one sixteenth," he said. "Then I know I can take off something on my next roll."

"And if you roll one-half?" I asked.

"Then you just take it off," he said.

I recorded Robert's strategy on the board:

Strategy for Roll #1

If you don't roll $\frac{1}{2}$, exchange one of the $\frac{1}{2}$ pieces for $\frac{1}{4}$, $\frac{1}{8}$, $\frac{1}{16}$, and $\frac{1}{16}$.

Some other students commented that they used the same strategy, but Claudia had a different approach. "I exchanged for just eighths and sixteenths," she said.

"How many of each?" I asked.

"Two eighths and four sixteenths," Claudia answered. I recorded Claudia's suggestion underneath Robert's:

$$\frac{1}{8}, \frac{1}{8}, \frac{1}{16}, \frac{1}{16}, \frac{1}{16}, \frac{1}{16}$$

"That doesn't work," Dan said.

"Yes, it does," Janie said. "Look. Two sixteenths make an eighth, so it's the same as four eighths, and that's a half."

Dan thought for a moment. "Oh yeah," he said.

"I don't agree that Claudia's idea is a good one," Davey said. "She has too many pieces to take off."

"So you think Robert's idea is better?" I asked.

"No," Davey said. "He has too many pieces, too. I exchanged for one fourth and two eighths." I recorded Davey's idea:

$$\frac{1}{4}, \frac{1}{8}, \frac{1}{8}$$

"What do you think about Davey's idea?" I asked the class.

Claudia was insistent. "He may have only three pieces, but one fourth is just as hard to get off as one half. You may as well leave the one half."

"But it's easier to get eighths off," Davey said, defending his choice.

I took the opportunity to talk about the probabilities of each of the fractions coming up when the die was rolled. "There's only one chance out of six to roll one-half when you roll the cube," I said. "Who can explain why that makes sense?"

I waited to see who would raise a hand. About half of the students did, and I called on Libby.

"There are six sides, and one-half is only on one of them," she said.

"Yes," I said. "A cube has six faces and each face has the same chance of landing up. Since one-half is written on only one face, it has a one in six chance." I used the correct terminology of *face* instead of *side*.

"And one-fourth has the same chance. It's written only once," Joey said.

"I agree," I said. "The probability of rolling one-half is one out of six. And there's also a one-sixth chance that you will roll one-fourth." I wrote on the board:

$$P(\tfrac{1}{2}) = \tfrac{1}{6}$$
$$P(\tfrac{1}{4}) = \tfrac{1}{6}$$
$$P(\tfrac{1}{8}) =$$
$$P(\tfrac{1}{16}) =$$

"What do you think the probability is of rolling one-eighth?" I asked. Hands shot up. I called on Sarah.

"It's two-sixths," she said.

"Why do you think so?" I prompted.

"Because one-eighth is on two sides," she said.

"It's the same for one-sixteenth," Sam said. "It's on there twice, too."

"Sometimes you should exchange one way and sometimes the other," Libby said. "You can get different rolls at different times."

I then introduced a variation on the rules for *Uncover*. When I had taught the game to a different class, one of the students, Jose, had raised a question. He had asked, "If I don't have a one-fourth piece on my board but I have two one-eighth pieces, and I roll one-fourth, can I take off the two one-eighth pieces?"

I hadn't addressed that possibility in the rules I had written, but in thinking about his question, I decided Jose's idea was mathematically sound. Also, looking for combinations of pieces would certainly support children's mathematical thinking. However, the suggestion hadn't come up in this class, so I explained Jose's idea.

"Any combination of pieces is fine as long as they add up to the fraction that comes up on the die," I told them.

"That's the way we played last night," Delia said. "It was my mom's idea."

"Ohhhh," Claudia said, always quick to understand a new situation. "Maybe you don't need to hold on to the one-half piece at all."

For the rest of the class period, I had them play *Uncover* with this new variation. For homework that night, I told the children they were to play either version of *Uncover* with someone at home and also to think more about what might be a good strategy for exchanging on the first roll.

DAY 4

I began class, as I had done on the two previous days, by having the students discuss their experiences from the night before. Instead of having a class discussion, however, I asked students to talk in small groups. In this class, the same students typically volunteered in whole-class discussions, and having students talk in small groups encouraged more of them to share their ideas. After the groups had the chance to talk, I called the class to attention.

Sam raised his hand, eager to report what his group had decided. He said, "We all liked the new way of playing better. It lets you think more." There was agreement from others in the class.

Lily had something different to report from her group. "We tried those strategies from yesterday and agree that they're all about the same," she said. There was an outburst of protest from others. I quieted the class and returned to Lily.

"Can you explain your group's reasoning?" I asked.

"Well, you don't know what you're going to roll and it's all luck, so it doesn't matter which way you go."

Josh waved his hand to disagree. "We know for sure that Davey's is better than Robert's because Davey only has three and Robert has four, and the chance of rolling one-eighth and one-sixteenth is the same, so Davey has a better chance."

"But it's still luck," Dan, a member of Sam's group, chimed in. I reminded Dan not to blurt out and then called on Jennifer.

"We agree with Josh's group, and we think that Claudia's idea was okay because her fractions are all more possible, but we still think that Davey will win. At least that's what happened when we played."

Joey had a suggestion to offer. He and Sam had played the game after school and added another rule. "It's like a fourth choice when you role," Joey explained. "If you want, you can put one of your partner's pieces back on his whole."

Sam added, "As long as there's room, you can do it. It's good in an emergency."

"It makes the game last longer, but it's better," Joey said.

Sam laughed. "Yeah, we finally made a rule that you can do it only ten times in a game. It's like having only so many time-outs."

The rest of the class was very interested in playing this version, but I had other plans for the rest of the period. When the other students played it later, however, it was a big hit and became *Uncover, Version 3.*

Introducing *Cover the Whole*

"You'll have a chance to try out Joey and Sam's game and also to test your theories," I said. "But now I'd like to introduce two other activities that you'll do with your fraction kits. They're not games but explorations that I think will help you learn more about fractions."

I wrote the names of the activities on the board:

Cover the Whole

Comparing Pairs

"Can we work with partners?" Claire wanted to know.

I replied, "You can talk with others, but you each have to do your own work and hand in your own papers." In learning situations, I want students to have as much support as possible, and talking with classmates is a way to provide that support. But I also want all students to have the experience of recording fractions, explaining their reasoning, and being responsible for their own assignments.

I began by explaining *Cover the Whole.* "In this activity, you cover your whole strip as you do when playing *Cover Up,* but you don't have to roll the die or play the game. Just make a train of pieces that covers the whole strip exactly." I took a moment and had each student cover his or her whole strip.

I then asked Libby what she had done. "Tell me the pieces you used, reading from left to right across your strip, and I'll record what you tell me." As Libby reported, I recorded the fractions on the board:

$$\frac{1}{4} \quad \frac{1}{4} \quad \frac{1}{4} \quad \frac{1}{8} \quad \frac{1}{8}$$

Then I added plus signs and = *1* to write a complete mathematical sentence:

$$\frac{1}{4} + \frac{1}{4} + \frac{1}{4} + \frac{1}{8} + \frac{1}{8} = 1$$

"Who can explain why it makes sense to put in plus signs and write 'equals one' at the end?" I asked.

"Because plus is adding and you're adding more pieces to the board," Mariah said.

"If you add them all up you get one," Davey added.

"Yeah," Joey said. "The two eighths make one fourth, and four fourths make a whole."

"Is this what we do?" Lily wanted to know. "It's easy."

"Yes," I answered. "You'll each cover your whole strip with pieces and record what you did in a complete mathematical sentence as I did for Libby's. You need to do this for at least five different combinations of pieces. Then there's one more step you need to do for each of your sentences. You have to shorten them, if it's possible. Watch as I shorten what Libby reported." I wrote:

$$\tfrac{3}{4} + \tfrac{2}{8} = 1$$

"Who can explain why this shorter sentence is equivalent to the longer one?" I asked.

"What does equivalent mean?" Sean asked.

"It means the same," Jennifer answered. "They're not exact, but they mean the same thing."

I added, "If I saw just the shortened sentence, I would still be able to figure out which pieces Libby had used." Sean seemed satisfied and there were no other questions. Because the students had experience playing *Cover Up* and *Uncover*, talking about fractions like three-fourths and two-eighths wasn't new, and the use of the correct notation was an easy connection for them to make.

The students worked for the rest of the period on *Cover the Whole*. (Figures 2–1 and 2–2 show what two students did with *Cover the Whole*.) A few who finished early returned to playing *Uncover*.

DAY 5

To begin class, I said, "I'm going to introduce two new activities for you to do with your fraction kits." I gathered the students so that they could see me use the fraction

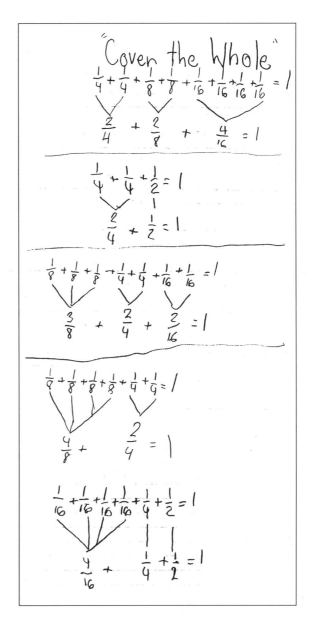

▲▲▲▲▲▲**Figure 2–1** *Delia had a unique recording system for keeping track when she shortened her sentences.*

pieces and also see the board. I wrote the names of the activities on the board:

Comparing Pairs
What's Missing?

To explain *Comparing Pairs,* I wrote an example on the board that was like those on the *Comparing Pairs* worksheet:

$$\tfrac{3}{8} \qquad \tfrac{9}{16}$$

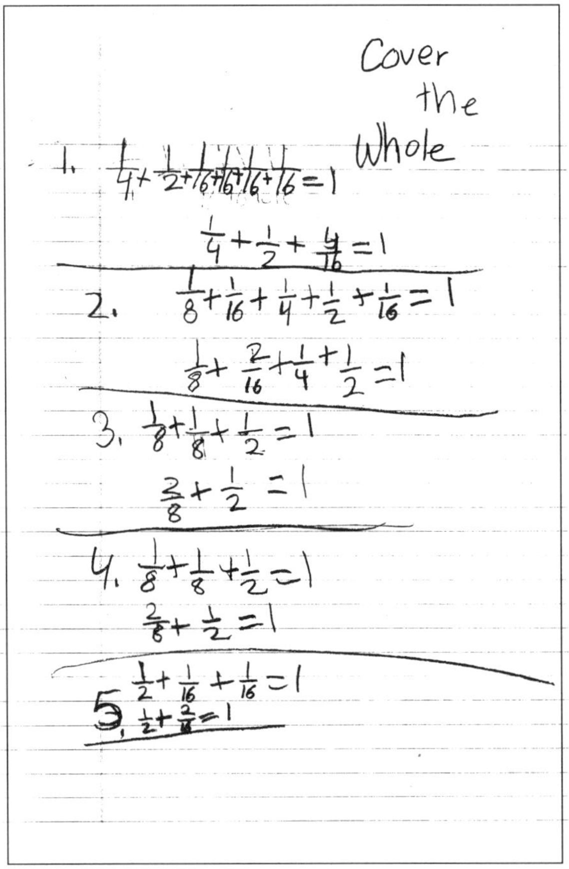

Cover the Whole

1. $\frac{1}{4} + \frac{1}{2} + \frac{1}{16} + \frac{1}{16} + \frac{1}{16} + \frac{1}{16} = 1$

   $\frac{1}{4} + \frac{1}{2} + \frac{4}{16} = 1$

2. $\frac{1}{8} + \frac{1}{16} + \frac{1}{4} + \frac{1}{2} + \frac{1}{16} = 1$

   $\frac{1}{8} + \frac{2}{16} + \frac{1}{4} + \frac{1}{2} = 1$

3. $\frac{1}{8} + \frac{1}{8} + \frac{1}{2} = 1$

   $\frac{2}{8} + \frac{1}{2} = 1$

4. $\frac{1}{8} + \frac{1}{8} + \frac{1}{2} = 1$

   $\frac{2}{8} + \frac{1}{2} = 1$

5. $\frac{1}{2} + \frac{1}{16} + \frac{1}{16} = 1$

   $\frac{1}{2} + \frac{2}{8} = 1$

▲▲▲▲▲▲**Figure 2–2** *Carol completed the assignment quickly and correctly.*

I began, "For each problem like this, you write the symbol for less than, greater than, or equal to in between the two fractions to make it a true statement. You can use your fraction kit pieces to figure out which sign to write." I wrote the three symbols on the board and reviewed them with the class:

= *is equal to*

> *is greater than*

< *is less than*

I then used a fraction kit to model for the class what to do, explaining as I arranged the pieces. "First I make a train for three-eighths using three of the one-eighth pieces. Below it I make a train that is nine-sixteenths long." I lined up nine of the one-sixteenth pieces. "I can see that the nine-sixteenths train is longer, so I know that nine-sixteenths is greater than three-eighths."

$\frac{1}{8}$		$\frac{1}{8}$		$\frac{1}{8}$				
$\frac{1}{16}$	$\frac{1}{16}$	$\frac{1}{16}$	$\frac{1}{16}$	$\frac{1}{16}$	$\frac{1}{16}$	$\frac{1}{16}$	$\frac{1}{16}$	$\frac{1}{16}$

"Who would like to come to the board and write in the correct sign?" I asked. I waited to see who would volunteer. When about half the students had raised their hands, I called on Carol. She came up and carefully wrote the "less than" sign. "I remember it's this one because less than goes like the letter *L*," she commented.

I then showed the class the worksheet on which I had written ten pairs of fractions for them to compare. "You'll see that there are spaces for two more problems," I said. "Make those up with any fractions you choose and then solve them." The problems students would make up would give me some information about their comfort with fractions.

"There's one more part to this assignment," I said. "When you've solved all of the problems, you have to explain three of them. Who can explain why nine-sixteenths is more than three-eighths?" Only a few students raised their hands. As I usually do when students seem hesitant, I asked the students to talk with their neighbors. I repeated the question before letting them begin talking. When I called the class back to attention, more hands were raised and I called on several students to reply.

Sam explained, "Well, it takes two sixteenths to make one eighth. So that means that you need four sixteenths to make two eighths, and four more to make three eighths." Sam seemed to understand the relationship between eighths and sixteenths, but he made an error in his thinking. After using four sixteenths to make two eighths, it would take only two more to make three eighths.

"How many sixteenths altogether would make three eighths?" I asked him.

Sam replied, "Two and two are four and four more . . . no, no, I mean two more. Wait, I'm mixed up."

Several students' hands went up. "Let's give Sam a chance to think," I said. "He has a good idea and just needs to look at it again. Take your time, Sam, and try again."

"Okay," he said. "It's six."

"Six what?" I probed.

"You need two, four, six of the six-teenths to make three of the eighths," he said, now with certainty.

I pointed to the problem on the board and said, "How does that help you explain this problem? Why is three-eighths less than nine-sixteenths?"

Sam said, "Because three-eighths is six-sixteenths, and nine-sixteenths is more." I nodded and recorded on the board:

$$\frac{3}{8} < \frac{9}{16} \text{ because } \frac{3}{8} = \frac{6}{16} \text{ and } \frac{9}{16} \text{ is more.}$$

"It would be helpful if you also wrote about how you knew that three-eighths is equal to six-sixteenths. Then I'll know more about how you are thinking. Sam, can you explain that part again?"

Sam said, "It takes two sixteenths to make one eighth, so you need four for two eighths and six for three eighths."

"That's good and clear to me," I said, and added to what I had written on the board:

$$\frac{3}{8} < \frac{9}{16} \text{ because } \frac{3}{8} = \frac{6}{16} \text{ and } \frac{9}{16} \text{ is more.}$$
$$\text{It takes } \frac{2}{16} \text{ to make } \frac{1}{8}, \text{ so you need } \frac{4}{16} \text{ for } \frac{2}{8}$$
$$\text{and } \frac{6}{16} \text{ for } \frac{3}{8}.$$

The struggle to get Sam to clarify his thinking was worth the effort, not only for him but for the others to hear.

"I have an easier way to explain," Jennifer said. "Nine-sixteenths is more than one-half and three-eighths is less than one-half." I nodded and wrote:

$$\frac{3}{8} < \frac{9}{16} \text{ because } \frac{9}{16} > \frac{1}{2} \text{ and } \frac{3}{8} < \frac{1}{2}.$$

I then said, "Both of these are fine. On your paper, you need to explain in some way that makes sense to you. If you are having difficulty, talk to a neighbor or ask me for help."

"Do we have to write for all of them?" Dan asked.

"No," I answered. "You have to write 'because' explanations for three of them, and then also for one of the problems you make up." (See Figures 2–3, 2–4, and 2–5 for examples of the work students produced for this activity.)

I then gave directions for *What's Missing?* Although the problems were different, the directions were the same—solve the problems, explain three of them, make up two of your own, and explain one of those. I did an example on the board using fractions that I knew would be easy for the students

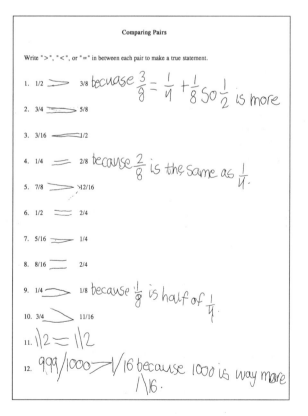

▲▲▲▲▲Figure 2–3 *For one of the problems he made up, Philip compared $\frac{999}{1000}$ to $\frac{1}{16}$.*

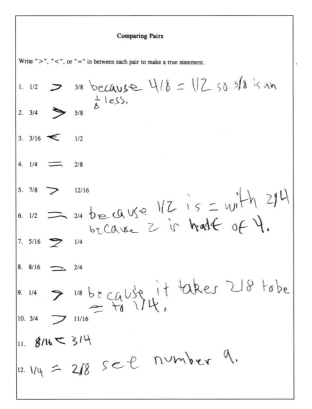

Comparing Pairs

Write ">", "<", or "=" in between each pair to make a true statement.

1. 1/2 > 3/8 because 4/8 = 1/2 so 3/8 is an 1/8 less.
2. 3/4 > 5/8
3. 3/16 < 1/2
4. 1/4 = 2/8
5. 7/8 > 12/16
6. 1/2 = 2/4 because 1/2 is = with 2/4 because 2 is half of 4.
7. 5/16 > 1/4
8. 8/16 = 2/4
9. 1/4 > 1/8 because it takes 2/8 to be = to 1/4.
10. 3/4 > 11/16
11. 8/16 < 3/4
12. 1/4 = 2/8 see number 9.

▲▲▲▲▲▲**Figure 2–4** *George used the same reasoning to explain two of the problems—#9 and #12.*

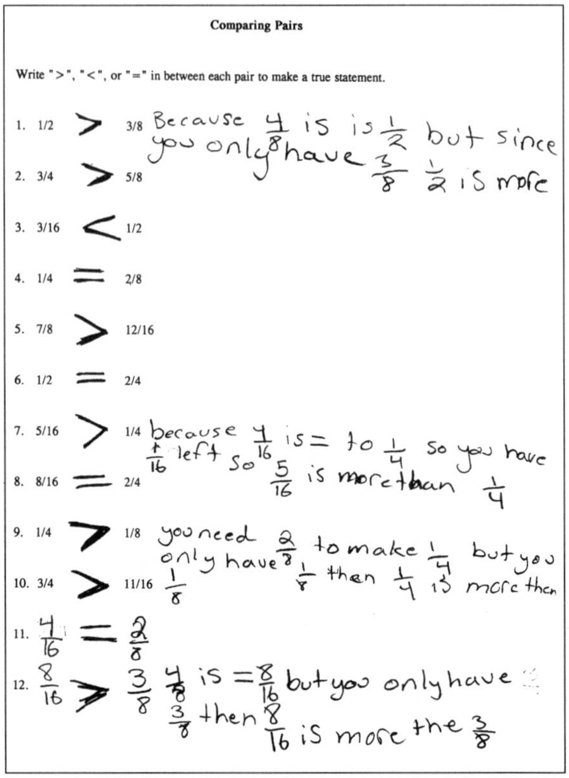

Comparing Pairs

Write ">", "<", or "=" in between each pair to make a true statement.

1. 1/2 > 3/8 Because 4/8 is is 1/2 but since you only have 3/8 1/2 is more
2. 3/4 > 5/8
3. 3/16 < 1/2
4. 1/4 = 2/8
5. 7/8 > 12/16
6. 1/2 = 2/4
7. 5/16 > 1/4 because 4/16 is = to 1/4 so you have 1/16 left so 5/16 is more than 1/4
8. 8/16 = 2/4
9. 1/4 > 1/8 you need 2/8 to make 1/4 but you only have 1/8 then 1/4 is more then
10. 3/4 > 11/16
11. 4/16 = 2/8
12. 8/16 > 3/8 4/8 is = 8/16 but you only have 3/8 then 8/16 is more the 3/8

▲▲▲▲▲▲**Figure 2–5** *Elizabeth wrote clear explanations about how she compared the fractions.*

to think about without the fraction pieces. I wrote:

$$\frac{1}{2} = \frac{\Box}{4}$$

"What number goes in the box to make this statement true?" I asked. Hands flew up and I called on Sarah.

"A two," she said. Then she added, "Should I explain?" I nodded.

"One-fourth is half of a half, so it takes two of them to make one-half." I wrote on the board:

$\frac{1}{2} = \frac{2}{4}$ because $\frac{1}{4}$ is half of $\frac{1}{2}$, so it takes $\frac{2}{4}$ to make $\frac{1}{2}$.

"Does anyone have another way to explain?" I asked. I called on Joey.

"It's kind of the same way," he said.

"Let's hear anyway," I replied.

Joey explained, "One-half is two times one-fourth, so you need two of them." I recorded his idea:

$\frac{1}{2} = \frac{2}{4}$ because $\frac{1}{2}$ is two times $\frac{1}{4}$, so you need $\frac{2}{4}$ to make $\frac{1}{2}$.

I gave one last direction. "Remember to write explanations for three of the problems I put on the worksheets, then also for one of your own." The students got to work and I circulated, observing, answering questions, and keeping students on task. (Figures 2–6 and 2–7 show how two students worked on this activity.)

Challenge Problems

At times at the beginning of class, or when a few minutes remained at the end of a period, I asked the children to close their eyes, visualize their fraction pieces, and answer questions as I posed them. The questions I asked were like the following:

How many eighths are there in one-half?
How many eighths are there in one whole?

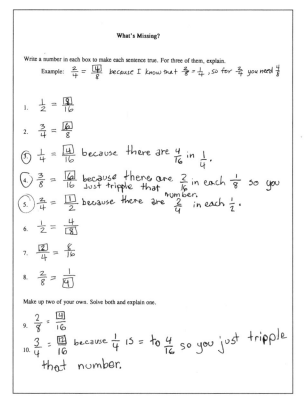

▲▲▲▲▲▲**Figure 2–6** *Marlo was the only student who used the idea of tripling to explain two of the statements.*

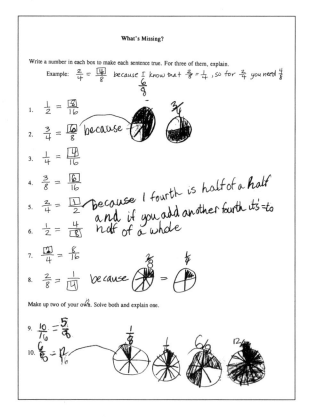

▲▲▲▲▲▲**Figure 2–7** *Ruthie used sketches for three of her four explanations.*

How many eighths are there in three-fourths?
How many sixteenths are there in one-half?
How many sixteenths are there in three-eighths?
How many eighths would be needed to cover two wholes?
How many fourths are in one-half?

Sometimes I would also ask students to explain their reasoning, noting when students didn't rely only on their fraction kits but also on the relationships between numerators and denominators.

For example, one day a few days later, I began class by saying, "Raise your hand if you know how many eighths there are in one-half without having to look at your fraction kit," I said.

"What do you mean?" Robert asked.

"If you were going to cover one of your one-half strips with one-eighth pieces, how many pieces would you need?" I asked. I called on Delia.

"I think it's four," she said.

"Is that a maybe answer or are you sure?" I asked.

"No, I'm sure," Delia said.

"How do you know?" I asked.

"Well, I know that two-eighths make one-fourth, and you need two one-fourths to make one-half, so you need four of the eighths," she said. I wrote on the board:

$$\frac{2}{8} = \frac{1}{4}$$
$$\frac{2}{4} = \frac{1}{2}$$
$$So \ \frac{4}{8} = \frac{1}{2}$$

Delia nodded to indicate she agreed with what I wrote. Davey had a different way to explain. "Eight of the eighths cover the whole strip, so if you cover up half of the strip, then you use only four of them."

"That makes better sense to me," Lily said.

"Does anyone have another way to explain?" I asked. No one volunteered.

"Here's another question," I said. "How many eighths would cover two whole strips?"

"We don't have enough for that," Tom said.

"We could share," Jennifer said.

"How many?" I asked. "Talk about this at your tables." Noisy conversation broke out and after a few moments hands were waving. I called on Joey.

"You'd need sixteen, because you need eight for one strip and then eight more for the other, and eight plus eight is sixteen." I wrote on the board:

$$\frac{8}{8} = 1$$

$$8 + 8 = 2$$

$$\frac{16}{8} = 2$$

"That looks weird," Claudia said.

"What looks weird?" I asked.

"The sixteen over eight," she said. "But I kind of get it."

"Me, too," Sarah said.

"I don't," Carol said.

"Can I explain?" Sam asked. I agreed.

"If you have one whole covered with eighths, then you use all of them, and that's eight," he said. "For two wholes you need eight more. And two eights make sixteen." I wasn't sure if Carol and some others understood, but I knew that they would have other opportunities to encounter this same idea. I continued with the lesson I had planned.

Questions and Discussion

▲▲

▲ *I noticed when I had my students cut their fraction kits that some of their pieces were uneven, and some students tried to trim their pieces to make them all the same size. How would you handle these situations?*

I've had these very things happen. Regarding the unequal pieces, I tell the students, "Measurement is never exact, so it's likely that your pieces won't be exactly the right sizes. There may be some difference, for example, among the sizes of your eighths. That makes it all the more important to think about the fractions and the fractional sizes of the pieces, rather than relying only on the paper pieces you've cut." I try to discourage students who want to be exact, trimming slivers off pieces that seem "off" to them. But even though I explain the futility of trimming, some students insist on doing so, as if their sense of order is somehow being violated by the inconsistencies. Still, I keep the emphasis on talking about the ideas of the fractions, not relying on the pieces alone for proof.

▲ *How do I deal with students who race through the games and don't pay attention to what their partners are doing?*

When I notice that happening, sometimes I talk with the particular pairs and sometimes with the entire class. I explain why they should pay attention to each other's moves. I say, "Not only is it good to check on what your partner does, but I'm trying to slow the game down enough so you also have time to think about the mathematics involved, such as what you'd like to roll next, or how many more rolls you think you'll need to cover your whole, or how much ahead one person is than the other. Remember the game is meant to help you learn about fractions. I want you to enjoy playing, but I also want you to do some thinking." I also reinforce the rules: "No grabbing for the die. Be sure to say 'Done' after you play. Pay attention to each other's pieces."

▲ **When you're observing the students play, how do you decide when to ask them about how much more they need to win, as you did with Andrew when he and Sam were playing and the class was watching?**

Because I'm interested in assessing what students understand, I want to find time to ask all of them. But I try to balance my need to probe their thinking with their need to experience the game, so I tread lightly. As an alternative, I sometimes give a written assignment, just a quick-write, and ask students to respond to questions such as "If I had one-half and one-sixteenth on my board, what would be the fewest rolls possible to cover it completely? What would the rolls be?" A class set of papers would give me a sense of the overall progress of the class as well as information about what individual students understand.

▲ **How do you know when it's a good time for a class discussion or when students need more time to play the game?**

Cover Up isn't very complicated or demanding. As soon as they've all grasped the rules and have had the chance to play five games or so, it's fine to have a discussion. With this class, even though *Cover Up* is a game merely of luck, the children seemed willing to play it more. I observe carefully to be sure that I introduce *Uncover*, which is a more challenging game, before their interest dissipates. *Uncover* invites more thinking, both about strategies for playing and about fractions.

▲ **At the end of the third day, you gave a homework assignment asking students to try the strategies other students had suggested. What if none of those strategies had come up?**

This is a good question and illustrates the benefit of teaching the same lesson to different classes. In another class where none of the students came up with strategies, I told the class about the ideas that students in other classes had had. I wrote on the board:

Possible Strategies for Roll #1

If you don't roll $\frac{1}{2}$, exchange one of the $\frac{1}{2}$ pieces for one of these sets of pieces:

1. $\frac{1}{4}$, $\frac{1}{8}$, $\frac{1}{16}$, and $\frac{1}{16}$
2. $\frac{1}{8}$, $\frac{1}{8}$, $\frac{1}{16}$, $\frac{1}{16}$, $\frac{1}{16}$, and $\frac{1}{16}$
3. $\frac{1}{4}$, $\frac{1}{8}$, and $\frac{1}{8}$

Then I gave the assignment of trying these strategies at home and seeing which they thought was best and why.

CHAPTER THREE
FRACTIONS IN CONTEXTS

Overview

Students develop understanding of the concept of one-half from real-world interactions long before they receive formal instruction about fractions in school. Building on what students already know, this lesson presents various situations and asks students to discuss whether each can best be described by "exactly half," "about half," "less than half," or "more than half." In addition to providing students further opportunities to think about one-half in real-world contexts, the lesson introduces them to estimating with fractions.

Materials

▲ optional: *Fractions in Contexts* worksheet, 1 per pair of students (see Blackline Masters)

▲ optional: *More Fractions in Contexts* worksheet, 1 per pair of students (see Blackline Masters)

▲ optional: *Raquel's Idea* worksheet, 1 per student (see Blackline Masters)

Time

▲ one class period

Teaching Directions

1. Write the following three statements on the board before class, or distribute a copy of them to each pair of students:

When pitching, Joe struck out 7 of 18 batters.
Sally blocked 5 field goals out of 9 attempts.
Of the 35 coins in Dick's bank, 14 were pennies.

2. Read the first statement aloud and ask: "Do you think Joe struck out exactly half, about half, less than half, or more than half of the batters?" Below the statements on the board, write the following, explaining the mathematical symbolism if necessary:

exactly half	$= \frac{1}{2}$
about half	$\approx \frac{1}{2}$
less than half	$< \frac{1}{2}$
more than half	$> \frac{1}{2}$

3. Ask students to explain their reasoning when they answer. Give all students who are interested the opportunity to respond.

4. Then read the second statement and ask: "Did Sally block exactly half, about half, less than half, or more than half of the field goal attempts?" Again, ask students to explain their reasoning when they answer, giving all students who are interested the opportunity to respond.

5. Continue with the third statement, following the same procedure you used for the first two statements.

6. Next ask the class if exactly half, about half, less than half, or more than half of the students are girls.

7. Write three more scenarios on the board or distribute copies for students to discuss in pairs or small groups:

Maria received thirteen birthday cards. Five of them arrived the day after her birthday.
Forty-five students signed up to work on the school paper. Twenty-seven of them were girls.
Twenty-five students in the class have pets. Twelve of them have dogs. Nine have cats. Six have fish.

8. After students have discussed the scenarios, have them present their ideas in a whole-class discussion.

9. Optional: For homework or as an assessment after students have had more experiences with fractions, give students the following problem:

Raquel thought about this statement: *When pitching, Joe struck out 7 of 18 batters.* She said that it was better to say that Joe struck out about one-third of the batters than to say that Joe struck out about one-half of the batters. "I think that seven-eighteenths is closer to one-third than one-half," she said. Do you agree or disagree with Raquel? Explain your reasoning.

Teaching Notes

As much as possible, it's helpful to relate children's study of mathematics to how we use and talk about mathematics outside of school. Not only does this help students see mathematics as useful and related to real-life situations, but it also helps them bring meaning to abstract concepts. This lesson presents students situations in several contexts that are familiar to them and asks that they analyze each to decide if it can best be characterized by "exactly half," "about half," "less than half," or "more than half."

The lesson is useful for introducing students to estimating with fractions and gives them experience with the idea that the precision required for answers to mathematical problems depends on the situation and the purpose for the communication. Also, the class discussions model how we more typically use fractions to communicate. One of the statements, for example, is *Sally blocked 5 field goals out of 9 attempts.* While it would be mathematically precise to state that Sally blocked five-ninths of the field goal attempts, it's more colloquial and may be just as sufficient to claim that she blocked more than half of the attempts.

The vignette that follows describes how I used the lesson to launch the study of fractions in a fifth-grade class. The lesson was a successful first fraction experience with these fifth graders, and I've had similar success presenting the lesson in the same way to fourth graders. I've also used the lesson with both fourth and fifth graders following other introductory experiences. The lesson is good preparation for the lessons in the "One-Half as a Benchmark" section.

The Lesson

▲▲

This was the initial lesson I taught to this particular class of fifth graders to launch instruction on fractions. I was interested in getting a sense of their understanding about and comfort with fraction concepts and also in introducing the idea of one-half as a benchmark for comparing fractions. When beginning to teach a new topic, I find it useful to do a general class assessment. I know that this isn't sufficient to give me information about what individual students know, but it's helpful for deciding on the direction to take for further instruction.

Before class began, I wrote three statements on the board:

> *When pitching, Joe struck out 7 of 18 batters.*
> *Sally blocked 5 field goals out of 9 attempts.*
> *Of the 35 coins in Dick's bank, 14 were pennies.*

I read the first statement aloud and asked the class, "Do you think Joe struck out exactly half, about half, less than half, or more than half of the pitchers?" Below the statements on the board, I wrote:

exactly half $\qquad = \frac{1}{2}$

about half $\qquad \approx \frac{1}{2}$

less than half $\qquad < \frac{1}{2}$

more than half $\qquad > \frac{1}{2}$

The "about" sign was new for the students. "It means 'is approximately equal to' and tells you that the answer is an 'about' number, not necessarily exact," I said.

As I always do in discussions like this, I asked students to explain their reasoning when they responded. I called on Paul first. He said, "It's less than half because seven and seven is fourteen, and that's less than eighteen."

Sophia said, "I think the same as Paul, but I used multiplication and did seven times two. That's fourteen, and it's smaller than eighteen."

Marika said, "Nine is half of eighteen, and seven isn't enough."

Emmy thought that "about half" was a better estimate. She was the only student who thought this. "It's pretty close because it's just two off from being exactly half," she said.

Noah thought that "less than half" made better sense. "But I did it with subtraction," he said. "I did seven take away eighteen and that's eleven and that's more." I didn't correct Noah's incorrect use of language ("seven take away eighteen"). Nor did I probe his thinking, although I was curious to hear more from him. However, I hadn't questioned Paul, Sophia, Marika, or Emmy about their ideas and didn't want to single out Noah. In this situation, I chose just to listen to students and form some initial impressions about what they did and didn't know about fractions.

After several other students expressed ideas that were similar to the ones already offered, I moved on to the next statement: *Sally blocked 5 field goals out of 9 attempts.*

Alma said, "It's more than half, because it would have to be ten tries to be half."

"I think it's just about half, because five is about half of nine," Josh said.

Sally looked at the situation from a different perspective. "Her father would definitely say she made more than half. He'd want to support her."

Chris, however, expressed a more numerically precise thought. He said, "You can't take half of nine because it's an odd number."

"Yes, you can," Raquel responded. "You can take half of any number. The answer is just in the middle."

"What is half of nine?" I asked.

"It's four and a half," Eli said. "I agree with Raquel that you can always take half of any number."

"But you can't count half of nine goals," Daniel argued. "That doesn't make any sense."

"Well, you should be able to take half of anything," Raquel insisted.

I offered my perspective on this. "Can you divide nine apples in half?" I asked. Most of the students nodded.

"Half of nine apples is four and a half apples," Ali said.

"What about nine balloons?" I asked. The students laughed.

"You'd wreck a balloon," Eli said.

"It would be stupid," Sally added.

"There are things that make sense to divide in half and things that don't," I said. "Things we do when we think about numbers don't always make sense when you think about them in real-life situations. It's important that we pay attention to how we use fractions as we learn about them."

Raquel's next comment shifted the direction of the conversation and surprised me. "I have something to say about the first sentence with seven out of eighteen," she said. "I think it's closer to one-third than one-half."

"Why do you think that?" I asked.

Raquel explained, "Because you can divide eighteen into thirds—six plus six plus six. And seven is just one away from six. But it's two away from nine, which is half. So it's closer to one-third than one-half."

"So if I had 'about one-third' on the list, you would have chosen that for the first statement," I said to Raquel. I made a mental note to mention Raquel's idea the next time I tried this lesson and see if it sparked ideas from any of the students. I'm always looking for ways to make whole-class lessons interesting to the more able thinkers while also being accessible to those with less experience. Raquel's question was a good way to do that in the future.

I then went on to the third statement: *Of the 35 coins in Dick's bank, 14 were pennies.* It seemed clear to most of the students that "less than half" was the best descriptor for the amount of coins that were pennies. The students' explanations were similar to the ones they gave for the other statements.

Raquel surprised me again with an observation. "I think that fourteen is two-fifths of thirty-five," she said. "Look, two sevens make fourteen, and three sevens make twenty-one, and fourteen plus twenty-one is thirty-five, so fourteen is two-fifths."

I thought for a moment about Raquel's reasoning. None of the other students, however, seemed interested. "I hadn't thought about that before, Raquel, but I agree with you," I said, to acknowledge her contribution. I didn't pursue it further and shifted the conversation.

"Who knows how many students there are in the class?" I asked. Many hands shot up.

"Let's say the number quietly together," I said, a technique I use when it seems that most children know an answer. There was a quiet chorus, "Twenty-five."

"Are exactly half, about half, less than half, or more than half of the students girls?" I asked, pointing to each descriptor on the board as I said it. As I suspected they would, most of the students stood up and began counting heads. This was fine with me, as the discussion had been going for almost half an hour and some students needed the chance to move a bit. A noisy argument erupted about how many girls and boys there were. Tess settled the argument by taking a class list and counting the names of girls.

"There are thirteen girls," she said, with a tone of authority.

"So that's about half," Noah said.

"It's just a little more than half," Katy said.

THREE MORE STATEMENTS

I quieted the class and told them what they were to do next. "I'm going to write three more situations on the board. Before we discuss them as a whole class, I'd like you to talk with a partner about them. For each, use the information to draw a conclusion using 'exactly half,' 'about half,' 'less than half,' or 'more than half.'" I wrote the statements on the board:

Maria received thirteen birthday cards. Five of them arrived the day after her birthday.

Forty-five students signed up to work on the school paper. Twenty-seven of them were girls.

Twenty-five students in the class have pets. Twelve of them have dogs. Nine have cats. Six have fish.

The students only needed about five minutes to talk about these statements. Having them talk in pairs not only gave more of them the chance to verbalize their ideas, but it also changed the pace of the lesson. I found with this class that the students' attention would wander if a class discussion went on too long. They would begin to drift off and stop attending to what was being said.

It was easy for the students to analyze the three situations, and when I called them back to attention, most were interested in reporting. Katy went first. "Maria received more than half of her birthday cards on her birthday," she said. That initially surprised some of the others, who had focused on the cards she had received the day after her birthday. Tess, for example, had concluded that Maria had received less than half of her birthday cards a day late.

For the next situation, Eli said, "More than half of the students who signed up for the paper were girls." Because the numbers were larger here, I took the opportunity to ask Eli how he had figured.

"I know that half of fifty is twenty-five, so twenty-seven had to be more than half of forty-five," Eli said.

Daniel had figured differently. "Half of forty is twenty," he said. "And half of five is two and a half, so twenty-two and a half people is less than twenty-seven girls." Others giggled at his use of "half" when referring to people. Daniel grinned, pleased with his mathematical "joke."

Emmy had another way to report. "Twenty-seven and twenty-seven add up to fifty-four," she began. "I know that because twenty plus twenty is forty and seven plus seven is fourteen and forty plus fourteen is fifty-four. So twenty-seven is more than half."

The discussion for the last situation went similarly.

EXTENSION/ASSESSMENT

Since this was my initial fraction lesson with this class, I didn't follow up on Raquel's comment about seven-eighteenths being closer to one-third than to one-half. Since then I've tried raising the question of whether seven-eighteenths is closer to one-third than to one-half in other classes, sometimes in the course of this first lesson and other times later, after students have had more experience with fractions. After using it in several situations, my preference is to wait a few weeks or so after teaching the lesson until the students have had more experiences with fractions. Then I open a class discussion with Raquel's question and have students write about it, either for homework or a class assignment. I wrote the following and duplicated copies for each student:

> *Raquel thought about this statement:* When pitching, Joe struck out 7 of 18 batters. *She said that it was better to say that Joe struck out about $\frac{1}{3}$ of the batters than to say that Joe struck out about $\frac{1}{2}$ of the batters. "I think that seven-eighteenths is closer to one-third than one-half," she said. Do you agree or disagree with Raquel? Explain your reasoning.*

When trying this in one class, I reminded the students about the previous lesson. I asked, "Do you remember when we discussed the statements about Joe striking out batters, Sally blocking field goals, and Dick collecting coins?" The students recalled the lesson and some remembered the exact numbers in the statements.

"I have a problem that I'd like you to consider about one of the statements," I said. I wrote on the board:

> *When pitching, Joe struck out 7 of 18 batters.*

"It was less than half," Bruce said.

"That was the most common conclusion when we discussed it," I said. "But in another class, Raquel, one of the students, had a different idea. She thought that seven-eighteenths was closer to one-third than to one-half."

The students were quiet for a moment. A few students raised their hands, but most didn't. Rather than call on those who had ideas, I said to the class, "Talk at your tables about this problem. Then we'll discuss it as a class."

The room got noisy as children put their heads together and talked. Conversations were animated at all but two tables, and I visited with each of those. At one, I just needed to prod the students to talk together, not think alone. At the other, I spent a few moments explaining the problem again to get them started. George, who was sitting at that table, finally said, "Oh, I get it," and he started the group conversation. When I called the class back to attention, several from each group held up hands, eager to respond. I called on Elizabeth.

She said, "We figured out that one-third of eighteen was six. So seven is one away. But nine is half of eighteen, and seven is two away." Reactions from some of the other students indicated that they hadn't followed Elizabeth's reasoning.

I said, "Let's back up and I'll write on the board what you're saying. Can you start again, Elizabeth?"

Elizabeth began again. "First we thought out that one-third of eighteen was six. We knew we were right because we did eighteen minus six and got twelve and twelve minus six is six, and there's six left. So six is one-third of eighteen and nine is one-half of eighteen, so seven is closer to six than to nine." I wrote on the board:

$\frac{1}{3}$ *of 18 = 6*

18 − 6 = 12

12 − 6 = 6

6 is $\frac{1}{3}$ of 18

9 is $\frac{1}{2}$ of 18

7 is closer to 6 than to 9

"Do you agree or disagree with Raquel?" I asked.

"Agree," answered Elizabeth, Bruce, Stanley, and Margaret in unison, all seated at the table together.

Theresa's hand shot up. "I disagree," she said.

"Tell us what you're thinking," I said.

Theresa said, "If you take seven plus seven plus seven, you get twenty-one, and eighteen plus three is twenty-one. But seven plus two is nine, and that's half of eighteen." I hadn't followed Theresa's reasoning. As I did with Elizabeth, I asked her to repeat what she said so I could write it on the board. I wrote:

$$7 + 7 + 7 = 21$$
$$18 + 3 = 21$$
$$7 + 2 = 9$$
$$9 \text{ is } \tfrac{1}{2} \text{ of } 18$$

I stood back and looked at what I had written. "Everything you said is true, " I said. "But I'm having difficulty understanding why that convinces you that Raquel is wrong."

Beth raised a hand. She was seated at a different table but thought she could help. She said, "If seven is one-third, then three sevens make twenty-one. But there were only eighteen batters and you'd need three more to get twenty-one. I agree with Theresa."

Sally had a counterargument. "Raquel said that seven was about one-third, so we wanted to find out what was *exactly* one-third of eighteen. I don't know why you are thinking about twenty-one. That's not even in the problem."

George entered the conversation. "I agree with Raquel because seven is less than half because nine and nine is eighteen and he only struck out seven. And one-third is less than half, so I think one-third is right."

Greg offered his idea. "It was almost close to one-half, but it was two less than one-half. I think that 'almost one-half' would be another choice."

Hannah raised a hand tentatively. "I'm not sure. I kind of agree with Elizabeth and I kind of agree with Theresa. I think they both can be right."

Encouraged by Hannah's comment, Lena offered, "I agree with everyone's idea. Either way it makes sense. But I think it's more on the side of being about a third of eighteen. It's closer because seven batters are farther from a half by two batters. It's only one up from six batters." Then Lena added, "I don't get how he could strike out seven batters. You can only strike out three batters in an inning."

The class got quiet. Then Jack spoke up. "That's right, but the problem doesn't say he did it in one inning. It could be a couple of innings." Lena agreed that this was possible.

Nicholas spoke next. "I thought that both Elizabeth's and Theresa's answers could work out. Theresa just looked at the problem in a different way. But now I think that Raquel is right because seven is closer to one-third than one-half, and she did say 'about one-third.'"

Theresa had been thinking and now waved her hand. "I changed my mind," she began and then added after a pause, "I think." She went on to explain. "If Joe hadn't struck out one batter, then he would have struck out exactly one-third. I think it's closer to one-third."

I ended the discussion and said to the class, "Now I'd like each of you to write about whether you agree or disagree with Raquel and explain your reasoning. That will help me understand how each of you thinks. If you're still confused about the problem, then tell me that on your paper but also explain what you understand so far. The more I know about your thinking, the better I can help you learn."

"Can we work together?" Charlotte asked.

"Yes," I replied. "But you each have to write your own paper. Remember, what's important is that you understand what you write and can explain it to someone else." I distributed a copy of the problem to each student and they got to work. (Figures 3–1 through 3–5 show how some students explained their thinking.)

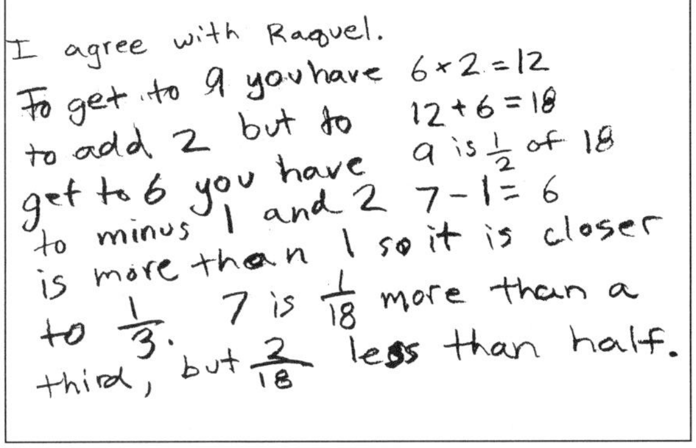

I agree with Raquel.
To get to 9 you have 6×2=12
to add 2 but to 12+6=18
get to 6 you have 9 is ½ of 18
to minus 1 and 2 7-1=6
is more than 1 so it is closer
to ⅓. 7 is 1/18 more than a
third, but 2/18 less than half.

▲▲▲▲▲▲**Figure 3–1** *Amy was the only student who indicated that 7 was $\frac{1}{18}$ more than $\frac{1}{3}$ but $\frac{2}{18}$ less than $\frac{1}{2}$.*

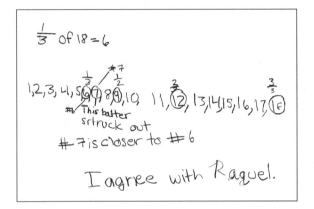

⅓ of 18 = 6

1,2,3,4,5,6,7,8,9,10, 11,12, 13,14,15,16,17,18
#6 This batter
strruck out
7 is closer to # 6

I agree with Raquel.

▲▲▲▲▲▲**Figure 3–2** *Sally thought about the problem by making a long line of color tiles using 6 red, 6 blue, and 6 yellow. On her paper, she recorded her thinking numerically.*

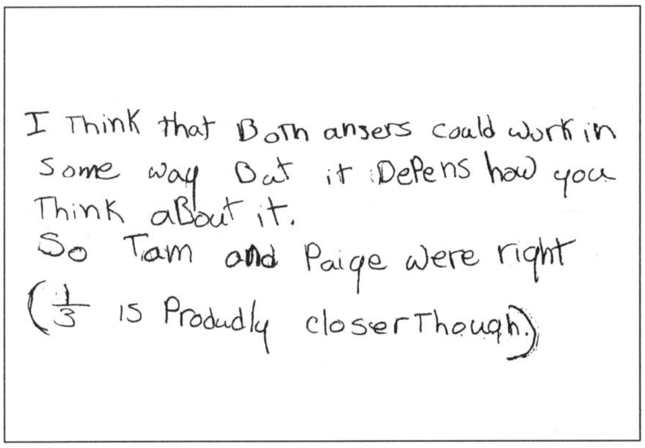

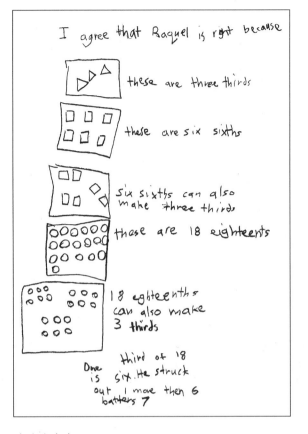

I agree that Raquel is right because

these are three thirds

these are six sixths

six sixths can also make three thirds

these are 18 eighteents

18 eighteenths can also make 3 thirds

One third of 18 is six. He struck out 1 more then 6 batters 7

▲▲▲▲▲▲**Figure 3–4** *Lawrence is most comfortable when he can "see" ideas, and he worked his way through the problem by drawing pictures.*

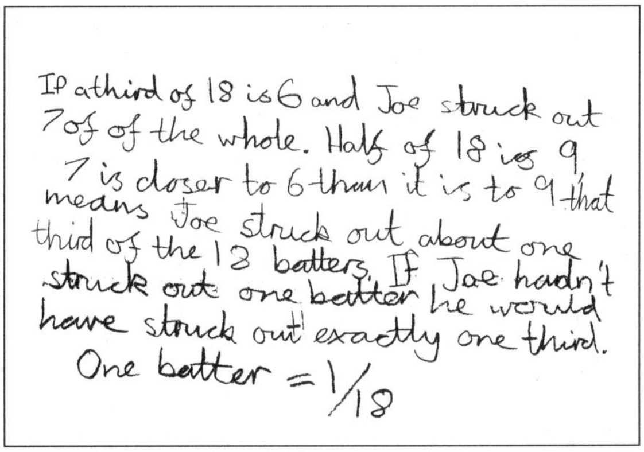

I Think that Both ansers could work in some way but it Depens how you Think about it.
So Tam and Paige were right
(⅓ is Probally closerThough.)

▲▲▲▲▲▲**Figure 3–3** *Beth's paper shows her uncertainty.*

If a third of 18 is 6 and Joe struck out 7 of of the whole. Half of 18 ies 9 7 is closer to 6 than it is to 9 that means Joe struck out about one third of the 12 batters. If Joe hadn't struck out one better he would have struck out exactly one third.
One better = 1/18

▲▲▲▲▲▲**Figure 3–5** *Theresa's paper shows how she changed her mind.*

Questions and Discussion

▲▲

▲ *If students disagree about how to classify a statement, how do you resolve the disagreement?*

My response depends on the situation. For some statements, more than one description can fit and, therefore, it isn't necessary to resolve differences in opinion. What's important is that students can justify the choices they make and explain their reasoning to the class. When a student response is clearly wrong and a student remains confused, I do my best to explain. However, in an introductory lesson such as this one, my goal is to gain information about children's knowledge and comfort with thinking about one-half.

▲ *Raquel seemed to be so much more advanced than the other students. At least, she would be advanced in my class. How did you meet her needs?*

At all times in the classroom, I strive to find activities that are accessible to all children while also having the potential to challenge students like Raquel, who think quickly and learn easily. Also, I try to think of extensions and challenges for activities that I present so that I can keep more able students involved and interested.

▲ *Why did you allow the children to work together if you were using the assignment as an assessment?*

I realized from the class discussion that only a few of the students were volunteering to participate. Others looked and listened but remained quiet. Some seemed confused. If more of the students had appeared confident, then I would have asked them not to work together. But with this class, giving them the assignment to do without any support didn't make sense to me. Even if they talked with one another, I felt that I could learn from their papers about what they understood. And by keeping their papers and giving the assignment again in a few months, this time asking them to work individually, I could measure individual students' progress.

CHAPTER FOUR
EXPLORING FRACTIONS WITH PATTERN BLOCKS

Overview

In this lesson, pattern blocks are used to offer students a way to think about halves, thirds, and sixths through comparing shapes and their areas. Students first look for all the different ways to construct a yellow hexagon using other pattern block pieces, a spatial problem-solving experience that also engages their logical reasoning skills. After solving the problem, they represent their solutions using fractional notation. Finally, they learn to play a game using the same pieces. Along with teaching them about fractions, the lesson builds students' familiarity with geometric shapes.

Materials

▲ pattern blocks, 1 bucket per group of three to four students
▲ fraction dice made from labeling the faces of cubes $\frac{1}{2}$, $\frac{1}{3}$, $\frac{1}{3}$, $\frac{1}{6}$, $\frac{1}{6}$, and $\frac{1}{6}$, 1 per pair of students
▲ rules for the game of *Wipeout* (see Blackline Masters)

Time

▲ two class periods

Teaching Directions

1. Organize students into small groups and distribute pattern blocks. If students have not had any prior experience with the blocks, provide time for them to explore the blocks. Talk with the students about the names of the pieces and list them on the board:

triangle
square
parallelogram or rhombus
trapezoid
hexagon

2. Pose the problem:

> *Use different combinations of pattern blocks to build hexagons that are the same size and shape as the yellow hexagon pattern block. Try to find all the possible ways.*

Offer one caution: "Don't count a different arrangement of the same pattern blocks as a different way. Look for different combinations of blocks."

3. Give students time to build the shapes. As you circulate, if you notice that a group has built duplicates, tell the group that some of its shapes are the same, but don't point out which ones they are. Instead, give the students the challenge of spotting them. Also, don't tell groups that there are seven different ways to build a shape congruent to the yellow hexagon. (If you count the hexagon as well, then there are eight ways.) Having the students try to figure out when they've found them all adds a logical reasoning dimension to the problem.

4. Stop the class when at least several groups have solved the problem. Ask students to describe solutions and record them on the board. For each, have other groups check that they built that arrangement and, if not, build it now.

> *2 red trapezoids*
> *6 green triangles*
> *3 blue rhombuses*
> *1 yellow hexagon*
> *1 red trapezoid, 1 blue rhombus, 1 green triangle*
> *1 red trapezoid, 3 green triangles*
> *2 blue rhombuses, 2 green triangles*
> *1 blue rhombus, 4 green triangles*

5. Model for the class how to describe one of the ways with fractions. For example, next to "2 red trapezoids" write: $\frac{1}{2} + \frac{1}{2} = 1$. Ask: "Who can explain why this describes a hexagon made from two trapezoids?" Emphasize that this representation assumes that the hexagon is worth one whole. Shorten the sentence: $\frac{2}{2} = 1$. If they have already done *Cover the Whole* with fraction kits (see page 22), remind them that changing $\frac{1}{2} + \frac{1}{2}$ to $\frac{2}{2}$ is like what they did when they shortened sentences.

6. Give the directions for an individual assignment: "Represent each of the ways you built the hexagon with fractions, first recording each block with a fraction and then combining fractions where possible." If you think it's needed, model representing another combination—one red trapezoid, one blue rhombus, and one green triangle. This introduces the fractions used for the other blocks.

7. The next day, continue students' experience with pattern blocks by teaching them how to play the game of *Wipeout*. (See Blackline Masters.) The game is similar to *Uncover*, a game they may have already learned to play with their fraction kits.

Teaching Notes

This lesson gives students practice with connecting fractional notation to a concrete experience.

The Lesson

▲▲

DAY 1

All of the students were familiar with the pattern blocks and eager to have the chance to work with them again. I began class by reviewing the names of the shapes.

I held up a yellow hexagon and said, "Raise your hand if you know the name of this shape." I looked around to notice who raised a hand. Most did. "Let's say the name together in a whisper voice," I said. I wrote *hexagon* on the board.

"What about this shape?" I asked, holding up a red trapezoid. "Raise your hand if you know its name." Fewer hands went up.

"Here's a clue," I said, writing *tr* on the board. More hands shot up. Again, I asked for them to whisper the name. I wrote *trapezoid* on the board.

Trent raised a hand. "I know another name," he said. "It's a quadrilateral."

"Yes," I acknowledged. "Quadrilateral is a name for a shape that has four sides." I then held up a blue rhombus. This time when the class whispered, I heard three different names. Some said, "Rhombus." Some said, "Diamond." Trent said, in a very loud whisper, "Quadrilateral." I wrote the three names on the board.

"I know another name," I said. As I started to write *parallelogram* on the board, several children guessed what the word was.

Margaret had a comment. "I call it a diamond because it's easier to remember."

"That's fine," I said. "But it's also important that you know the other names as well."

After I had listed *triangle* and *square*, and pointed out that the tan block was another version of the blue block, I posed the problem to the class and explained how they were to work. "For this problem, you are to find different ways to put blocks

together and build hexagons that are exactly the same size and shape as the yellow hexagon." I held up two trapezoids and showed the class how they fit together to make a hexagon.

"As you find ways, build them on your table so that I can see which ones you've found. Don't stack them up, because then I won't be able to see what combinations of blocks you used."

"Do we each do our own?" Jonathan asked.

"No," I said. "The task is for your group to find them all. If you find a way on your own, set it in the middle of the table and check to be sure it's not a duplicate. Also, talk about how you know for sure you think that you've found them all." The students were ready to get started, but I gave them one more direction before I distributed the blocks.

"Don't count a different arrangement of the same pattern blocks as a different way. Each way you find should use a different combination of blocks."

I asked for a volunteer to explain what they were to do. Marlo volunteered and did a good job. I then distributed the blocks and the students got to work.

As I circulated, at times I noticed duplicates on a table. In these cases, I would say, "I can see two that are the same." Then I'd leave it to the students to find the match. Also, I had to remind a few tables that once they had used two blue rhombuses and two green triangles, they couldn't use this combination of blocks again even if they arranged them differently.

After about ten minutes, I called the class to order. I said, "Put all of the blocks that you haven't used to build hexagons back in the container and set the container aside." I knew that some groups would need blocks to build shapes they had missed, but I didn't want extra blocks on the table to distract them.

Once the students had done this and were again quiet, I commented, "I noticed that you all built hexagons with red, blue, and green blocks, but not the orange squares or tan rhombuses."

"I tried but they didn't work," Frank said.

"Me, too," Philip added.

"Can you do it?" Marlo asked.

"No," I said, "the angles on those blocks don't cooperate very well, and they won't fit together to make the yellow hexagon."

"I made another hexagon with them," Trent said, holding up two tan rhombuses.

"Yes, that shape has six sides and that makes it a hexagon," I said. "But it's not the same shape hexagon as the yellow block." Some reached for blocks to build what Trent did, but I called them back to attention to explain what we were going to do next.

"I'm going to go around the room and give each group a chance to describe one way you built the hexagon," I said. "I'll record on the board. When it's your group's turn, you have to identify a way that I haven't already recorded. Also, when I write a way on the board, check to be sure you also built it."

Drew reported first for his table. "One hexagon," he said with a grin.

"Yes, that's one way," I responded and wrote on the board:

1 yellow hexagon

Cindy went next. "One red, one blue, and one green," she said. I asked her for the names of the shapes as well as the colors. As she gave them, I recorded on the board:

1 red trapezoid, 1 blue rhombus, 1 green triangle

I continued going around the room until I had listed all eight possibilities:

1 yellow hexagon

1 red trapezoid, 1 blue rhombus, 1 green triangle

2 red trapezoids

6 green triangles

3 blue rhombuses

1 red trapezoid, 3 green triangles

2 blue rhombuses, 2 green triangles

1 blue rhombus, 4 green triangles

I then said, "Watch as I write a mathematical sentence on the board and raise your hand when you think you know which of the arrangements the sentence describes." I wrote on the board:

$\frac{1}{2} + \frac{1}{2} = 1$

About half of the students raised their hands. After waiting to see if any other students would also respond, I called on Diego. "It's two trapezoids because they both equal one-half and that makes a whole," he said.

"You're right," I said. "That's the one I was describing. Who knows how to combine the fractions to shorten the sentence?" I called on Ruthie.

"You could write 'two-halves equals one whole,'" she said. I recorded on the board:

$\frac{2}{2} = 1$

"Show a thumb up if you understand why these sentences describe the hexagon built from two trapezoids or a thumb down if you're confused or not sure," I said. About a quarter of the class showed thumbs down, so I gave another example. This time I wrote on the board:

$\frac{1}{3} + \frac{1}{3} + \frac{1}{6} + \frac{1}{6} = 1$

I called on Cynthia, who was waving her hand enthusiastically. However, once she had the floor, she got flustered. After a few false starts, she turned to Jonathan, who was sitting next to her. "I think Jonathan knows," she said.

I looked at Jonathan and he indicated that he was willing to explain. "It's the one with two triangles and two rhombuses," he said. "It works because the triangles are sixths since six of them make a hexagon and three rhombuses make a whole so rhombuses have to make a third."

Cara raised a hand. "You could change that to two-thirds plus two-sixths," she said. I nodded and wrote on the board:

$\frac{2}{3} + \frac{2}{6} = 1$

I then said to the class, "On a sheet of binder paper, list all of the ways you built the hexagon, and next to each one write a fraction sentence that describes what you built. And then shorten each fraction sentence if you can." (Figures 4–1 and 4–2 show how two students worked on this assignment.)

The students got to work. It took some effort to keep them all on task. The pattern blocks are very intriguing to the students. But by the end of class, all of them had managed to record sentences for each of the hexagon arrangements. I told students who finished early that they could continue exploring with the blocks.

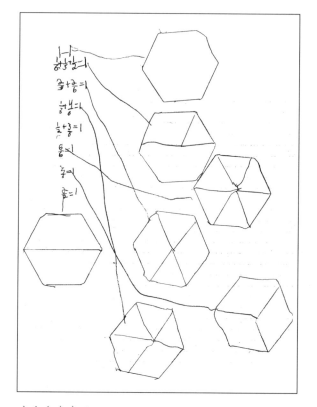

▲▲▲▲▲▲**Figure 4–1** *Diego traced the pattern block pieces to show the hexagons he recorded.*

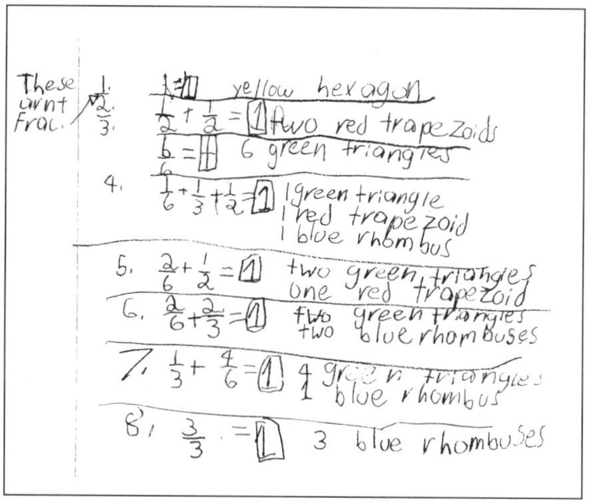

[Figure 4–2 content, handwritten student work:]

```
These          1. [1]  yellow hexagon
arn't      1/2·2/3
Frac.          2. 1/2 + 1/2 = [1] two red trapezoids
               3. 6/6 = [1]  6 green triangles
          4.
             1/6 + 1/3 + 1/2 = [1]  1 green triangle
                                     1 red trapezoid
                                     1 blue rhombus
          5.  2/6 + 1/2 = [1]  two green triangles
                                one red trapezoid
          6.  2/6 + 2/3 = [1]  two green triangles
                                two blue rhombuses
          7.  1/3 + 4/6 = [1]  4 green triangles
                                1 blue rhombus
          8.  3/3 = [1]  3 blue rhombuses
```

▲▲▲▲▲▲**Figure 4–2** *Drew indicated that the sentence describing the yellow hexagon didn't use fractions.*

DAY 2

The next day I again used the pattern blocks, this time introducing a game to the students that would give them experience thinking about halves, thirds, sixths, and the relationships among them.

"Today you'll learn to play the game of *Wipeout*," I told the students. "It's a game for two players that is similar to the game of *Uncover* that you played with your fraction kits, but you play this game with pattern blocks."

I asked for a volunteer to play with me while the others watched. Most of the class was interested, and I chose Nickie. She joined me at the front of the room and the others gathered around to watch.

"The idea of this game is to be the first to get rid of your blocks," I said. "When one person wipes them all out, the game is over. To start, each of us takes one, two, or three hexagons. We can decide how many to use, but we both have to take the same number." I asked Nickie, "How many should we play with?"

She thought for a moment and then said, "Two."

"Okay," I said. "Let's each take two yellow hexagons."

Exploring Fractions with Pattern Blocks   43

I then showed them one of the dice I had prepared. "These have different fractions on them than the dice we used for the fraction kit games," I explained. I read off the fractions on the faces, "There's one one-half, two one-thirds, and three one-sixths."

As the children generally did before playing *Cover Up* or *Uncover,* Nickie and I each rolled the die to see who got the larger fraction and would go first. I did, and I explained the rules as I took my turn.

"On your turn, you roll the die and then you have one of three choices," I said. I rolled the die and got one-third.

"Which block is worth one-third?" I asked the class.

"The rhombus," several answered.

"Here are my three choices," I continued. "I could remove a rhombus, make an exchange that's equivalent, or do nothing. I can't remove a rhombus since I don't have one, so I think I'll exchange. Nickie, you have to watch what I do and see if you agree."

"Oh, I get it," Cynthia said. "It's the same as *Uncover.*"

I exchanged both of my hexagons, one for a trapezoid, a rhombus, and a triangle, and the other for two rhombuses and two triangles.

"Is that okay with you?" I asked Nickie. She nodded. I then passed the die to her and she took her turn.

Since the rules were familiar to the students, after we each took two turns, I organized the students to play with partners. The playing went smoothly and the students were engaged. From their play, they began to internalize the relationships among the fractions, that one-half is one-sixth more than one-third, that one-third is equivalent to two-sixths, that two-thirds is equivalent to four-sixths, and so on. (See Figure 4–3.)

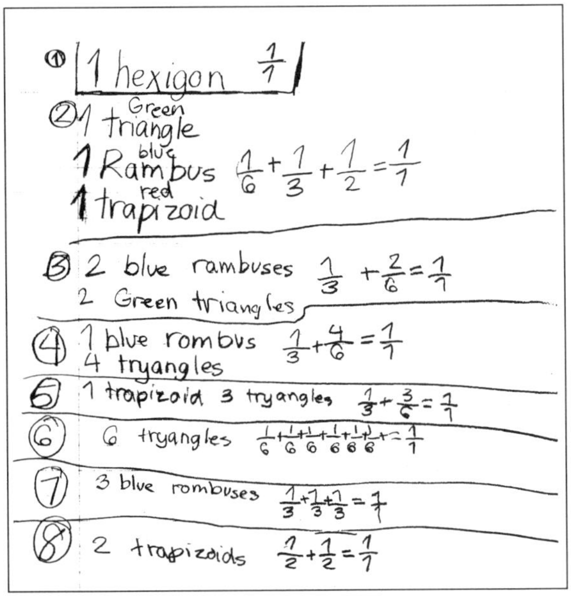

▲▲▲▲▲▲**Figure 4–3** *Cara's spelling was inconsistent, but her mathematical representations were correct.*

Questions and Discussion

▲▲

▲ *If my students haven't had a good deal of experience with pattern blocks, what's a good beginning activity?*

Ask the students to explore the blocks and figure out how many different colors and shapes there are. Also, ask them if they can "tile" their desktops with the blocks, fitting them together so that they cover the surface. After students have had time to do this, have a discussion about what they noticed about the blocks. Record what they report on a chart and add to it as students make other discoveries.

▲ *It's hard for me to get the class to stop playing with the blocks and attend to problems. What can I do?*

Try giving the class a short amount of time at the beginning of class for free exploration. Tell them the amount of time you'll give for this. You might want to set a kitchen timer and tell them when it rings that they have to stop their own explorations and attend to the problem you have for them to solve. Also, giving a one-minute warning before you stop them can help.

CHAPTER FIVE
DRAWING FRACTIONAL PARTS OF SETS

Overview

This lesson provides students practice representing fractions by making sketches. It's more typical to provide children experience with dividing circles, squares, and rectangles into fractional parts, but it's also important to provide them experience representing fractional parts of sets of objects. This lesson asks children to illustrate several statements about fractions. The activity also provides students experience with equivalent fractions.

Materials

▲ *Drawing Pictures for Fractions* worksheet, 1 per student (see Blackline Masters)

Time

▲ one to two class periods

Teaching Directions

1. Write on the board: $\frac{1}{2}$ *of the squares have an X in them.*

2. Ask: "Who thinks he or she can draw something on the board to illustrate this statement?" Have a child come up and draw and then ask the others to show their agreement, disagreement, or confusion with thumbs up, down, or sideways. Ask the student who drew to explain. Repeat with students who have other ideas about how to illustrate the statement.

3. Repeat for another statement: $\frac{3}{4}$ *of the circles have an X in them.*

4. Repeat again: $\frac{3}{5}$ *of the triangles are shaded in.*

5. Distribute *Drawing Pictures for Fractions* worksheets for an individual assignment.

Teaching Notes

A particular benefit of this activity is that there are many ways to represent each of the statements that children are asked to consider. For example, it's possible to draw different numbers of squares to illustrate the statement $\frac{1}{2}$ *of the squares have an X in them.* After one student draws and explains, having others provide different interpretations builds understanding of equivalent fractions. When one student puts Xs in four of eight squares and another in three of six squares—both valid solutions—it illustrates the statement while also showing that one-half can be represented as four-eighths and three-sixths. Children need many experiences to understand how different fractions can represent the same fractional parts.

While it's not essential, this lesson is best done after students have experienced the *Fractions as Parts of Sets* lesson (see pages 1–9).

The Lesson

▲▲▲

I began class by writing on the board:

$\frac{1}{2}$ *of the squares have an X in them.*

"Who would like to draw something on the board to illustrate this statement?" I asked the class. More than half of the students volunteered and I called on Cynthia. She came to the board and drew the following:

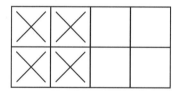

I asked the others to show with their thumbs if they agreed, disagreed, or weren't sure. Most students agreed, but several indicated they either disagreed or weren't sure. I asked Cynthia to explain.

She said, "I drew eight boxes and half of them have Xs. I split them in four and four and put Xs in four of them." I asked the class to again show thumbs. No one indicated that he or she disagreed, but some still held their thumbs sideways to show their confusion.

"Can someone explain in a different way and see if that helps make it clear?" I asked. I called on Cara.

"Normally you see it as one square and you cut it in half," she said. "But since she drew eight squares . . . . " Cara paused and then said, "I'll start again. There are eight squares and four plus four is eight, so Cynthia put Xs in four of them because that's half." I wrote on the board:

There are eight squares.
4 + 4 = 8
4 is $\frac{1}{2}$ of 8

Trent raised a hand to explain. His explanation was essentially the same as Cara's. He said, "She drew eight boxes. One-half of eight is four, so she drew Xs in four of the eight squares so that half of the squares would have Xs."

Margaret also volunteered. "Draw the eight squares up and down instead of sideways and put Xs in the four squares at the top," she said.

"Like this?" I asked, drawing on the board:

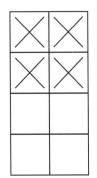

Margaret nodded and said, "See, you can see that you put Xs in half of them. That's four-eighths and that's the same as one-half." I wrote on the board:

$$\frac{4}{8} = \frac{1}{2}$$

"I was just trying to confuse people with eight squares," Cynthia said.

"Well, you did confuse some people," I answered. "But that's all right because we sometimes learn best after first being confused."

"I have something to add," Bruce said. "If half of the squares have Xs and half don't, then you have to have two equal parts. So Cynthia's works."

"Yes," I said. "An important idea is that halves have to be equal parts. Thanks for bringing it up, Bruce."

I then moved the lesson forward by saying, "Would anyone else like to come up and make a different drawing to show squares with Xs in half of them?" I picked Marlo. She drew the following:

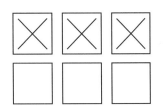

Most of the students agreed, but Kevin, Drew, Jose, and Philip indicated with their thumbs that they were confused. Marlo

explained, "It's actually just about the same as Cynthia's. Three and three is six, so half of six is three. So in other words, you could say that I did three-sixths, and that's the same as one-half." I wrote on the board as Marlo explained:

$3 + 3 = 6$
$\frac{1}{2}$ of 6 is 3
$\frac{3}{6} = \frac{1}{2}$

Marlo added, "You can see that three squares have Xs and three don't."

"Can I do one?" Jonathan asked. I agreed, and he came to the board and drew the following:

Some of the students laughed. Cindy exclaimed, "Oh, my gosh!"

"I split that square in half so half has an X and half is blank," Jonathan explained.

"Can you think of another fraction besides one-half that describes what you drew?" I asked him.

"It's two and a half . . . two and a half over something," Jonathan said.

"How many squares did you draw?" I prompted.

"Oh," Jonathan said. "It's two and a half over five."

"That's two and a half–fifths," I said and I wrote:

$$\frac{2\frac{1}{2}}{5}$$

Robert raised a hand. "I noticed something," he said. "Four and four is eight, three and three is six, two and a half and two and a half is five. They all work like that."

"What does that tell you?" I asked him.

"They're all halves," he said.

"The same patterns hold for one-half," I pointed out. "One and one adds up to two." I then wrote a different statement on the board using a fraction that wasn't a unit fraction. I wrote:

$\frac{3}{4}$ *of the circles have an X in them.*

Alanandra came up first. She drew four circles and marked them as follows:

"I did it pretty much like Jonathan," she said. "I split that circle in half and put X in half of it." Alanandra then looked back up at the sentence and said, "Uh oh, that's not right." She adjusted her drawing:

"How do you know that's right?" I asked her.
"Because it's four circles and three have Xs in them and that's three-fourths." The others all showed thumbs up to show their agreement.
Trent came up next. He drew the following:

He turned to the class and began an explanation before students had a chance to hold up their thumbs. "Okay," he said. "I drew eight circles and six out of them have Xs in them. Now, let's group them by twos. The first two have Xs, the second two have Xs, the third two have Xs, and the last two are blank. So there are four groups of two and three of them have Xs. Now, does anyone have questions?" Trent has a rather professional delivery style and it took a good deal of concentration for me not to grin.
A chorus of confusion broke out in the class. I quieted the children and said, "Your explanation makes good mathematical sense, Trent, but perhaps someone else can help by giving a different explanation."

"Can I try and explain in another way?" Trent asked me. I agreed.
"First let's look at it as six-eighths," he said. "It's pretty much the same thing as three-fourths." Trent turned to me and asked, "Can I draw circles to show the groups?" I agreed. Trent drew circles to make the groups of two clearer:

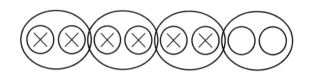

"Oh, now I get it," Jose said.
"Me, too," Sethie added.
"You said that six-eighths is *pretty much* the same as three-fourths," I said to Trent. He nodded.
"Do you think they are *exactly* the same or just *pretty much* the same?" I asked.
Trent thought for a minute and then answered, "Pretty much."
"Is six-eighths *always* pretty much the same as three-fourths?" I probed.
Trent paused for a moment and thought. "No, I don't think they're always the same," he said and returned to his seat.
Marlo came up to make another drawing. She drew three circles, made a ring around them, then drew three more circles and a ring around those, and repeated this twice more. She numbered the groups and put Xs in the circles in the first three groups.

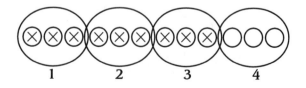

"I did four groups and put Xs in three of them," she said.
"How many circles did you draw and how many Xs?" I asked.

Marlo had to count to figure this out. "Twelve circles and nine Xs," she said. "So it's nine-twelfths." I wrote on the board:

$$\frac{9}{12} = \frac{3}{4}$$

"I can make an easier drawing," Ruthie said. She came up to the board to draw.

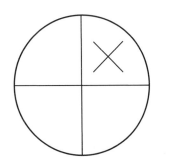

Ruthie looked at me. I said, "I think that Ruthie's drawing illustrates a different sentence." I wrote on the board:

$\frac{3}{4}$ of one circle do not have Xs.

"Oh," Ruthie said. "I meant to draw three Xs." She added two Xs to her drawing.

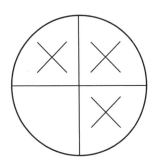

I said, "That shows three-fourths of one circle, and that's a fine way to picture three-fourths. We can think of three-fourths of one circle, as Ruthie did, or of a set of circles, as Alan, Trent, and Marlo did."

"Ruthie's is like three-fourths of a pizza is pepperoni and the rest is cheese," Cynthia offered.

Margaret added, "Three-fourths is the same as fifteen-twentieths. Can I show this?" I agreed and Margaret came to the

board. She drew squares instead of circles, but her mathematics was correct.

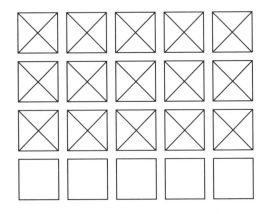

I repeated the same experience for one more statement. I wrote on the board:

$\frac{3}{5}$ of the triangles are shaded in.

After this, I gave the students an assignment for them to start in class and finish for homework. I asked them to work individually so I could check on each student's ability to make drawings to interpret fractional parts of sets.

DAY 2

I began class the next day by asking the students to share their solutions to the assignment they had completed for homework. "See how your solutions are the same or different," I told them. "After you've had a chance to talk among yourselves, we'll have a class discussion."

As the students talked, I went around to check that they had done the homework. All but two had; one had been absent and the other had no excuse. However, by engaging in discussions at their tables, these students were able to have some experience with the assignment, even though they hadn't done it themselves. I interrupted the class after a few minutes.

When I called the class to attention, I asked, "Who had an unusual way to illustrate the first statement and show that two-fifths of a set of circles are shaded?" Lawrence came to the board, drew ten circles in two rows of five, then shaded in four of them.

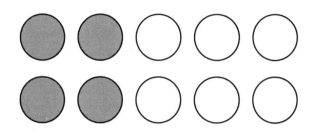

After pausing for a moment, he said, "You can draw another group, too." He then added another row of five circles and shaded in two more.

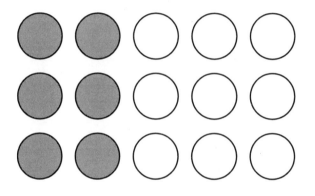

"Did anyone solve this problem the way Lawrence did?" I asked.

"I did it Lawrence's first way," Seth said. "But I colored in different circles."

"How many circles did you color in?" I asked.

"The same amount, but not the first ones," Seth answered.

"I drew only five circles," Jose said.

"I drew twenty," Margaret added.

I then said, "It looks to me that what Lawrence drew on the board shows six-fifteenths. But Lawrence gave it as an illustration for two-fifths. What do you think about that?" I wrote $\frac{6}{15}$ next to the $\frac{2}{5}$ that Lawrence had written.

Sethie said, "I think it shows both. If you double the . . . what's the number on the top called?"

"It's the numerator," I said and took a moment to write on the board:

$$\frac{numerator}{denominator}$$

Sethie continued, "If we double the numerator and we double the denominator, we'll still have the same."

I pointed to $\frac{2}{5}$ and asked Sethie, "If you double two, what do you get?"

"Four," she answered.

"And if you double five?"

"Ten," she said. I wrote on the board:

$$\frac{4}{10}$$

"But that's not six-fifteenths," I said. Sethie was confused. She had figured out that doubling the numerator and denominator resulted in a fraction worth the same, but she hadn't extended the rule further.

"They're the same," Trent said, referring to two-fifths and six-fifteenths. "You didn't double them, you tripled them because two plus two plus two is six and five plus five plus five is fifteen."

Marlo added, "I say it works if you double them, or triple them, or quadruple them, or whatever."

Lawrence then wanted to add some more information. "It doesn't matter how many you have as long as you shade in two groups of them and leave three groups unshaded."

"What do you think about that, Sethie?" I asked.

"Well, I kind of get it," she responded.

"Maybe talking about the others will help," I said. I continued the discussion and had the students present solutions for the other statements. (See Figures 5–1 through 5–4.) For each, I began with one student offering a solution and then talked about alternatives. Some children based all of their reasoning on the drawings; others concentrated on the particular numbers in the numerators and denominators. From discussions like these, I hope to broaden all children's understanding.

Draw pictures to show the following fractional parts:

1. 2/5 of a set of circles are shaded
2. 4/5 of the squares are red
3. 3/4 of the triangles are blue
4. 1/3 of the balls are footballs
5. 4/9 of the fruit are apples

▲▲▲▲▲▲Figure 5–1   *On his paper, Seth counted 2 cherries with their stems connected as 1 piece of fruit.*

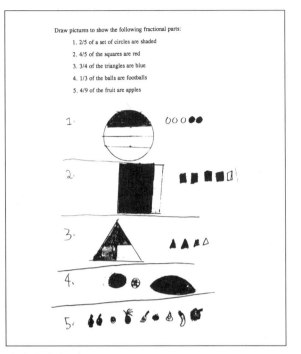

Draw pictures to show the following fractional parts:

1. 2/5 of a set of circles are shaded
2. 4/5 of the squares are red
3. 3/4 of the triangles are blue
4. 1/3 of the balls are footballs
5. 4/9 of the fruit are apples

▲▲▲▲▲▲Figure 5–3   *Drew showed two solutions for the first three problems, mixing parts of sets with parts of wholes. However, he erroneously divided the circle and triangle into parts that were not equal.*

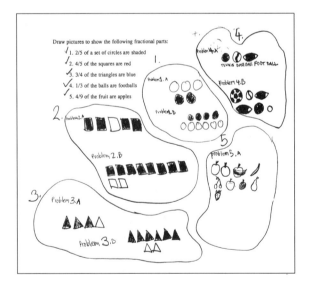

Draw pictures to show the following fractional parts:

1. 2/5 of a set of circles are shaded
2. 4/5 of the squares are red
3. 3/4 of the triangles are blue
4. 1/3 of the balls are footballs
5. 4/9 of the fruit are apples

▲▲▲▲▲▲Figure 5–2   *Margaret showed two solutions for all but the fifth problem.*

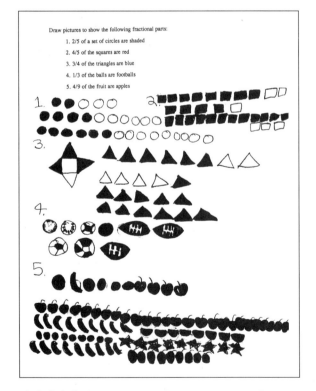

Draw pictures to show the following fractional parts:

1. 2/5 of a set of circles are shaded
2. 4/5 of the squares are red
3. 3/4 of the triangles are blue
4. 1/3 of the balls are footballs
5. 4/9 of the fruit are apples

▲▲▲▲▲▲Figure 5–4   *Theresa's paper shows her understanding of representing fractional parts of sets.*

Questions and Discussion

▲ *What do you do about students who are having difficulty understanding equivalent fractions?*

The idea of equivalence with fractions is a complex one and I don't expect understanding to come quickly for most students. I provide the students with repeated learning opportunities. All children learn in their own ways and on their own time tables. The teaching challenge is to find learning activities that provide students different ways to think about the same idea that also are interesting to students whose understanding is solid. The same idea crops up in most of the lessons in this book.

▲ *How do you handle the situation with students like Drew, who divide circles and triangles into unequal parts?*

One approach is to build a problem-solving experience around the issue and have children approximate the areas of the different segments using squared paper. Another approach is to open the solution for class discussion so students have the chance to talk about the areas of the various segments. If you do this, be sure not to point out a particular student as being wrong, but focus on what can be learned from investigating the mathematical situation.

CHAPTER SIX
INTRODUCING ONE-HALF AS A BENCHMARK

Overview

The May 1999 issue of *Teaching Mathematics in the Middle School* included an article by Barbara J. Reys, Ok-Kyeong Kim, and Jennifer M. Bay titled "Establishing Fraction Benchmarks." The article began: "The use of benchmarks, such as 0, $\frac{1}{2}$, and 1, for comparing the size of fractions is not emphasized very often in instruction" (530). The article also stated: "To begin to use benchmarks as a natural and instinctive process, students benefit from intentional modeling and prompting by the teacher" (532). The following lesson suggests a way to introduce one-half as a benchmark and then provide students practice using one-half to compare fractions.

Materials

▲ none

Time

▲ fifteen to twenty minutes, to be repeated

Teaching Directions

1. Ask students what they think a benchmark is. If they don't have ideas, explain that a benchmark can be thought of as a standard against which we can judge things. You might also talk with them about how whole-number benchmarks—ten, one hundred, and one thousand—can be useful.

2. Write two fractions on the board, one less than one-half and the other greater than one-half, for example, $\frac{2}{5}$ and $\frac{4}{7}$.

3. Ask: "How could thinking about the benchmark of one-half help you decide which of these fractions is larger?" Give all students who are interested the opportunity to respond. Ask students to explain their reasoning when they answer.

4. For further experiences, identify other pairs of fractions for students to compare using one-half as a benchmark, choosing one fraction that is greater than one-half and another that is less than one-half. It may be simple for some students to compare the fractions, but the opportunity to explain helps more able students cement their understanding and helps students who are just learning to formulate their ideas. Following are some pairs of fractions to use:

$$\frac{3}{8} \qquad \frac{5}{9}$$

$$\frac{2}{3} \qquad \frac{5}{12}$$

$$\frac{2}{5} \qquad \frac{4}{7}$$

$$\frac{7}{12} \qquad \frac{45}{100}$$

$$\frac{13}{25} \qquad \frac{4}{9}$$

Teaching Notes

It's common to hear children say, "My half is bigger than your half." While it makes sense for children to use this colloquial interpretation of one-half when they share things, it doesn't make sense mathematically. Children also use one-half in a non-mathematical sense when they talk about their birthdays. At some time after turning seven, children consider themselves to be seven and a half. The moment isn't precise but occurs somewhere in between being seven years old and turning eight.

This lesson brings children's attention to one-half in a different way, by using it as a reference to judge the sizes of other fractions. If children have had experience thinking about whole-number benchmarks, such as ten, one hundred, and one thousand, the idea of such a reference may not be new. If, however, students haven't had experience using benchmarks previously, this is a good way to introduce them to the benefit of how certain landmark numbers can be particularly useful.

I've learned from doing this activity over time in different classes the importance of encouraging and listening to children's explanations. While my ideas about one-half are well developed and entrenched, students' thinking isn't, and they often have unique ways to consider problems. It was surprising to me when a student stated, with confidence, that "four-sevenths is half of a seventh more than one-half." I've learned when confronted by ideas like this one to encourage discussion and give the student who offered the idea another chance to explain. Also, there are times when students' ideas are initially confusing to me—it's hard to concentrate at the same time on teaching and on thinking about a new math idea. If the idea about four-sevenths is new to you, you'll see how it played out in the particular class described below.

The Lesson

▲▲

To begin class, I told the students that I wanted to help them think about one-half as a benchmark fraction. I asked them what they thought a benchmark was.

"It's an important number to remember," Joey said.

"It's kind of like something you can use to figure other things out," Kim added.

"It's something you really know," Martin added.

"The numbers ten and one hundred are examples of benchmarks because they are important to how we represent numbers by ones, tens, hundreds, and so on," I said.

"There are ten pennies in a dime and one hundred pennies in a dollar," Lily said. "They're important numbers in money."

"We have ten fingers," Jeremy added.

I then said, "When we think about fractions, one-half is a useful benchmark."

I wrote two fractions on the board:

$$\frac{2}{5} \quad \frac{4}{7}$$

I asked, "How could thinking about the benchmark of one-half help you decide which of these fractions is larger? Who has an idea about this?" I waited a bit to give students a chance to think and then called on Rebecca.

"I think four-sevenths is more because four-sevenths is more than one-half and two-fifths is less than one-half," she said.

"How do you know that four-sevenths is more than half and that two-fifths is less than half?" I probed.

"Because four and four makes eight, and that's more than seven, and two and two are four and that's less than five," Rebecca answered.

Joey had a different way to explain. "Three and a half is half of seven," he said. "So four-sevenths is more than half. And two and a half is half of five, so two-fifths is less than half."

Mariah added, "I think that four-sevenths is one-half of a seventh more than one-half and two-fifths is one-half of a fifth less than one-half." The reaction in the class indicated that most of the students didn't follow Mariah's reasoning.

"Can you tell a little more about your idea?" I asked Mariah.

She began tentatively. "Well, first I thought that you can't have half with sevenths, but then what Joey said gave me an idea. He said that four-sevenths is more than

half. And I know that three-sevenths is less than half because three and three makes only six. So half has to be in the middle."

"I don't get it," Michael said.

"Me either," Sam added.

"Oh, I see," Rebecca said. "Three and a half is in the middle, like Joey said."

Mariah added, "So four-sevenths is half of a seventh more."

"I think I get it," Claire said.

"Well, I don't!" Michael said again.

"Let me see if I can help," I said. I wrote on the board:

$$\frac{3}{7} \quad \frac{1}{2} \quad \frac{4}{7}$$

"Three-sevenths is less than one-half," I said. "Who can explain why that's true?" I called on Claire.

"Three and three are only six," she said.

"Half of seven is three and a half," Josh added.

"Who can explain why four-sevenths is greater than one-half?" I then asked. Several students offered ideas like Joey and Rebecca had earlier.

"If I want to write a fraction with sevenths that is worth exactly one-half, and three-sevenths is too small but four-sevenths is too large, what fraction can I write?" Mariah's hand shot up. So did Sam's and Andrew's. I waited a bit. Josh raised a hand, then Claire, Pamela, Kim, and Rebecca. I called on Rebecca.

"It has to be three and a half sevenths," she said.

"You can't do that!" Tom said.

"Sure you can! Watch," I responded. I wrote on the board, above the $\frac{1}{2}$:

$$\frac{3\frac{1}{2}}{7}$$

The students seemed fascinated by what I had written. I explained, "This is called a complex fraction. Do you know what *complex* means?" Several students had ideas.

"It means complicated," Lily said.

"Really hard," Sam added.

"That fraction looks hard," Jeremy said.

"I don't get it," Michael said.

"Look, Michael," Tom said. "It's the same as the others. The top is half the bottom, so the fraction is a half."

I explained further, "We're used to seeing fractions with whole numbers for the numerators and denominators. A complex fraction has a fraction in either the numerator or denominator, or in both. You'll learn more about these fractions in high school."

Before returning to the discussion about comparing four-sevenths and two-fifths, I added, "So Mariah's idea is that four-sevenths is just one-half of a seventh more than three and a half sevenths. Let's see if you have any other ideas about how to compare four-sevenths and two-fifths."

I'm never quite sure how to handle conversations like this one. Mariah's idea was clear to her and I knew that some of the other students would benefit from hearing it. However, there's always the risk that students like Michael will be left behind. My classroom approach is not to avoid conversations that might be difficult for some students, but to keep them open, handle them lightly, and be sure to return to the ideas that all students can handle. I called on Martin next.

He said, "I know that four-sevenths is bigger than two-fifths because four times seven is twenty-eight and two times five is only ten and twenty-eight is more than ten." Here was another sticky situation to deal with. While Martin's computations were correct, doing the multiplication had no bearing on comparing the two fractions. It's not unusual for students to present an erroneous idea like this, and I'm careful first to acknowledge their attempts to make sense of a situation. Then, in order to help a student see that his or her conjecture isn't correct, I try to offer a counterexample, one that points out that the conjecture is flawed. Thinking of such contradictions is often hard in the midst of teaching, but I thought of one in this instance.

"What about comparing one-half and one-seventh?" I asked Martin. "Do you know which is larger?" I chose these two fractions because unit fractions, those with numerators of one, are easy for students to compare.

Martin answered, "One-half is more because sevenths are smaller pieces."

I continued, "But if I use the method you suggested for comparing four-sevenths and two-fifths, I'd come to the opposite conclusion. I'd think: one times two is two and one times seven is seven. And since two is less than seven, one-seventh is more than one-half. But we know that one-half is more than one-seventh."

"Yeah, that's true," Martin said. "It doesn't work."

"When you have an idea that works in one example but not in another, then it's not a reliable idea for reasoning," I said. Martin nodded.

Kim had an idea. "I know that two-fifths is the same as four-tenths," she said. "So if I look at four-tenths and four-sevenths, then I know that four-sevenths is more because sevenths are bigger pieces than tenths."

There were no other ideas for comparing four-sevenths and two-fifths, so I left the discussion and continued with the next part of the lesson I had prepared. I planned to return to this sort of discussion from time to time to help students become comfortable thinking about using one-half as a benchmark, presenting other pairs of fractions in which one fraction was greater than one-half and the other less than one-half.

Questions and Discussion

▲▲▲

▲ *Why do you always pick fractions so that one is greater than one-half and the other is less than one-half? Wouldn't it be a good idea to pick fractions more randomly?*

I've grappled with this question myself. I generally don't like to narrow the focus of a mathematical investigation, and in that spirit I could choose fractions without the restriction I suggested in this lesson. However, from my experience with students, I've learned that practice with a particular idea can be useful. In this case, the practice is with deciding if a fraction is more or less than one-half. This may be simple for your students so you won't need to spend much time on it, but comparing fractions to one-half may be more difficult or not as obvious for some of your students. As in all situations, use your judgment.

Also, using the benchmark of one-half is one of a collection of strategies that students benefit from when learning to compare fractions. While it works particularly well with fractions that straddle one-half, it's not as useful for other fractions. As students build a repertoire of strategies for comparing fractions, it's appropriate and important to present a mix of problems so that they can decide which strategies are more effective.

▲ *You didn't offer the students the option of using manipulatives or making drawings to help them think. Wouldn't this be helpful?*

Using manipulative materials and making sketches are valuable tools for learning and thinking about fractions. However, it's also important for students to learn to approach fractions abstractly and build their own mental models for bringing meaning to fractions. Children have had a significant amount of experience with the idea of one-half, so it's a concept that is well suited for pushing them to think more abstractly.

CHAPTER SEVEN
MORE OR LESS THAN ONE-HALF

Overview

This activity requires just part of a class period and can be repeated from time to time. Students are shown a fraction, decide if it's more or less than one-half, and explain their reasoning. This focus on one-half helps establish it as an important and useful benchmark. Also, the lesson can provide practice with mental computation of whole numbers as students compare numerators and denominators.

Materials

▲ none

Time

▲ ten to twenty minutes, to be repeated

Teaching Directions

1. Write a fraction on the board for students to compare to one-half.

2. Ask: "Is this fraction more or less than one-half?" Tell students that they are to explain their reasoning and also listen to the reasoning of others. Also tell them that they should try to think of as many different ways as possible to explain.

3. After each student response, ask: "Does anyone have another way to explain that?" Continue until all students who want to explain have had a chance to do so.

4. Repeat the lesson from time to time, either as a warm-up at the beginning of class or when you have some time left at the end of a period.

Teaching Notes

Students benefit from many opportunities to explain their thinking. Talking about their ideas and hearing the ideas of others help children develop, extend, and cement their understanding. The focus of this lesson is fairly narrow—deciding if fractions are more or less than one-half. But the usefulness extends beyond the practice of comparing fractions with this important benchmark by providing students experience with explaining their reasoning.

This lesson is a good filler when you have a few extra moments at the end of class, before dismissing for recess or lunch, or to ease into a math lesson. At times I'd write a fraction on the board and ask the class for three different ways to explain why it was more or less than one-half. Other times I'd ask students to quickly write an explanation, then I'd start at one end of the room and ask a student to read what he or she had written. My directions to the class were, "Listen to the explanations everyone reads. When it's your turn, if you explained in a different way, then read yours. Otherwise, just say, 'I pass.'" After one or two times with this, some students struggle to find unique ways to explain and, in this way, continue to challenge themselves.

The following section describes how I used the lesson in a fifth-grade class early in the school year.

The Lesson

▲▲

From time to time, I'd do an activity with the class called *More or Less Than $\frac{1}{2}$*. I used this activity when I had some time left at the end of a period or as a warm-up at the beginning of class. I'd write a fraction on the board and ask if it were more or less than one-half. Students who answered also had to explain their thinking. After each student's response, I'd ask, "Does anyone have another way to explain that?" In this way, students focused not only on answering and explaining their reasoning but also on trying to think of different ways to explain answers. I'd continue discussing the fraction until all students who wanted had had a chance to explain.

Here's how the activity went with a class of fifth graders in the fall of the year. I wrote on the board:

$$\frac{2}{3}$$

"Is this more or less than one-half?" I asked.

Davy began by saying, "There are three thirds in a whole, and two-thirds is more than halfway to the whole."

"How do you know it's more than halfway?" I probed. Davy wasn't sure.

I said, "Listen to other ideas, and see if they can help you explain more." I called on Ramon next.

"On a measuring cup, the line for two-thirds is above the one-half line," Ramon said. "It's like halfway to a whole cup after half a cup."

Leslie asked to come to the board. She drew a circle and divided it into three equal-size wedges. She said, "If you had a cookie cut into thirds like this, you can see that one-third is less than one-half. If there were two people and you each took one-third, then you'd have to share some more to get one-half each. So one-half is one-third plus some more."

Rachel's explanation was more abstract. "If two-thirds was the same as one-half, then two would have to be half of three. But it's more, so two-thirds has to be more."

One day, I chose one and one-quarter for the fraction. When I wrote it on the board, some students laughed and others blurted out comments: "Simple!" "That's easy." "No-brainer." Practically every student raised a hand.

"More or less?" I asked. "Let's all say the answer softly together." That took care of the answer.

"Who can explain why one and a fourth is more than one-half?" I then asked. Again, there were lots of volunteers.

Daniel said, "It's obvious, because one-half is less than one and one and a fourth is more than one, so it has to be more than one-half."

Sadie said, "It's more than twice as big, because one-half and one-half are one and one and a fourth is even more than that."

"On the number line, they're on different sides of one," Emma said. "That shows one-half is less."

Even for an obvious solution, students may think in different ways. Listening to their thinking often gives me new insights into students' understanding. Also, sometimes students think in ways I hadn't thought of, giving me new ways to look at the mathematics.

For this activity, I sometimes selected fractions with larger numerators and denominators, at times choosing fractions that were easy to analyze, such as $\frac{61}{100}$ or $\frac{400}{1000}$, but at other times choosing fractions that also offered a mental computation challenge, such as $\frac{127}{260}$, $\frac{89}{180}$, even $\frac{267}{498}$. The students seemed to like stretching their thinking to decide if fractions like these were more or less than one-half.

Questions and Discussion

▲▲

▲ *What do you do when a student offers an idea that others don't understand?*

This lesson encourages students to think in their own ways, thus making it a lesson that can meet the needs of a wide range of understanding and confidence among students. However, it happens from time to time that a student gives an explanation that others can't follow. Often this is a way for a more capable student to try out new thinking. Sometimes I ask the student to try explaining again. At other times I'll respond, "I hadn't thought of that way before. Let me think about it and we can talk later." My goal is to acknowledge the contribution while also being careful not to make others feel deficient if they don't follow the reasoning.

▲ *You suggest using fractions with large numbers in the numerators and denominators. But fractions like $\frac{127}{260}$ or $\frac{267}{498}$ really have no real-world connection. Why do you think they're important?*

I realize that these fractions don't connect to real-world contexts or to any of the manipulative materials we use. But I think it's fine, and a good idea, to extend what students are learning and ask them to think about ideas more abstractly. Playing with fractions in this way can stretch students' mathematical imaginations.

CHAPTER EIGHT
WHEN IS A FRACTION WORTH ONE-HALF?

Overview

In this lesson, students are asked to come up with as many different ways as they can to explain why a fraction is equivalent to one-half. The lesson also engages the students with algebraic thinking as the methods they suggest are translated to generalizations using variables to represent numerators and denominators.

Materials

▲ none

Time

▲ one class period

Teaching Directions

1. Write on the board a fraction that is equivalent to one-half, for example, $\frac{6}{12}$, $\frac{4}{8}$, or $\frac{5}{10}$.

2. Tell the students that you're interested in all the different ways they can come up with to explain why a fraction is equivalent to one-half.

3. As each student reports, record his or her idea on the board and then model for the class how to represent the idea algebraically. Post the list for a class reference.

4. Ask the class for other fractions that are equivalent to one-half.

5. When you're satisfied that they all understand, give them ten fractions and ask them to decide if each is less than, equal to, or greater than one-half and to explain their reasoning for each. This is suitable for a class assignment or for homework. If you think it's necessary, give an example to the class first before students get to work. Write $\frac{4}{7}$ on the board for them to discuss.

Teaching Notes

This lesson is most appropriate after students have had opportunities to compare fractions to one-half, as suggested in the lessons *Introducing One-Half as a Benchmark* and *More or Less Than One-Half.* Students should be able to identify, correctly and with confidence, whether a fraction is more than, less than, or equal to one-half. This lesson asks students to extend their thinking from evaluating specific fractions to describing their reasoning for all fractions.

Modeling how to represent their thinking algebraically provides the students experience with seeing how variables can be used to describe their ideas. The lesson also models the usefulness of algebra as a way to express arithmetic generalizations.

The Lesson

▲▲

After the class had experience comparing two fractions by using one-half as a benchmark, I wrote on the board:

$$\frac{6}{12}$$

"Raise your hand if you can explain why this fraction is equivalent to one-half," I said. I waited until every student had raised a hand. While the question was trivial for most students, I planned to build on their understanding and have a class discussion about different ways to determine that a fraction is equivalent to one-half. Also, I planned to compile the explanations they'd offer into a list and represent them algebraically, thus giving the students experience with using variables to describe general numerical relationships.

Before calling on any students to respond, I gave a direction. "Be sure to listen to what others say and see if your idea is the same or different. If you have a different way, then raise your hand again. I'm interested in seeing how many different ways we can come up with to explain what makes a fraction equivalent to one-half."

Jake reported first. "You add the top twice and see if it makes the bottom," he said.

I knew, or thought that I knew, what Jake was stating. But his response gave me the chance to push for more clarity

from him and, therefore, model for the students how to be more precise in their explanations.

"Tell me what you mean with the fraction I wrote on the board," I said.

"You go six plus six and you get twelve," he said.

"Oh," I said. "You added six to itself." Jake nodded his agreement.

"That works," I confirmed. "Can you say your idea again, but this time use the words *numerator* and *denominator* instead of *top* and *bottom?*"

Jake said, "You go numerator plus numerator and see if the answer is the denominator." He stumbled over pronouncing *denominator* but finally got it out correctly. I then wrote on the board:

If the numerator plus the numerator equals the denominator, then the fraction is worth $\frac{1}{2}$.

"Does this explain your idea, Jake?" I asked. He agreed.

"Who has a different way to decide if a fraction is worth one-half?" I asked. I called on Rosie.

She said, "Do the numerator times two and see if the answer is the denominator." I wrote on the board:

If the numerator times 2 equals the denominator, then the fraction is worth $\frac{1}{2}$.

I looked at Rosie to see if she agreed with what I had written. She nodded.

"I have another way," Donald said. "If the numerator goes into the denominator two times, then the fraction is one-half." I wrote:

If the numerator goes into the denominator two times, then the fraction is worth $\frac{1}{2}$.

Before taking other suggestions, I said to the class, "My hand gets tired writing down your ideas. One of the benefits of mathematics is that we have symbols to describe ideas and don't have to use words all of the time. The symbols are like short-cuts. See if you understand how I can record Jake's, Rosie's, and Donald's ideas in mathematics, not English."

I turned to the board, explaining as I wrote. "Instead of writing *numerator* and *denominator* over and over, I'll just use a shortcut for each: n and d. Who can explain why this makes sense?" I had written:

$\frac{n}{d}$

n = numerator
d = denominator

Carl answered, "You just used the first letter."

"They're like initials," Connie added.

"Look at this fraction," I said, writing $\frac{3}{4}$ on the board. "For this fraction, n is three and d is four."

"But it's not one-half," Steven said.

"No, it's not," I agreed.

"I don't get why n is three and d is four," Gena said.

"Who can explain?" I asked. I called on Peter.

"Because three is the top number in the fraction, so it's the numerator," he said. "And four is the bottom number, so it's the denominator."

"But the fraction you wrote—n over d—isn't a real fraction," Gena said.

The idea of algebraic variables was new for these students and I tried to explain. "It's

not a specific fraction," I said. "Suppose you went home and told your mom that your teacher gave you homework. If it were math homework, then you'd be referring to me. But if it were science homework, or a book report, or something for art, then you'd be talking about a different teacher. 'Teacher' is a general description; 'Ms. Burns' would be a specific description. In the same way, 'n over d' is a general name that could mean any fraction, but 'six-twelfths' refers to a specific fraction because you now know what numbers you're thinking of for the numerator and denominator."

I wasn't sure if Gena understood, but I pressed on. "Watch as I translate Jake's idea into a mathematical shortcut. If it makes sense to you, it sure will save us some writing energy." I wrote on the board next to the sentence I had written to describe Jake's idea:

Jake: If $n + n = d$, then $\frac{n}{d} = \frac{1}{2}$.

I continued, "And watch what I could write for Rosie's idea." I wrote:

Rosie: If $n \times 2 = d$, then $\frac{n}{d} = \frac{1}{2}$.

"I'm liking this recording much better," I said. "Let's test them and see if they make sense for six-twelfths, with n equal to six and d equal to twelve."

Jake said, "Mine works, because six plus six is twelve."

"Mine, too, because six times two is twelve," Rosie said.

"What could I write for your idea, Donald, using n's and d's?" I asked.

Donald thought for a moment and then asked, "Can I come up and write it?" I agreed. He came up and used the notation for whole number division to record. He wrote:

$n\overset{2}{\overline{)}d}$

This notation for division isn't standard to algebraic representation, which I wanted Donald and the others to know. But I also wanted to honor Donald's contribution, which was correct in concept, but not in convention. "What you wrote makes sense to me," I said. "See if this way also describes your idea. It's the way you'll usually see your idea in math books." I wrote:

Donald: 2

If $n\overline{)d}^{\;2}$ or $d \div n = 2$, then $\frac{n}{d} = \frac{1}{2}$.

I then returned to the discussion of other ways to see if a fraction were equivalent to one-half. I called on Gena, who now seemed more confident.

Gena said, "If the numerator is half of the denominator, then it works." I wrote on the board:

Gena: If $n = \frac{1}{2}$ of d, then $\frac{n}{d} = \frac{1}{2}$.

George had another idea. "If you can divide the denominator by two and get the numerator, then it's one-half." I recorded:

George: If $d \div 2 = n$, then $\frac{n}{d} = \frac{1}{2}$.

The class was then silent and I thought that the children had exhausted all of the possible ways. Then Zack raised his hand.

"I have an idea," he said. "Take the numerator and divide it by two. And then times that answer by four and you get the denominator." I repeated what Zack said, recording with symbols:

Zack: If $n \div 2 \times 4 = d$, then $\frac{n}{d} = \frac{1}{2}$.

I stepped back from what I had written. Zack was grinning, "See, it works." Some of the others were impressed; others were confused.

"I need some punctuation on what I wrote," I said and added parentheses:

Zack: If $(n \div 2) \times 4 = d$, then $\frac{n}{d} = \frac{1}{2}$.

"This reminds me to do what Zack said first, to divide the numerator by two, and then multiply by four," I explained.

"Hey, does that always work?" Tommy wanted to know.

"Try fifty-hundredths," Jake said.

"Okay," Zack said. "Fifty divided by two is twenty-five and twenty-five times four is one hundred."

"Try ten-twentieths," Connie said.

Zack obliged. "Ten divided by two is five and five times four is twenty."

Tommy's hand shot up. "Try three-sixths," he said.

Zack said, "Three divided by two . . . oops . . . wait a minute. Oh, I know, three divided by two is . . . " He stumbled and lost his confidence. "Wait, I need paper," he said.

George, who had already reached for paper, shouted, "It works! Look, three divided by two is one and a half, and that times four works. One and a half four times is three and three, and that's six. So it works." Zack didn't look sure but seemed relieved. Some followed George's reasoning, but many of the others were completely lost.

"Is it right?" Emily asked me.

"When we're not sure about something, we call it a 'conjecture.' This is Zack's conjecture."

I didn't go further with this because I didn't want to lose sight of the focus on one-half for the rest of the students. Instead, I said, "Raise your hand when you have in mind another fraction that's equivalent to one-half." After a moment, all but Jonathan and Connie had raised their hands.

"Do you have a fraction, Jonathan?" I asked. He nodded and raised a hand. So did Connie.

I started around the room having students tell me fractions, and I recorded their suggestions on the board. When I called on Addison, he said, "One hundred–two hundredths." There was an outbreak of giggles followed by a rash of other fraction suggestions that caused even more giggles: "Five hundred–one thousandths." "One thousand–two thousandths." "One million–two millionths." I wrote each of these on the board:

$$\frac{500}{1,000}$$

$$\frac{1,000}{2,000}$$

$$\frac{1,000,000}{2,000,000}$$

Ali took another direction when it was her turn. "Seven and a half–fifteenths," she said. I wrote on the board:

$$\frac{7\frac{1}{2}}{15}$$

Others followed with similar fractions. (We had talked in this class before about complex fractions. Otherwise, I might have suggested a fraction like this to introduce the idea to the class.)

I then asked, "So how many fractions do you think you could write that are equivalent to one-half?"

"Infinity!" several answered at the same time.

"I agree," I said. "There are an infinite number of fractions that are equivalent to one-half. Representing your ideas algebraically as I did on the chart is a handy way to refer to many, many fractions."

I then gave the class an assignment. "I'm going to write ten fractions on the board," I explained. "Decide if each is equal to one-half, less than one-half, or more than one-half. On your paper, explain your reasoning for each. Let's try an example." I wrote on the board:

$$\frac{4}{6}$$

"Thumbs up if you think it's equivalent to one-half and thumbs down if you think it's not," I said. Everyone's hand showed thumbs down.

"Who could explain why it's not equal to one-half using Jake's idea?" I said, pointing to it on the board. I called on Alison.

"Four and four is eight, and eight is more than six," she said.

"How would Rosie explain?" I asked. Rosie's hand shot up and I gave her the chance to reply.

"Four times two is eight and that's too big," she said.

I continued this way for each of the methods I had recorded. Not only did this help the students focus on one another's ideas, it also gave me a chance to reinforce the use of algebraic notation.

"Is four-sixths more or less than one-half?" I asked. "How can you tell?"

Carl answered, "It's bigger, because four and four is too much. It's too many sixths."

I then listed on the board the ten fractions the students were to consider:

1. $\frac{4}{8}$
2. $\frac{6}{13}$
3. $\frac{3}{5}$
4. $\frac{3}{6}$
5. $\frac{7}{10}$
6. $\frac{8}{15}$
7. $\frac{25}{50}$
8. $\frac{25}{51}$
9. $\frac{25}{49}$
10. $\frac{1,000}{2,000}$

As the students worked, I transferred the algebraic representations of their ideas to a chart and posted it for future reference. (See Figures 8–1 and 8–2 for examples of how students worked on this assignment.)

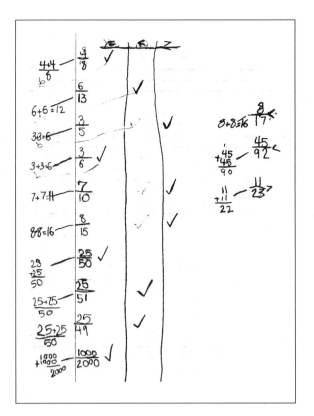

▲▲▲▲▲Figure 8–1 Brett used a chart to present the answers.

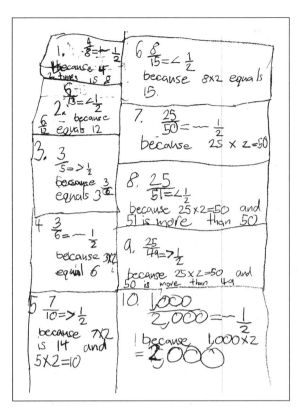

▲▲▲▲▲Figure 8–2 Tommy's paper shows his understanding.

Questions and Discussions

▲▲

▲ *My students haven't had experience with algebra. Should I do something first about that before introducing this lesson?*

Any new ideas are best learned by connecting them to what students have already experienced. In that light, this lesson may serve as a good way to introduce students to using variables to represent arithmetic generalizations that they themselves made. Using *n* and *d* for *numerator* and *denominator* may help students become comfortable using algebraic notation in this situation.

▲ *I notice that you did all of the algebraic recording. Could you expect students to do some?*

This depends on the students' prior experience with representing their thinking algebraically. The class I described had not had such prior experience. Therefore, I took the opportunity to model for them how to represent their ideas using variables. My goal was that after a number of such experiences, students would come to see algebraic representation as a useful and convenient way to describe their thinking.

When Is a Fraction Worth One-Half? 67

CHAPTER NINE
HOW MUCH MORE TO MAKE ONE-HALF?

Overview

In this lesson, students tackle the problem of figuring out for various fractions how much more they would need to add to make one-half. Rather than relying on particular computational procedures, the lesson focuses students on using patterns to arrive at answers. In this way, the emphasis of the lesson is kept on students' thinking and reasoning.

Materials

▲ none

Time

▲ two half-hour sessions

Teaching Directions

1. Ask: "If I have one-fourth of something, how much more do I need to make one-half?" Ask students to answer and explain.

2. Ask: "If I have one-eighth of something, how much more do I need to make one-half?" Again, ask students to answer and explain.

3. List on the board the unit fractions with denominators from two to twelve. Next to one-fourth and one-eighth, record as shown to indicate the fractions needed to make one-half.

$$\frac{1}{2}$$
$$\frac{1}{3}$$
$$\frac{1}{4} + \frac{1}{4} = \frac{1}{2}$$
$$\frac{1}{5}$$

$$\frac{1}{6}$$
$$\frac{1}{7}$$
$$\frac{1}{8} + \frac{3}{8} = \frac{1}{2}$$
$$\frac{1}{9}$$
$$\frac{1}{10}$$
$$\frac{1}{11}$$
$$\frac{1}{12}$$

4. Remind the students that patterns form the basis of mathematical ideas. Tell them that they're going to figure out for each fraction listed how much more is needed to make one-half. Ask students to look for patterns in the answers they find and discuss what they notice. It's most likely that the fractions with even denominators will be easier for the students, while the other fractions will pose difficulties. If this happens, leave the list incomplete and return to it for further discussion after a week or so. During that time, encourage students to keep thinking about solutions. Finally, with the class's help, complete the list.

Teaching Notes

This lesson is appropriate once students are comfortable comparing fractions with one-half. As an assessment sometime prior to beginning the lesson, ask the first question suggested in the teaching directions: "If I have one-fourth of something, how much more do I need to make one-half?" If students can't easily answer this question and explain their reasoning, then I don't recommend that you continue with the lesson at this time. Instead, provide students with concrete experiences and additional opportunities to think about fractional relationships. Similarly, check students' response to the second question: "If I have one-eighth of something, how much more do I need to make one-half?" Again, if students are shaky answering this one, wait until they've had more experience with fractions.

The lesson described here occurred in two sessions, but it's possible to teach the lesson in one class period if students are able. In my experience, however, waiting provides gestation time for the students' thinking. Waiting also models for students how mathematicians often work—leaving a problem and then returning to it at a later time.

The Lesson

▲▲▲

I began class one day by asking, "If I have one-fourth of something, how much more do I need to make one-half?" This question was easy for the students; most raised their hands right away and others followed after a moment.

"You need one-fourth," Claire said. She then explained, "One-half is the same as two-fourths, so if you only have one-fourth, then you need one more."

Jeremy explained in a different way. "If you divide a half in half, you get a fourth. So the other half of the half is another fourth." Several of the students expressed confusion, so Jeremy came up to the board to show what he meant. He drew a circle and divided it into fourths.

"See," he explained again, "half of a half is a fourth, so if you have a fourth, you need another one."

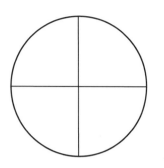

Rosie had another way to explain. "You can tell from the fraction kit," she said. "When you play *Uncover,* you can exchange a half for two of the fourths pieces." Rosie was referring to one of the games the class had learned to play using the fraction kits they had made. (See Chapter 2, "The Fraction Kit," for the rules to *Uncover* and other games with fraction kits.)

I then said, "I have another question to ask. If I have one-eighth of something, how much more do I need to make one-half?" Again, hands shot up, although a little more slowly this time. I waited, then called on Matthew.

"You need three-eighths," Matthew said. "Like Rosie said, when you play *Uncover,* you can trade in a half for four-eighths. Take away one of them and you have three-eighths left."

"Or you could use a fourth and an eighth," Gena added.

I turned to Matthew. "Is a fourth and an eighth the same as three-eighths?" I asked him. He nodded yes.

"How are you sure?" I probed.

"Because a fourth is two-eighths, and one more makes three," he answered.

I then wrote a list of unit fractions on the board:

$$\frac{1}{2}$$
$$\frac{1}{3}$$
$$\frac{1}{4}$$
$$\frac{1}{5}$$

$$\frac{1}{6}$$
$$\frac{1}{7}$$
$$\frac{1}{8}$$
$$\frac{1}{9}$$
$$\frac{1}{10}$$
$$\frac{1}{11}$$
$$\frac{1}{12}$$

"Everything in mathematics depends on patterns," I said. "What patterns do you notice in the list of fractions I wrote on the board?"

"They go in order," Tom said.

"Tell me more about that," I said.

"The denominators go two, three, four, five, like that," he clarified.

"I agree," I said. "The denominators increase by ones. Does anyone notice anything else?"

There was no immediate response. Finally Sam said, "They go in order in a different way. They go down. One-half is the biggest and one-twelfth is the smallest."

"Yeah, they go down by ones," Connie added. I let Connie's comment go, even though it wasn't mathematically correct. While the denominators decreased by one, the fractions didn't, but calculating the differences between fractions would be too hard for the students at this point.

"There are all ones on top," Zack said.

No one else volunteered, so I said, "You've noticed several patterns in the list of fractions I wrote. Now I'd like to make another list of fractions next to this list with each fraction in the second list telling how much more you need to get to one-half."

"What do you mean?" Tom asked.

"Let me show you with one-fourth and one-eighth," I said. To clarify, I added to what I had already written:

$$\frac{1}{2}$$
$$\frac{1}{3}$$
$$\frac{1}{4} + \frac{1}{4} = \frac{1}{2}$$
$$\frac{1}{5}$$
$$\frac{1}{6}$$

$$\frac{1}{7}$$
$$\frac{1}{8} + \frac{3}{8} = \frac{1}{2}$$
$$\frac{1}{9}$$
$$\frac{1}{10}$$
$$\frac{1}{11}$$
$$\frac{1}{12}$$

"Let's figure out what we need to add to each of the other fractions in the list to make one-half," I said. "And let's see what patterns come up or maybe even use patterns to figure out ones that are hard. Does anyone know any others?"

"You don't need anything for the top one," Kim said.

"What about the others?" I asked.

"I know about one-sixth," Rebecca said. "You need two-sixths more because one-half is the same as three-sixths."

Sam said, "Hey, I know about one-third, because I know that it's the blue block and you need a green triangle to make one-half." Sam was referring to pattern block pieces. "The green is one-sixth, so you need one-third more." I recorded Rebecca's and Sam's ideas on the list.

$$\frac{1}{2}$$
$$\frac{1}{3} + \frac{1}{6} = \frac{1}{2}$$
$$\frac{1}{4} + \frac{1}{4} = \frac{1}{2}$$
$$\frac{1}{5}$$
$$\frac{1}{6} + \frac{2}{6} = \frac{1}{2}$$
$$\frac{1}{7}$$
$$\frac{1}{8} + \frac{3}{8} = \frac{1}{2}$$
$$\frac{1}{9}$$
$$\frac{1}{10}$$
$$\frac{1}{11}$$
$$\frac{1}{12}$$

"One-twelfth is easy," Mariah said. "Six-twelfths is half, so you need five-twelfths."

"One-tenth is easy, too," Tommy said. "You need four more tenths to make five-tenths." I added these ideas.

$$\frac{1}{2}$$
$$\frac{1}{3} + \frac{1}{6} = \frac{1}{2}$$

$$\frac{1}{4} + \frac{1}{4} = \frac{1}{2}$$
$$\frac{1}{5}$$
$$\frac{1}{6} + \frac{2}{6} = \frac{1}{2}$$
$$\frac{1}{7}$$
$$\frac{1}{8} + \frac{3}{8} = \frac{1}{2}$$
$$\frac{1}{9}$$
$$\frac{1}{10} + \frac{4}{10} = \frac{1}{2}$$
$$\frac{1}{11}$$
$$\frac{1}{12} + \frac{5}{12} = \frac{1}{2}$$

"I see a pattern, kind of," Zack said. "Look, one, two, three, four, five on top and four, six, eight, ten, twelve on the bottoms."

"I see it!" Michael said. "But it's only for the even fractions."

"You mean the pattern holds for the fractions with even denominators," I said. Michael nodded.

"I don't see it," Lily said.

"Maybe it would help if I rearrange the list," I said. I made changes to organize the list a bit differently.

$$\frac{1}{2}$$
$$\frac{1}{3} + \frac{1}{6} = \frac{1}{2}$$
$$\frac{1}{4} + \frac{1}{4} = \frac{1}{2}$$
$$\frac{1}{5}$$
$$\frac{1}{6} + \frac{2}{6} = \frac{1}{2}$$
$$\frac{1}{7}$$
$$\frac{1}{8} + \frac{3}{8} = \frac{1}{2}$$
$$\frac{1}{9}$$
$$\frac{1}{10} + \frac{4}{10} = \frac{1}{2}$$
$$\frac{1}{11}$$
$$\frac{1}{12} + \frac{5}{12} = \frac{1}{2}$$

"What should I write next to one-half?" I asked.

"Zero," several answered at once.

"Would that fit the pattern?" I asked.

"It fits part of the pattern," Claire said. "It goes five, four, three, two, one, so then comes zero."

I said, "One-half plus zero more halves adds up to one-half." I wrote as I said this:

$$\frac{1}{2} + \frac{0}{2} = \frac{1}{2}$$

Students had several comments. "That's cool." "It's weird." "Can you do that?" "What are we going to do about the rest of the fractions?" I asked. The students were stumped. Rather than continue, I decided to leave what we had done on the board and return to it at a later time. "Mathematicians don't solve every problem they come up against right away," I said. "Sometimes it helps to think about something for a while. I'll leave what I've written on the board and we'll come back to it another time when someone has an idea. In the meantime, I'll make just one list again so we don't have to use too much room on the board." I rearranged the list again:

$$\frac{1}{2} + \frac{0}{2} = \frac{1}{2}$$
$$\frac{1}{3} + \frac{1}{6} = \frac{1}{2}$$
$$\frac{1}{4} + \frac{1}{4} = \frac{1}{2}$$
$$\frac{1}{5}$$
$$\frac{1}{6} + \frac{2}{6} = \frac{1}{2}$$
$$\frac{1}{7}$$
$$\frac{1}{8} + \frac{3}{8} = \frac{1}{2}$$
$$\frac{1}{9}$$
$$\frac{1}{10} + \frac{4}{10} = \frac{1}{2}$$
$$\frac{1}{11}$$
$$\frac{1}{12} + \frac{5}{12} = \frac{1}{2}$$

THE NEXT WEEK

Over the next several days, I occasionally reminded the students about the list we had begun, suggesting from time to time that they take a look and think some more. Also, I prodded a few of the students who I thought could make headway with this challenge. My plan was to reopen the discussion after I had a sense that at least a few students had some ideas. I knew that the problem would remain beyond the grasp of some of the students, but I thought that they could benefit from hearing others' ideas.

One morning, Sam came to me. "I figured out one of the fraction problems."

"What are you thinking?" I said. We walked over to the chart.

"I was thinking about what we had talked about with sevenths, that half was three and a half sevenths," he began. "So if you have one-seventh, then you could add on two and a half more and you'd have three and a half–sevenths. And that would be one-half." Sam was referring to a conversation the class had had during the lesson *Introducing One-Half as a Benchmark*.

"So tell me again what we need to add to one-seventh to get one-half," I said.

"Two and a half more," he said. I wrote on the chalkboard:

$$\frac{1}{7} + \frac{2\frac{1}{2}}{7} = \frac{3\frac{1}{2}}{7} = \frac{1}{2}$$

"That's it," he said. "Am I right?"

"It makes good sense to me," I said. "How about if we talk about your idea with the whole class? Is that okay with you?" I asked. Sam agreed.

"We'll wait until tomorrow," I said. "I'd like to continue with what I planned for today. Besides, this will give you time to see if you can convince anyone else about your idea."

Several of the students had noticed Sam and me talking and interest in our conversation grew. Lily came to me after recess and said, "Is it true that Sam figured out the fraction thing?"

"He has a really interesting idea. We'll talk about it tomorrow," I answered. "Have you thought about it?"

Lily rolled her eyes. "It's not my cup of tea," she said.

I realized that Sam's idea would be hard for some of the students, but I decided to go ahead with the lesson. I told the class that we would discuss the list the next day and that we'd begin with Sam's idea.

If Sam hadn't come to me, I would have taken one of two approaches. One would have been to play the role that Sam did, offering the idea for one-seventh or another of the fractions with odd denominators, then giving the class several more days to ruminate. Or I'd pull aside a small group of students who I thought would understand, offer them an idea, and then give them the assignment of thinking further before a class discussion.

The next day the class discussion went as I predicted, with some students understanding well, others understanding partially, and some confused. Some of the students had been able to use Sam's idea and apply it to the other fractions on the list. With their help, I completed the list so it looked like this:

$$\frac{1}{2} + \frac{0}{2} = \frac{1}{2}$$
$$\frac{1}{3} + \frac{1}{6} = \frac{1}{2}$$
$$\frac{1}{4} + \frac{1}{4} = \frac{1}{2}$$
$$\frac{1}{5} + \frac{1\frac{1}{2}}{5} = \frac{2\frac{1}{2}}{5} = \frac{1}{2}$$
$$\frac{1}{6} + \frac{2}{6} = \frac{1}{2}$$
$$\frac{1}{7} + \frac{2\frac{1}{2}}{7} = \frac{3\frac{1}{2}}{7} = \frac{1}{2}$$
$$\frac{1}{8} + \frac{3}{8} = \frac{1}{2}$$
$$\frac{1}{9} + \frac{3\frac{1}{2}}{9} = \frac{4\frac{1}{2}}{9} = \frac{1}{2}$$
$$\frac{1}{10} + \frac{4}{10} = \frac{1}{2}$$
$$\frac{1}{11} + \frac{4\frac{1}{2}}{11} = \frac{5\frac{1}{2}}{11} = \frac{1}{2}$$
$$\frac{1}{12} + \frac{5}{12} = \frac{1}{2}$$

Andrew said, "It's a pattern with halves in it—one, one and a half, two, two and a half, three, three and a half. It's counting by halves."

"But it doesn't work up there at the top," Tom said.

Rebecca almost jumped out of her seat. "Yes! It does!" she shouted. The others looked at her, surprised at the outburst. "Can I come up?" she asked me. I agreed.

"You have to change the one-sixth," she said, pointing to $\frac{1}{3} + \frac{1}{6} = \frac{1}{2}$ on the chart.

"One-sixth is half of a third, so you could write it like this." She wrote on the board:
$$\frac{\frac{1}{2}}{3}$$

There were admiring "ooohs" and "aaahs" from some students and grumbling and confusion from others.

"Oh yeah," Andrew said. "That makes the pattern work." To clarify this, I added to the list:

$$\frac{1}{2} + \frac{0}{2} = \frac{1}{2}$$
$$\frac{1}{3} + \frac{1}{6} = \frac{1}{2} , \ \frac{1}{3} + \frac{\frac{1}{2}}{3} = \frac{1\frac{1}{2}}{3} = \frac{1}{2}$$
$$\frac{1}{4} + \frac{1}{4} = \frac{1}{2}$$
$$\frac{1}{5} + \frac{1\frac{1}{2}}{5} = \frac{2\frac{1}{2}}{5} = \frac{1}{2}$$
$$\frac{1}{6} + \frac{2}{6} = \frac{1}{2}$$
$$\frac{1}{7} + \frac{2\frac{1}{2}}{7} = \frac{3\frac{1}{2}}{7} = \frac{1}{2}$$
$$\frac{1}{8} + \frac{3}{8} = \frac{1}{2}$$
$$\frac{1}{9} + \frac{3\frac{1}{2}}{9} = \frac{4\frac{1}{2}}{9} = \frac{1}{2}$$
$$\frac{1}{10} + \frac{4}{10} = \frac{1}{2}$$
$$\frac{1}{11} + \frac{4\frac{1}{2}}{11} = \frac{5\frac{1}{2}}{11} = \frac{1}{2}$$
$$\frac{1}{12} + \frac{5}{12} = \frac{1}{2}$$

I ended the discussion at this point. Some of the students were pleased and excited and some sat quietly, not understanding. Lily was still rolling her eyes.

"I'll leave the chart up," I said. "All of it may not make sense to you now, but I know that with some time, you will be able to understand what we've done. This is complicated and advanced thinking. Students usually don't encounter fractions with fractions in the numerator until high school, so if what's on our list doesn't make sense now, don't worry. You'll have plenty of chances to think about problems like this as you continue to study fractions."

Questions and Discussion

▲▲

▲ *If the students rely on patterns to come up with answers, how can you be sure that they understand what the fractions really mean?*

There's no single path for students to learn, and a focus on patterns in this lesson offers an alternate approach for helping students develop their understanding of fractions. It's possible that some students will focus merely on the patterns and not connect them to the meaning of fractions, but that isn't a harmful risk. Thinking about patterns is mathematically important in itself and, in this context, at the very least plants the notion of using patterns to make sense of fractional relationships.

▲ *It seems that the lesson gives students missing addend problems with fractions. Shouldn't this be done after they've learned to add fractions?*

While the problems ask students to identify missing addends, the lesson doesn't focus on students applying a particular procedure for adding or subtracting. Rather, the students are expected to reason using all of the ideas and tools they've accumulated. The experience is useful for building a foundation of understanding fractional relationships on which more formal instruction in adding and subtracting fractions will rest.

▲ *What do you do for the students who aren't able to understand what is going on? Don't you worry about them?*

I know that confusion and partial understanding are natural to the process of learning. I also know that all students don't learn at the same time or in the same way. While a lesson like this can pose difficulties for some students, other lessons will be easier for them. What's important is that I establish a classroom environment that recognizes differences and is committed to helping all students learn. I'm not worried that math is sometimes hard for some students. I try to communicate to students that while they may not understand something yet, I'll work to find ways to help them learn.

CHAPTER TEN
HALVING SQUARES

Overview

In this lesson, students explore different ways to divide squares into halves. For each square they divide, they shade one of the halves and must be prepared to justify how they are sure that the section they shaded is truly one-half. One idea that emerges from this activity is that while the two halves of the square have to be the same size, they do not have to be the same shape. This investigation provides students a way to think about halves geometrically and also gives them experience with the concept of area.

Materials

▲ *Halving Squares* worksheet, at least 1 per pair of students (see Blackline Masters)

Time

▲ one class period

Teaching Directions

1. Draw a square on the board and ask for a suggestion about how to divide it into halves. Call on a student, divide the square according to the suggestion made, and shade one of the halves. Repeat for two or three more squares, each time asking students for a suggestion for cutting the square in half in a different way. Following are typical suggestions that students give.

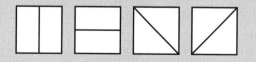

2. Tell the students that they will work in pairs and explore different ways to divide squares in half. Show them the *Halving Squares* worksheet and give the following directions: "Working with a partner, divide each square on the worksheet into halves and shade one of the halves. You should be able to cut on the lines you draw and have the part you shaded be the same size as the rest of the square. Divide each square in a different way. Also, be prepared to explain why you're sure each section you've shaded in is equal to one-half."

3. As the students work, draw three more squares on the board as shown. These will be useful for a later class discussion and also can spark children's ideas while they are working on their worksheets.

4. After fifteen or twenty minutes, interrupt the students for a class discussion. Ask pairs to look over their worksheets and each choose a square to share that they think is unique.

5. Draw a square on the board and invite a pair to come up and divide it as they did on the square they chose from their worksheet. Ask them to explain how they are sure that the shaded portion is one-half. Invite the class to challenge or comment. Repeat for other pairs of students.

6. Ask students to consider the three squares that you drew on the board while they were working. Refer to the second two squares to reinforce the idea that halves don't have to be the same shape, but they have to be the same size. It may help to ask the children to think about each square as a square of chocolate that they are going to share. Remind them that it's possible to have the same amount of chocolate without having same-shape pieces.

Teaching Notes

An important mathematics concept for children to learn is that all halves of the same whole are the same size. If a whole is divided into two parts, and the parts are different sizes, then the parts are not mathematical halves. Two halves can only be different sizes when they are halves of two different wholes. Half of a grapefruit, for example, is typically larger than half of an orange.

While halves of same-size wholes must be the same size, they don't necessarily have to be the same shape. Think about making two sandwiches using slices of bread from the same loaf. Suppose you cut each sandwich in half a different way, cutting one on the diagonal to make triangular halves and the other down the middle to make rectangular halves. The halves from the two sandwiches are different shapes, but they each represent half of the same-size sandwich and, therefore, are the same size. You'd have the same amount to eat no matter which shape you chose.

When they divide squares, some children may at first think that the two halves have to be identical; that is, the halves have to be congruent pieces. It's important to help them realize that as long as the areas of the two pieces are the same, then the pieces are halves. The following description of the lesson presents one way to do that.

Typically in the lesson, students at first think only of several ways to divide a square in half, but with some encouragement they begin to see that there are many other possibilities. A realization that can emerge from the lesson is that there are an infinite number of ways to divide a square into halves.

The Lesson

▲▲▲

I drew a square on the board and asked the class, "Who can tell me how to divide the square into halves?" Many hands shot up and I called on Jose. I was pleased to see that he had volunteered, as he usually is reticent about participating. However, Jose got flustered and forgot his idea. I repeated my question, and he still wasn't able to respond.

"How about I let someone else answer now and you can take a turn a little later," I said gently. Jose looked relieved. I called on Trent.

"You can put a line through it," he said.

"Where shall I draw the line?" I asked.

"In the middle," he said.

"Where do I start?" I asked. It takes experience and practice for the children to be precise in their explanations.

"Start on the middle of the left and draw a horizontal line," Trent then said.

"Ah, that helps me understand what you were thinking," I said. I drew a line to divide the square.

I then drew another square next to this one and asked, "Who can tell me how to divide this square into halves in a different way? Jose, would you like to try now?"

Jose nodded and said, with confidence, "You go diagonally."

"Okay, but starting from which corner?" I asked.

"Up on the left," he said. I divided the square as he suggested.

I drew another square and asked for a suggestion to divide it in half. I called on Marlo.

"You draw an up-and-down line," she said. "I always forget the word."

"Do you mean vertical?" I asked.

Marlo answered, "That's it, you draw a vertical line down the middle." I did this, then stopped to write *horizontal, diagonal,* and *vertical* on the board.

When I drew a fourth square, from previous experience I had expected that a student would suggest drawing a diagonal line in the other direction, but when I called on Jonathan, I could tell from the smile on his face that he had another idea. "Start at the top but a little bit in and then go on a slant, I mean a diagonal, and get to the bottom but not to the corner but a little bit in." I wasn't clear about what Jonathan was explaining.

"Where on the top do I start?" I asked.

"Near the corner but in," he said. "Can I just come up and show you? I really don't know how to tell." I agreed. Jonathan came up and drew a line to divide the square.

I turned to the class. "Thumbs up, down, or sideways to show that you agree, disagree, or aren't sure if Jonathan divided the square in half." Some students saw clearly that they were halves, but others weren't sure. Carla offered an explanation.

"You can see they're both the same, just one is upside down. If you cut it apart, you could turn it and check." she said. Several students responded with "Oh yeah," or "I see it now."

"You can't cut the board," Jonathan said.

I ignored his comment and said, "If you want to be sure, then drawing it on paper, as you'll be doing soon, and cutting it apart can sometimes help you tell that the two pieces of a square really are halves."

"Can I do one?" Cynthia asked. I agreed and drew another square on the board.

"Start in the middle of the top and draw a back-and-forth line down the middle like a zipper," she directed. I drew a vertical zigzag line.

"That's it," Cynthia said.

"What do you think?" I said to the class. All thumbs were up.

I then gave directions for the assignment they were to tackle. I showed the class the worksheet I had prepared with six squares on it. "You'll work with a partner," I said. "Try to figure out how to divide each of these squares in half a different way."

"Can we use the ways on the board?" Margaret wanted to know.

"No, see what other ways you can find," I answered. "After you divide a square, shade in one of the halves." I returned to the board and shaded one of the halves in each of the squares to model this for the students.

I gave final directions. "When I look at squares you've divided, I'll look first to see if it's clear how I might cut the square on the lines you drew. Then I'll look to see if the part you shaded is the same size as the other part of the square." I assigned partners, having

students work with the people sitting next to them and rearranging a few who were at tables that had an odd number of students.

OBSERVING THE STUDENTS

The children got to work quickly, anticipating that the activity would be fun to tackle. A few relied on ideas already on the board, drawing a diagonal in the opposite direction or a line as Jonathan had done but horizontally. Many did versions of Cynthia's zigzag suggestion, some in more intricate patterns. Others used curvy lines to divide squares.

When I noticed that some students were running out of ideas, I went to the board and drew three more squares, divided each into two sections, shaded in one of them, and put a question mark next to each to indicate to the students that they might think about whether I had drawn halves. I drew these squares to help students generate other ideas, but I also planned to use the squares for a class discussion.

As I circulated, looking at what students were doing, I reminded several pairs of students to shade in one-half of their squares. An error that several pairs of students made was to divide a square creatively, but in a way that didn't clearly show where it should be cut. Jose and Philip had such an example, as did Frank and Nickie.

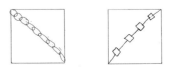

I asked each pair to shade the part that they thought was one-half. Jose and Philip abandoned their idea, but Frank and Nickie were able to make an adjustment to correct what they had initially drawn.

After about fifteen minutes, when several of the pairs had divided all six squares, I interrupted the students and told them they had just a few moments to finish what they were doing and that it wasn't necessary for them to have completed the entire worksheet. I then called the class to attention for a class discussion. If time remained afterwards, I'd have had them continue working on their papers. I've found that a class discussion can help spark students' thinking. Also, I wanted to discuss the shapes I had drawn.

A CLASS DISCUSSION

I began the class discussion by asking each pair to look over their paper and choose one square that they'd like to share with the class. "Choose one that you think is particularly unique," I said.

"What's unique?" Frank asked.

"It means really different," Trent said.

While giving partners a few moments to make their choices, I erased the first five squares I had drawn on the board to make room for their ideas. I left on the board, however, the three squares I had drawn while they were working. I drew a square on the board and asked for a volunteer to share. Kevin came up first and drew one of his and Diego's ideas.

He said, "You can tell the halves are the same because there are five bumps on the shaded side and five bumps on the plain side, and the line is in the middle." The other students agreed.

I drew another square on the board and Carla came up. It was hard for her to draw on the board and she erased and started over several times, apologizing as she did so. Finally she had a fairly good replica of what she and Trent had done.

George came up then and divided the next square I drew. "I took this idea from what you drew on the board over there," he said, indicating the squares I had drawn while they were working. "Ours isn't as fancy."

I then focused the class on the first of the three squares I had drawn. "What do you think of the first square I divided? Do you think the part I shaded is worth one-half?" I asked. This seemed clear to the students.

"What about the second square?" I asked. There was disagreement about this. A few students sketched it on paper and got out scissors to cut the pieces. Meanwhile, Cindy came to the board and divided the shaded part.

"If you cut up the diamond like this," she explained, "then it has four triangles, and each one has a partner, so it has to be half."

"Oh, look!" Diego said, excitedly. "You can just fold in the corners." Diego had divided a square on his worksheet as I had and had cut it out. Before cutting on the lines, he saw that he could fold in the corners. Others were impressed and several wanted to try it for themselves to check. One benefit of using concrete materials is that children can have an actual physical check of their ideas. I gave the students a little time to do this and talk among themselves. Then I called them back to attention.

"What about my third square?" I asked.

"That definitely doesn't work," Ruthie said.

"Do you think the part I shaded is too much or too little?" I asked her.

"You can't divide it that way and tell," she answered.

"I think you can," Jonathan said. "It looks like you could fold over the edges."

"But they wouldn't touch," Carla said.

"It has to be possible. You can divide things any way you want," Trent said.

"I think it's too hard to figure out," Marlo said.

"You might be right," I said. "This is hard for fourth grade, but let me see if I can help you." I drew another square and also drew lines to make it a 10-by-10 grid.

"There are ten small squares across and ten down," I said. "Do you know how many small squares there are altogether in the square I drew?" Several knew immediately that there were one hundred; others needed a little more time to think before coming up with an answer.

When there was agreement, I said, "Imagine that this is a block of chocolate with lines in it so I can break it into little squares. If I were going to share this with you so we each had half, how many little squares would you get?" A few children made guesses—thirty, forty, and thirty-five. I was surprised that the correct answer wasn't obvious for the fourth graders. Then Trent said, "It has to be fifty." Everyone immediately agreed.

"You could split it down the middle," Drew said.

"Or across," Margaret added.

"I can split it in any way as long as we both get fifty small squares," I said. "Let me think." I outlined a 7-by-7 square and shaded it in.

"How many small squares in this 7-by-7 piece?" I asked. "How could you figure that out?" Several students said that you needed to do seven times seven. Conversation broke out and when I called them back to attention, we agreed that there were forty-nine pieces in the square in the middle.

"But you'll be cheated because you don't have fifty," Carla said.

"Yeah, we'll have fifty-one," Jonathan said.

"I could give you one of mine," Carla said. She asked to come to the board. I agreed and she added a square onto the shaded part. "Your piece has a teeny handle," she said.

"We did it," Trent said with satisfaction.

Diego raised his hand. "It's the same as the one you did before," he said, referring to the square he had drawn and cut out. "The square on this one is the same as the diamond on the other." Again, conversation broke out.

"If I tilt my head," I said, "then I can see that the diamond is really a square, and I agree that they're about the same size. You can try this for yourselves. Or try to think of other ways to divide squares on your worksheet into halves."

Questions and Discussion

▲▲

▲ *What's the value of students dividing squares into halves that are different sizes or even different numbers of pieces?*

It's important to help children become as flexible as possible in their math thinking. A risk of using just one model for introducing fractions is that children can erroneously think of fractions in one way, as pieces of a circle or parts of a rectangle. In the same way, when we focus on dividing a particular shape, it's valuable to stretch students' thinking beyond considering congruent pieces. In this case, dividing squares helps introduce the idea that halves must have the same area but not identical shapes.

▲ *Why didn't you present the ideas of the squares you drew and divided before they got to work? Wouldn't that have helped give them more ideas?*

I wanted the students to have some firsthand experience grappling with the challenge of dividing squares into halves before I asked them to focus on my ideas. When children have had experience with an idea, I find that they're better prepared to absorb new information. They can connect the new information to what they've already done and discovered. Also, for these fourth graders, I find that keeping whole-class discussions shorter and getting them directly involved is more effective.

▲ *Would it be a good idea to ask students to find more ways for homework?*

Yes, it's a fine idea to give each student a fresh worksheet and ask him or her to find other ways to divide the squares into halves. This not only gives them extra practice but also gives them the experience of tackling the challenge on their own without the help of partners.

CHAPTER ELEVEN
SHARING COOKIES

Overview

In this lesson, students share "cookies" among three, four, and six people. The cookies are actually paper circles that students can fold and cut as they explore how to divide them equally. From this exploration, students learn about dividing different quantities into equal shares and also have the opportunity to see relationships among halves, thirds, fourths, and sixths.

Materials

▲ *Circles for Cookies* worksheet, duplicated on white paper, approximately 2 sheets per student (see Blackline Masters)

▲ *Sharing Cookies* worksheets for sharing among 3, 4, and 6 people, each duplicated on a different color paper (not white), approximately 2 sheets of each per student (see Blackline Masters)

▲ optional: *Fractions with Cookies* worksheet, 1 per pair of students (see Blackline Masters)

▲ scissors

▲ paste or glue

Time

▲ two class periods

Teaching Directions

1. Draw on the board a replica of the sheet for sharing cookies among four people. In the box for the number of cookies to share, write a *4*. Also, draw four circles on the board to represent the four cookies.

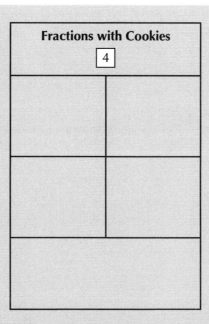

2. Ask: "How would you share four cookies among four people?" The problem will be trivial for the class. Model for the students how to record by drawing a circle in each of the spaces on the board, checking off one of the "cookies" you drew as you do so. Also, record below: *Each person gets one cookie.*

3. Then ask: "How would you share five cookies among four people?" Redo the worksheet, write a *5* in the box, and draw five circles for the cookies. Ask students to explain their thinking, giving more than one student the chance to respond if each reasoned differently. Record again by drawing a circle and a fourth of a circle in each space. Record below in several ways:

Each person gets 1 cookie and $\frac{1}{4}$ of a cookie. Each person gets $1\frac{1}{4}$ cookies. Each person gets $\frac{5}{4}$ cookies.

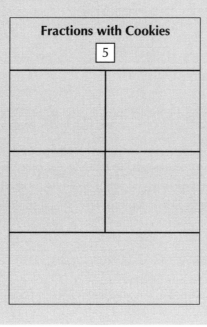

4. Repeat for sharing one cookie among three people. Cross out one of the boxes on the worksheet on the board so that there are only three places to place cookie shares. Talk with the class about how to share the cookie and have students explain their reasoning. Then draw one-third of a cookie in each space and record: *Each person gets $\frac{1}{3}$ of a cookie.*

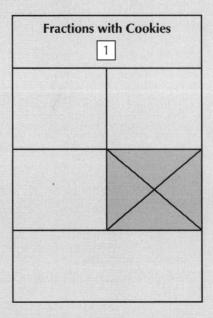

5. Next ask: "How can you share four cookies among three people?" Again, have students explain, draw the cookie shares, and record: *Each person gets $1\frac{1}{3}$ cookies.*

6. Model with one last problem: "How can you share seven cookies among six people?" Alter the worksheet on the board so that it has six spaces. For this example, not only record the answers but also record explanations from at least two of the students to model for the class how they are to write when they work on their own.

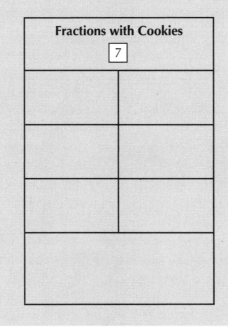

7. Show the class the three versions of the worksheet for sharing among three, four, and six people. Explain the activity. Write the directions on the board or distribute copies:

Fractions with Cookies

1. Do five worksheets, one of each version and two others of your choice.
2. Use no more than 20 cookies for any one worksheet.
3. Cut "cookies" into equal shares and paste them in the appropriate places.
4. Record how much each person gets. Explain your reasoning.
5. For each sheet, choose a number of cookies that is not a multiple of the number of people.

Discuss the last direction with the class to be sure that the students understand what multiples are.

Teaching Notes

A version of the *Sharing Cookies* activity appears in *A Collection of Math Lessons, Grades 3–6*, a book I wrote more than ten years ago. In that version, third graders concentrated on sharing cookies among only four people. That's also the way I've introduced the activity with fourth graders who were just beginning to think about fractions.

I decided to restructure the activity into a more complex version for these fifth graders because they had more prior experience with fractions than the third and fourth graders I previously did the activity with. They had already worked with fraction kits and pattern blocks, and this exploration gave students a different context in which to confront the ideas they were learning about fractions.

The Lesson

▲▲▲

DAY 1

In preparation for the lesson, I duplicated three versions of a worksheet for sharing cookies among three, four, and six people. I duplicated each version on a different color paper, making enough copies so that there was one for every two children. Also, I duplicated circles that would be the cookies on white paper. Using colors for the activity sheets would make the white circles clearly visible and, therefore, easier to use for later class discussion.

To begin the class, I drew on the board a replica of the sheet for sharing cookies among four people. In the box for the number of cookies to share, I wrote a *4*. I also drew four circles on the board to represent the four cookies.

"How would you share four cookies among four people?" I asked. Hands shot up and there were titters and comments of surprise at this easy question. I called on Shannon.

"They'd each get a cookie," she said.

"I agree," I said. As I drew a circle in each of the spaces on the board, I checked off one of the cookies I had drawn on the board. Then I recorded below: *Each person gets one cookie.*

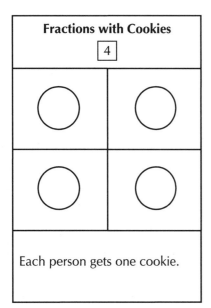

Fractions with Cookies

4

Each person gets one cookie.

While this example was trivial mathematically, I used it to establish the routine for how students were to use the worksheets when they worked on their own. Explicit directions and modeling when introducing something new help avoid confusion later, and I've learned to err through overkill rather than make assumptions that lead to later distractions.

I erased the check marks I had made next to the cookies and what I had recorded on the worksheet. I added a circle to the four on the board so I had five cookies represented. "How would you share five cookies among four people?" I asked. Again, I chose a question that I thought would be easy. Most hands shot up, but not immediately from all of the students.

"You can't do that," Robert said.

"Yes, you can," Lara countered. "Just divide a cookie."

"Oh yeah," Robert said.

"Oh yeah," Dan also said.

This was a quick exchange, done softly, so I didn't reprimand the students for speaking out, even though I'd been struggling to

get them to raise their hands during lessons and wait to be called on. Instead, I waited until the room was quiet and all hands were raised. I called on Claudia.

"They each get a cookie and a quarter of a cookie," she said. Others agreed. I drew one cookie in each space, again checking off these circles I had drawn on the left. One cookie was left. I looked at Claudia.

"Just divide that one into fourths and put a fourth in each space," she said.

I did what Claudia suggested. As I drew a fourth of a circle in each space, I said, "You won't have to draw when you do this activity. You'll have paper cookies to cut and paste." Then I asked, "What should I write for how much each person gets?" I called on Delia.

"Each person gets one cookie and a fourth," she said.

"A fourth of what?" I asked. I'm always pushing the children to define the whole.

"A fourth of a cookie," she added. I wrote:

Each person gets 1 cookie and $\frac{1}{4}$ of a cookie.

"I know a shortcut way to write each person's share," I said. "When you have a whole number and a fraction, you can write it like this." I wrote:

Each person gets $1\frac{1}{4}$ cookies.

Dan raised his hand. "I have another way to write it," he said. "Each person gets five-fourths." I recorded on the board:

Each person gets $\frac{5}{4}$ cookies.

"Explain how you got that," I said to Dan.

His response was precise. "If you cut up one cookie, you get four fourths, and one more makes five fourths."

"That works," I agreed. "Any comments or questions?" There were none.

I erased what I had recorded, again leaving just the worksheet. I then did two examples with sharing cookies among three people—first sharing one cookie and then sharing four cookies. I crossed out one of the boxes on my replica of the worksheet so that there were only three places to draw cookie shares, just as I had done on the worksheets they were going to use. For the first example, I drew one circle to the side and wrote a *1* in the box on the worksheet.

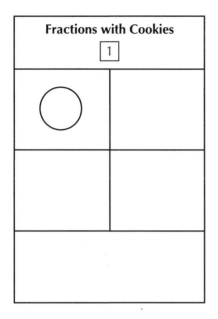

"How would you share one cookie among three people?" I asked.

After all hands were raised, I called on Grant.

"They each get a third," he said.

I drew lines to divide the circle I had drawn into thirds and then drew a third in each of the spaces, commenting aloud that drawing the letter *Y* was a good way to approximate thirds. I've found that students often are initially confused by dividing a circle into thirds and it warrants discussion. (Beware, however, that some students try to draw the letter *Y* when dividing a square into thirds! See page 141 for *The Y Problem,* an assessment that relates to this.)

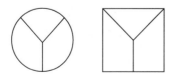

Some of the students criticized that the thirds I drew didn't "look right." I responded,

"It would be easier if I cut and pasted paper circles, as you will. It's hard to draw." I recorded on the board:

Each person gets $\frac{1}{3}$ of a cookie.

For my second example, sharing four cookies among three people, I drew four circles on the board. I purposely chose this example to avoid having them figure out how to share two cookies among three people, as they would have to do with sharing two or five cookies. I wanted to have the students tackle thinking about sharing two cookies among three people when they were working in pairs and had the circles in hand. While whole-class instruction is useful for helping students understand what they are to do, it's not the best setting to have students grapple with a problem that might be difficult without having, as in this instance, the opportunity to get their hands on their own cookies. (In retrospect, it might have been a good pedagogical strategy to ask them to share two cookies among three people and guide them to see how that answer should be twice as much as the answer for sharing one cookie among three people.)

"How would you share four cookies among three people?" I asked.

From the quick response of hands, I assessed that this was also easy for them. I called on Libby to answer, and she did so correctly. I quickly drew the cookies in the spaces and recorded: *Each person gets $1\frac{1}{3}$ cookies.*

Next I introduced the problem of sharing seven cookies among six people. I altered the worksheet on the board so that it had six spaces. For this example, not only did I record their answers, but I also recorded explanations from two of the students to model for the class what I expected them to write when they worked on their own. Also, writing verbatim what the students say is a way to help students realize that what they write can be directly linked to how they explain their reasoning.

From Delia's explanation, I wrote: *Each person gets $1\frac{1}{6}$ cookies. There are 6 cookies, so each person gets 1. Then divide the last cookie into sixths and each person gets $\frac{1}{6}$.*

From Davey's explanation, I wrote: *Each person gets $\frac{7}{6}$. Each person gets 1 whole and $\frac{1}{6}$, and 1 whole is 6 sixths, and another sixth is $\frac{7}{6}$.*

I left these two explanations on the board for students to refer to when they were working independently.

I then showed the class the three versions of the worksheet and explained the activity. As I gave the directions, I wrote them on the board:

Fractions with Cookies

1. *Do five worksheets, one of each version and two others of your choice.*

2. *Use no more than 20 cookies for any one worksheet.*

3. *Cut "cookies" into equal shares and paste them in the appropriate places.*

4. *Record how much each person gets. Explain your reasoning.*

5. *For each sheet, choose a number of cookies that is not a multiple of the number of people.*

"What do I mean by this last direction?" I asked. "What's a multiple?"

Some hands went up. I called on Maggie.

"A multiple is like two, four, six, eight, like that," she said.

"I agree that the numbers you said— two, four, six, eight—are all multiples of two," I responded. "So what's a multiple?"

"It's something you get when you multiply," Josh said.

I nodded and paraphrased. "A multiple of a number is the product of multiplying the number by some number. Who remembers what we call the numbers you multiply?" Several students remembered "factor."

"When you share cookies among four people, what numbers aren't allowed?" I asked.

Jennifer answered, "Four, eight, twelve, sixteen, twenty."

"That's right," I said. "Those are multiples. If you can divide a number into another evenly, without a remainder, then the larger number is a multiple of the smaller one. Four can be divided into all of the numbers Jennifer said. I don't want you to use four, eight, twelve, sixteen, or twenty cookies for this sheet because then there wouldn't be any need to think about fractions. Pick numbers that aren't multiples so that you'll have to use fractions to share all the cookies evenly."

I distributed one of each color sheet and a sheet of cookies to each pair of students, put the rest of the sheets on the supply table, and had the students begin work.

Observing the Students

I circulated as the students worked. I observed Josh and Robert sharing four cookies among six people. Josh had cut all of the cookies into halves and had glued a half in each of the six spaces. There were two halves left.

"Oh, I know," he said. "Let's cut each of these into thirds." Robert agreed and they each snipped a half into three pieces.

"They're each a sixth," Josh said to me, noticing I was paying attention to what they were doing. "They each get one-half and one-sixth."

"How do you know each of those small pieces is one-sixth?" I asked.

"Because three make a half and three make the other half, so there are six from a whole," he answered.

Robert was frowning. "What are you thinking?" I asked him.

"We should have started by cutting all of the cookies in thirds," he said. "Then each person would get two-thirds."

Josh stopped gluing the sixths in place to consider this. "Yeah," he said. "That would work."

"So is two-thirds the same as one-half plus one-sixth?" I asked.

Both boys were stopped by this question. "It has to be," Josh said after a moment.

"What do you mean?" Robert asked.

"Can you explain why they have to be the same?" I asked Josh.

Josh shook his head. "I don't think so."

"Oh, look," Robert said. "It's the same. They're both four-sixths. The half is three-sixths and one more is four-sixths. And two-thirds is four-sixths if I cut them each in half."

"Oh," Josh said, nodding. (See Figure 11–1.)

I next went to check on Joseph, who was working with Sean. I knew that Joseph was having difficulty with fractions. In general, Joseph learns at a slower pace than the others and seems comforted when he knows that someone will help him if he has difficulty. He's a willing student, but he needs encouragement as well as a good deal of extra assistance. His partner today, Sean, is a clever student but is prone to play

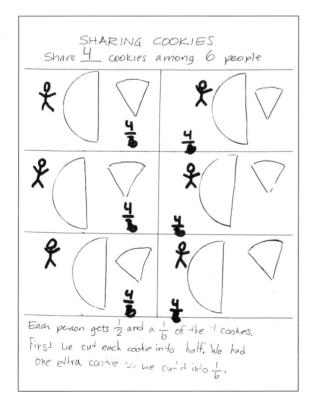

▲▲▲▲▲▲Figure 11–1 *Robert and Josh figured out that $\frac{1}{3}$ of $\frac{1}{2}$ is $\frac{1}{6}$.*

whenever he can. He seems younger than the others, but he is a good worker and is invested in doing well.

Joseph and Sean were on their first problem, working on sharing ten cookies among four people. They had already divided the cookies by pasting two cookies and an additional half cookie in each space. Sean was busily writing at the bottom of the sheet.

Sean looked up and said to me, "Joseph glued and I'm writing." I've worked hard with students to be sure that both students are involved when working in pairs, and Sean wanted to assure me that this was the case.

"How did you decide on using ten cookies?" I asked.

Sean kept on writing and Joseph answered. "It was Sean's idea."

"How did you feel about using ten cookies?"

"Okay," Joseph said, in a noncommittal tone. I wasn't sure how he felt.

"Can you explain how you divided up the cookies?" I probed.

"We put the whole ones in the spaces and had two left over. Then we made halves," Joseph answered.

I looked at their paper and noticed that the halves had pencil lines on them, as if the boys had contemplated dividing them into fourths. I commented on what I noticed. Sean looked up from his writing.

He said, "Well, at first I thought we should cut them into fourths since there were four people, but then I realized we didn't have to, that we could just make halves and we would have four of them."

I looked at Joseph's face but still got no clue about his thinking. "Can you tell me how much each person's share is?" I asked Joseph.

He looked down at the paper and answered, "Two cookies and a half of a cookie." Sean was now through writing. I picked up the paper.

"Joseph, how about reading aloud what Sean wrote so you and I can be sure we agree with it?" Joseph did this. Sean had written:

Each person gets 2 cookies and $\frac{1}{2}$ of a cookie. We went around to each square and put one cookie in each untill we had 2 cookies in each square, but we had 2 cookies left wich we cut $\frac{1}{2}$'s and we had 4 $\frac{1}{2}$'s left. We put the $\frac{1}{2}$'s in the squares.

"That's what we did," Joseph said after reading.

"Let's do sharing with six people next," Sean said, reaching for another worksheet. "How many cookies should we use, Joseph?"

"You pick," Joseph said.

Sean thought for a minute. Then he grinned and said, "Let's do nine cookies."

"How come nine?" I asked.

"I know I can do that," he said. "I can tell it will be easy."

"Do you know how much each person will get?" I asked.

"I think one and a half, but I'm not sure," he said. "Let's cut out the cookies, Joseph."

"Remember to talk about what you're doing," I said. "And after one of you does the writing, the other one should read it aloud so that you can both check that you agree." I left the boys to work.

Even though I didn't get much information from Joseph about his thinking, Sean's comments helped me see how he was thinking and that he knew how to choose a problem he was sure of being able to do.

I noticed Jennifer and Davey working together on their first problem, sharing sixteen cookies among three people. "We thought a problem with a big number would be interesting," Davey told me. They worked efficiently, cutting out circles quickly and overlapping one on the other on their sheets until they had pasted five in each section. As Davey pasted them down, Jennifer cut the remaining circle into thirds. Jennifer then recorded:

Each person gets $5\frac{1}{3}$ cookies. There are sixteen cookies if you leave out one cookie thats 15 and 15 ÷ 3 = 5 and there's one cookie left cut it into thirds and it's even.

I left once they decided on their next problem, to share eighteen cookies among four people.

Time for math was over, so I had the students gather up their work and have it ready for the next day. I said, "When we start math tomorrow, just get back to work where you left off."

DAY 2

At the beginning of class the next day, I told the students to get back to their cookie problems. I circulated to make sure they had all gotten started again, encouraging a few and solving the problem of Josh and Robert's missing work. (It was in Robert's cubby.)

Then I went to see how Dan and Grant were doing. In contrast to the large numbers of cookies that Jennifer and Davey had been choosing, Dan and Grant chose small numbers—first sharing two cookies among four people and then sharing two cookies among three people. Now they were completing work on sharing two cookies among six people. They had pasted down the cookies but hadn't recorded yet.

"How come you chose those problems?" I asked the boys.

"We wanted to see how they would come out," Dan said.

"And we thought they'd be easy," Grant said, grinning.

"How did they come out?" I asked. "Let's take a look." They placed the three sheets next to one another on the table.

"Look, there's two pieces in each part on all of them," Grant said.

"What do you mean?" Dan asked.

"See, on this one, they each get two-thirds," Grant said, pointing to the sheet on which they had shared two cookies among three people. He then added, pointing to the other worksheets, "And on this one they got two-fourths and on this one they got two-sixths."

"But the pieces are smaller when there are six people," Dan said.

"Does that make sense?" I asked.

Grant answered. "There are more people, so they get less."

I left the boys and turned to Maggie and Shannon. They were sharing six cookies among four people and had correctly pasted one circle and a half of a circle in each section. However, they had written:

Each person gets $1\frac{1}{4}$ cookies. We had 6 cookies and we gave a cookie to each person, then we had 2 cookies left and four people.

I pointed to one of the sections on the worksheet with one whole cookie and half of a cookie pasted in it. "How much is in this section?" I asked.

"A cookie and a half," Shannon answered. I looked at Maggie and she nodded her agreement.

"I agree," I said. "But I'm confused by what you wrote below." The girls both read what they had written.

"Ohhh, I think it should be one and one-half," Shannon said.

Maggie had done the writing and defended what she had recorded, "But there are four people, so they each get a quarter of what there is."

"But they got a cookie and a half," Shannon insisted.

"See, they each get a quarter," Maggie said to us. "One and a half is a quarter of six cookies."

"Now I'm confused," Shannon said.

"You're both thinking right," I said. "But there's a problem with how you recorded your thinking mathematically, Maggie. If you look at what you pasted down, it shows that each person gets one and a half cookies. I agree that you divided the cookies into

four equal shares so you have quarters. You could say each person gets one quarter of the cookies altogether."

"So I'm wrong?" Maggie asked.

"Your thinking is correct," I responded. "But what you wrote doesn't mathematically express what you explained."

"Oh, I know now," Maggie suddenly said. "They each get one and a half cookies." She reached for their paper to make the change.

"That's what I thought," Shannon said, watching Maggie make the change.

Later when I checked their work, I noticed that they had done another paper sharing eleven cookies among four people. In each section, they had pasted two whole cookies, a half of a cookie, and a quarter of a cookie. They had written:

Each person gets $2\frac{3}{4}$ cookies. We put 2 cookies, we had 3 cookies left over. We cut 2 cookies in $\frac{1}{2}$ and the last cookie in $\frac{1}{4}$'s.

They had combined all of the pieces and correctly expressed that each person got two and three-fourths cookies. (See Figure 11–2.)

I left the girls and moved over to check on Jennifer and Davey, who were talking about sharing eighteen cookies among four people. They had shared the whole cookies, pasting four in each place, and had cut the two remaining cookies into halves.

"Let's cut them into fourths," Jennifer said.

"We don't have to," Davey said. "We have enough halves."

"But we're dividing them for four people," Jennifer said. "We need fourths."

"You don't have to have fourths," Davey protested.

"But you always have fourths if you divide something for four people," Jennifer stated.

Davey shrugged, overpowered for the moment by Jennifer's insistence. Jennifer cut the halves into fourths and placed two fourths in each space.

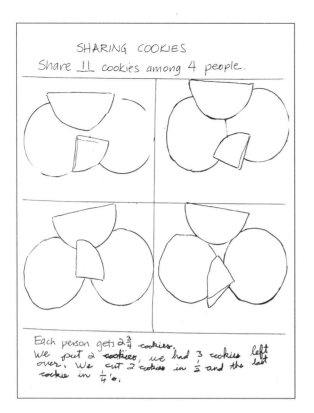

SHARING COOKIES
Share 11 cookies among 4 people.

Each person gets 2¾ cookies.
We put 2 ~~cookies~~, we had 3 cookies left
over. We cut 2 cookies in ½ and the last
cookie in ¼'s.

▲▲▲▲▲▲Figure 11–2 *When they shared
11 cookies among 4 people, Shannon and Maggie
realized that* $\frac{1}{2}$ *plus* $\frac{1}{4}$ *was the same as* $\frac{3}{4}$.

"Here, glue these down," she said, pointing to the circles while she started to write.
She wrote:

Each person gets 4 cookies and $\frac{2}{4}$ *cookies
because 4 × 4 is 16. There [are] 2 cookies left
over so we cut them in 4ths and it is equal.*

"I have a question," I said. Jennifer and
Davey looked up. "If I said that each person
gets four and a half cookies, would I also be
right?"

"Yes," Jennifer said. "One-half is the
same as two-fourths." I looked at Davey; he
nodded his agreement.

"So I'm interested in why you cut the
cookies into fourths instead of pasting
down halves," I said.

"She just wouldn't leave them alone,"
Davey said.

"Well, what you've done is correct," I
said. "But I'm curious about why you cut
them."

"It's just clearer this way to me," Jennifer
said. I realized that Jennifer's thinking that
she needed four equal shares was mixed
with her thinking about fourths of a circle. I
wasn't concerned about this because she
seemed clear that one-half and two-fourths
were equivalent. (See Figure 11–3.)

I watched Jennifer and Davey talk about
sharing four cookies among six people.
They quickly cut three of the four cookies
each in half and pasted one-half in each
section. Then they took the last cookie, cut
it into sixths, and pasted one-sixth in each
section. Jennifer wrote:

Each person gets $\frac{1}{2}$ *and* $\frac{1}{6}$ *of a cookie.*

"Can you find one fraction to write that
means the same as one-half and one-sixth
together?" I asked.

"That's hard," Davey said.

"No, it's not," Jennifer said. "It's like we
did with the fraction kit and found one frac-

SHARING COOKIES
Share 18 cookies among 4 people.

Each person gets 4 cookies and ¾ cookies because
4×4 is 16. There 2 cookies left over so
we cut them in 4ths and It is equal.

▲▲▲▲▲▲Figure 11–3 *Jennifer and Davey
were interested in problems with large numbers
of cookies.*

tion for a long train. Look, a half has three-sixths, so it has to be four-sixths altogether."

"Oh, okay, I get it," Davey said.

"Explain it to me in your own words," I said to Davey, to be sure that he understood.

"There are six-sixths in a whole, so a half has three, and one more makes four-sixths," he responded. Jennifer added to the bottom of their paper: *This is the same as $\frac{4}{6}$ of a cookie.*

When I looked at Lara and Delia's work, I noticed a recording error on their paper. They had correctly shared eleven cookies among six people, pasting in each section one whole cookie, one-half of a cookie, and one-third of a cookie. They wrote:

Each person gets $1\frac{1}{2}\frac{1}{3}$ cookies. Since each person gets $\frac{1}{1}$ there are 5 cookies. We cut 3 cookies in half and 2 cookies in 3rds. So each person gets $1\frac{1}{3}\frac{1}{2}$ cookies.

Their error wasn't from lack of conceptual understanding, but of incorrect use of fractional notation, or punctuation. They should have written either: *Each person gets 1, $\frac{1}{2}$, and $\frac{1}{3}$ cookies* or *Each person gets $1 + \frac{1}{2} + \frac{1}{3}$ cookies* or *Each person gets $1\frac{1}{2}$ cookies and $\frac{1}{3}$ more.*

I explained to the girls, "You don't need the 'and' when there's a whole number and a fraction, but with two fractions next to one another, you have to include either 'and' or a plus sign." This information isn't lodged in conceptual understanding of fractions, but in the social conventions of the symbolization, and this is an example of when the only way to teach is by telling. The girls couldn't discover this; they had to learn about it from some source outside of themselves—me, a classmate or other person, or a book.

I then asked the girls what one fraction they could use to combine one-half and one-third so they didn't need the "and." They didn't have an immediate answer.

"Talk about it and I'll check back in a while," I told them. (When I checked back

later, they were still stuck. "It's too hard," Delia said. I told them not to worry, that I'd be helping them with problems like that over the next several weeks.)

I checked back in with Sean and Joseph. The boys were now working on sharing ten cookies among six people. They were cutting out the ten cookies in preparation for sharing them.

"I think this is going to be hard," Sean said. Joseph didn't comment or react but kept on cutting. I left them to work, but Sean came in a bit and asked me for help. "I don't know how to explain what we did," he said.

I joined the boys and looked at what they had done. They had pasted one circle in each of the six sections. They then cut one-third out of each of the four remaining circles, leaving four pieces that were two-thirds of a circle and four pieces that were one-third of a circle. They pasted the two-thirds pieces in four of the sections, and pasted two of the one-third pieces in each of the other two sections. So far, they had written: *Each person gets 1 and $\frac{2}{3}$ cookies. First we put 1 cookie in each square and had three cookies left.*

"If you started with ten cookies, and put one in each of the six sections, then I don't understand why you would have three cookies left," I said.

"Oops," Joseph said. "We had four." Sean made the change on the paper.

"So how do I write about how we cut the rest?" he asked.

"Tell me what you did," I suggested.

"We drew on each circle to make thirds and then we cut out one third and then we pasted them down," Sean said.

"Start by writing that," I said. "Then read it aloud and see if you need to add more. Come and ask me to check and see if you need more details." As I always do, I tried to find ways to encourage them to talk about their ideas as a precursor to writing. It usually seems to help. (See Figure 11–4.)

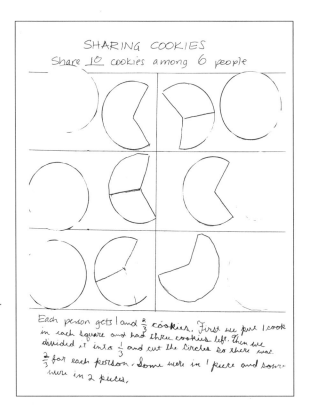

SHARING COOKIES
Share _10_ cookies among 6 people

Each person gets 1 and 2/3 cookies. First we put 1 cookie in each square and had three cookies left. Then we divided it into 1/3 and cut the circles so there was 2/3 for each person. Some were in 1 piece and some were in 2 pieces.

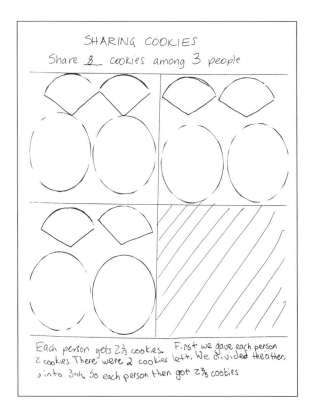

SHARING COOKIES
Share _8_ cookies among 3 people

Each person gets 2 2/3 cookies. First we gave each person 2 cookies. There were 2 cookies left. We divided the other into 3rds. So each person then got 2 2/3 cookies

▲▲▲▲▲▲Figure 11–4 *After sharing 9 cookies among 6 people, Sean and Joseph tackled sharing 10 cookies among 6 people.*

▲▲▲▲▲▲Figure 11–5 *Lara and Delia were clear about how they shared 8 cookies among 3 people.*

At times I also encourage pairs to talk with other pairs when they're working on the same problem. For example, I noticed that when Josh and Robert shared two cookies among three people, in each section they pasted one-half of a cookie and one-sixth of a cookie. They wrote: *Each person gets $\frac{1}{2}$ and $\frac{1}{6}$ of a cookie. First we cut the cookies in half and their was one $\frac{1}{2}$ left so we cut it in thirds and each piece was $\frac{1}{6}$.* When Dan and Grant did the same problem, however, they had cut both cookies into thirds and pasted two of the thirds in each section. They wrote: *Each person gets $\frac{2}{3}$ of the cookie. If 3 people have 1 cookie they each get $\frac{1}{3}$ because we broke it into 3 parts. Then we did it again.*

I asked the four boys to look at the two papers together and let me know what they thought. They got into a huddle. A few minutes later, Robert came over to me.

"We did it," he said.

"What did you decide?" I asked.

"We're both right," Robert answered. "That was cool."

I did the same with two other pairs of students. Claudia and Libby had shared four cookies among six people by cutting all six cookies into thirds. That gave them twelve thirds. They pasted two of the thirds in each section. Jennifer and Davey, as I explained earlier, had solved the same problem by pasting one-half of a circle and one-sixth of a circle in each section. (See Figures 11–5 and 11–6 for two ways students solved the same problem.)

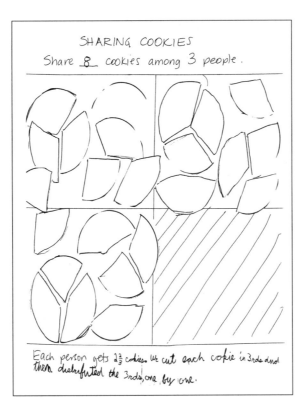

SHARING COOKIES

Share _8_ cookies among 3 people.

Each person gets $2\frac{2}{3}$ cookies. We cut each cookie in 3rds and then distributed the 3rds, one by one.

▲▲▲▲▲▲Figure 11–6 *Dan and Grant had a different solution for the same problem that Lara and Delia did.*

Questions and Discussion

▲▲▲

▲ *What will you do differently when you teach this activity again?*

I liked the way this activity went. When I do it again, I might have students do the same problems and save the opportunity for them to choose their own numbers of cookies for the menu later. But I liked what resulted from this activity. It seemed accessible to all and at the same time challenging for those who were able.

▲ *Did you think about whether or not the fifth graders really needed to cut and paste the "cookies"? Did you consider making that optional for them?*

I've learned from experience not to worry about an activity being too babyish for the students because they have to cut, paste, or work with manipulatives. I've found that students don't object, unless the cutting, pasting, or working with materials seems like meaningless busywork. In this case, the circles provide a way for students to tackle the problems, and what students do with the circles gives me insights into their thinking. In this class, none of the students questioned whether or not they had to cut and paste circles. If they had, I would have explained my reasons—that I thought the circles would give them a way to think about the mathematical ideas and that how they cut the circles would give me important information about how they are thinking about fractions. I'd also tell the students that even as an adult, I need to "see" what I'm doing and rely heavily on sketches to help with math problems.

▲ *Why did you have students choose the number of cookies they would share for the problems?*

I'm always on the lookout for ways to blend instruction and assessment in lessons so that when children are involved in learning activities, I have the opportunity to gain insights into how each of them is thinking. Giving students the chance to set parameters for problems gives me information about their comfort levels and the challenges they're willing to take on.

▲ *Don't you think that if the students all did the same problems, you could more easily have a class discussion later?*

Yes, I guess that's true. As a matter of fact, when I circulated around the room, I looked for common problems that we could discuss. So, upon reflection, I could have assigned some problems in common, maybe giving them three specific ones to try, and then let them do two of their own choosing. This is one of those professional judgment calls for which there's no right answer and probably no wrong choice either.

▲ *You asked students to solve problems of dividing cookies among three, four, and six people. How come you skipped five people?*

I find that it's too hard for the students to divide circles into fifths and then be able to discern the fifths from sixths. With circles, the shapes of halves and fourths are easily recognizable. Thirds are, also, with a little practice. Sixths are related to thirds, so students have a way to cut them. Fifths, however, are more difficult. I don't think that every material is suitable for all possible fraction situations. We'll get to fifths in another way. The context of money is more natural and suitable, I think, since a nickel is one-fifth of a quarter and twenty cents is one-fifth of a dollar.

▲ *What do you talk about with students as you observe them working on this activity?*

When circulating around the room, I offer help when asked, always focusing my help on getting the students to reason for themselves. A good deal of the help I give is helping students get down in writing what they've done. Most important is that students can explain what they're doing and why it makes sense. Hearing students explain gives me insights into their understanding, and having the opportunity to talk about their ideas helps students confirm and often extend their thinking. With this activity, I first look at students' worksheets to check for correctness. If an answer is wrong, I talk with the students about it. Also, I look to see if there are ways I can challenge their thinking further, starting with what they've done.

CHAPTER TWELVE
HOW MUCH IS BLUE?
A PATTERN BLOCK ACTIVITY

Overview

In this activity, students are shown a design made with thirteen pattern block pieces—three green triangles, six blue parallelograms, three red trapezoids, and one yellow hexagon. The problem they solve is: "What fractional part of this design is blue?" The challenge of this problem for students is that they must think about both the fractional parts of the total design and the areas of the individual pattern block pieces. Along with finding the answer, students have to explain their reasoning.

Materials

▲ pattern blocks, enough so that each child can build the design and have extra blocks as well, about 1 bucket per 6 students

▲ *Pattern Block Design* worksheet, 1 per student (see Blackline Masters)

▲ optional for extension: *Pattern Block Triangle Paper* worksheet, 1 per student (see Blackline Masters)

Time

▲ two class periods, plus extra time for students to solve one another's puzzles

Teaching Directions

1. On chart paper or on an overhead transparency, draw the design as shown (see next page) so all students can see it.

2. Discuss with the students what they know about pattern blocks. Then write on the board the problem the students are to solve: *What fractional part of this design is blue?* Ask the children to think about the problem quietly by themselves before you begin a class discussion.

3. After a few moments, begin a class discussion by asking: "Who has an estimate of what the answer might be?" Discuss their ideas.

4. Then give each student a copy of the design drawn to the actual size of pattern blocks. (See Blackline Masters.) Also, distribute pattern blocks. Give the class directions: "Prepare your papers by writing the question at the top. Figure out the answer by using the blocks, drawing pictures, or doing whatever will help you. Then write about how you reasoned." If you have students work in pairs, it's still a good idea for each to write an individual paper.

5. Circulate as the students work, giving help as needed.

6. The next day, have students who are willing report how they solved the problem. To extend the experience, give the following directions: "Each of you should make your own design using an assortment of green, blue, red, and yellow pattern blocks. Draw your design on pattern block paper and then pose a question: What fractional part of the design is _____? (Choose one of the colors.) On a separate sheet, record the answer and explain your reasoning."

7. Check the students' papers for accuracy. Then either devote class time for all students to figure out answers to one another's designs or organize the designs and answers into two folders and use them for a choice activity.

Teaching Notes

In the November 1995 issue of the NCTM journal *Teaching Children Mathematics* (Volume 2, Number 3), Janet H. Caldwell, professor of mathematics at Rowan College in New Jersey, wrote an article titled "Communicating About Fractions with Pattern Blocks." After reading the article, I tried the activity and found it effective for engaging students and assessing their understanding.

An interesting aspect of the problem is that while six of the thirteen blocks are blue, the blocks of different colors are each different sizes. Therefore, it's not true that six-thirteenths of the design is blue. In order to solve this problem correctly, students have to consider the area of each of the pieces.

For this activity, the students should have access to pattern blocks. As with all manipulative materials, it's important that students are comfortable and familiar with the blocks before being asked to focus on this problem. They should have had prior experience exploring pattern blocks and the relationships among them. If this is not the case, then I recommend first trying the introductory activities presented in Chapter 4, "Exploring Fractions with Pattern Blocks."

The Lesson

▲▲▲

DAY 1

To prepare for the lesson, I drew on chart paper an enlarged version of the design made from pattern blocks and posted it for all of the students to see.

"It's a rocket!" Sam said.

"Maybe it's a kite," Michael added.

I didn't comment on the boys' remarks but addressed the class. "What do you know about pattern blocks?" I asked. The students were familiar with pattern blocks and I wanted to focus their attention on them before presenting the problem.

"Two greens make a blue," Emma said.

"And six greens make a yellow," Nick added.

"You can make a yellow in lots of different ways," Sean said.

"Not so many ways," Amy responded. "Just six, I think. Or maybe seven." Earlier we had investigated the different combinations of red, blue, and green pattern blocks that could be used to build the yellow hexagon. Then, considering the hexagon as the whole, we assigned fractional values to each of the other pieces. (See the *Exploring Fractions with Pattern Blocks* lesson, pages 39–45.)

"I know the names of the shapes," Alma said. She then correctly recited them, "Triangle, parallelogram, hexagon, and trapezoid."

"I remember that you can use a red one and three triangles to make the yellow hexagon," Ramon said.

Some hands were still raised, but I said, "You seem to know about the pattern blocks, so rather than hearing more ideas, let me tell you about the problem I'd like you to solve."

I directed their attention to the chart paper. "The problem is about this design. I'll write it on the board." Writing the problem as well as giving it orally is helpful for children who don't always absorb what they hear. I read as I wrote:

What fractional part of this design is blue?

"First think about this quietly by yourself," I said. "Then we'll have a class discussion about your ideas."

The room got quiet. After a few moments, I asked the class, "Who has an estimate of what the answer might be?" About seven or eight students raised their hands immediately. I waited, and several more students raised their hands. I called on Sarah.

"I think it's a little less than half," Sarah said.

"Why do you think that?" I asked.

Sarah replied, "See, first I tried to count the blocks, but it was hard to do from here. So then I just looked at it and it looks like it's less than half." There were some murmurs of agreement from the class.

"Any other ideas?" I asked. I called on Paul.

"I counted, and I think it's six-thirteenths," Paul said.

"What did you count?" I asked.

"The blocks," Paul answered. "There are thirteen blocks and six of them are blue, so I would write six over thirteen."

Sophie chimed in, "I don't think that can be." She turned to me and asked, "Can I explain?" I nodded.

Sophie then turned to Paul. "You can't do that, Paul," she said. "You can't count all the blocks as the same because they're different sizes so they're not equal. The sizes have to be equal in fractions."

Paul thought for a moment and then said, "Oh yeah." He didn't seem convinced, however.

"Do you have an idea about an answer?" I asked Sophie.

"I'm not sure yet," she answered. "But I started figuring it out. I think it would be easier to figure with the blocks. Then I could cover the design in greens." Several children agreed.

"I was going to cover it in blues," Daniel added.

"That's what I was going to do," Sean said.

"Me, too," several others added.

"Could we try it with the blocks?" Amy asked.

The children were getting excited. I quieted them by asking for their attention and then explaining what they were to do. "I'll give each of you a copy of the design drawn to the actual size of pattern blocks. Also, I'll give a bag of pattern blocks to each group. While I do this, you can get your papers ready by each writing at the top of your paper your name, the date, and the question. Then you can figure out the answer by using the blocks, drawing pictures, or doing whatever will help you. Finally, you need to write about how you reasoned."

"Can we work together?" Tina asked.

"You can talk about your ideas with one another," I said. "But you each should write your own paper. Remember, it's fine to use an idea you get from someone else, as long as it makes sense to you and you can explain it with your own words." I distributed the pattern blocks as the students organized their papers.

Observing the Students

I circulated as the students worked, answering questions, prodding for more information, and refocusing students when necessary.

Paul asked me, "Should I write about what I thought first and then give another idea?"

"That would be good," I said. "Then I'll have a record of how you changed your thinking."

After first writing about the idea he had presented to the class, Paul covered the design with green triangles. He then added to his paper: *there were 30 triangles. then, I thought, "If I added 2 triangles together, and there are 6 diamonds, then I will just divid 30 in half which is 15." So $\frac{6}{15}$ is blue.* (See Figure 12–1.)

Sophie worked quickly, doing what she had said she would—covering the design

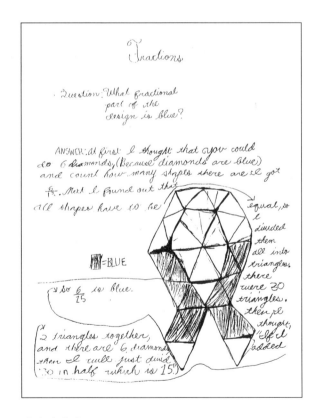

▲▲▲▲▲▲**Figure 12–1** *Paul described his original idea and then his revised idea.*

with green triangles. She counted them to find that thirty triangles covered the design. Sophie wrote: *I think that it could be $\frac{12}{30}$ because if you divide all the peices into triangles there are 30, and there are twelve triangles for 6 blues. $\frac{12}{30} = \frac{6}{15}$.*

Daniel and Sean worked together to cover the design with blue parallelograms. "It doesn't work exactly," Daniel said.

"What do you mean?" I asked.

"Look," Sean explained. "You can't really cover it. You'd have to cut a blue one in half to make it really fit. But we used triangles." The boys had discovered that the shape of the design makes it impossible to cover it entirely with blue parallelograms. They had used fourteen blue parallelograms and two green triangles.

"What are you going to do now?" I asked.

"No problem," Daniel said. "It's the same as fifteen blues so the answer is six-fifteenths. We're done."

"So you're ready to write now," I said as a reminder. The boys nodded and reached for their papers.

Alma and Amy worked together and came up with an answer of two-fifths. They had rearranged the thirteen blocks in the design into five hexagons, each the same size as the yellow pattern block hexagon. The six blue blocks formed two of the hexagons.

Alma had written:

We maid the blocs so that there were 5 hexagons, and 2 of the hexagons were blue and that is all the blues. Answer $\frac{2}{5}$ is blue.

The five hexagons were on her desk. (See Figure 12–2.)

Because Sophie had finished her paper by then, I told her that Alma and Amy thought about the problem in a completely different way and figured out that the design was two-fifths blue.

"Are they right?" Sophie asked.

"Go take a look at what they did and see if you agree," I answered. Emma went with Sophie, and in a moment I heard their comments of admiration. The girls returned to

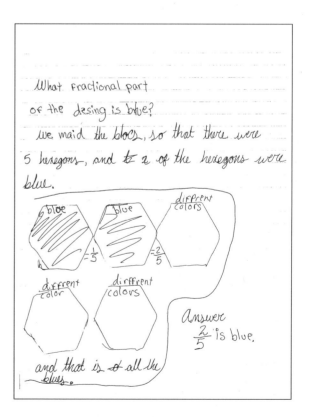

▲▲▲▲▲▲Figure 12–2 *Alma and Amy solved the problem by rearranging the 13 blocks into 5 hexagons, using 6 blue blocks to form 2 of the hexagons.*

their desks to rearrange their blocks into hexagons.

Katy brought her paper to me with a sly smile. I read what she wrote:

I say a little bit more than a third of the drawing is blue. I know this because I divided the whole drawing into diamonds. After I did that I counted the diamonds and got 15 and know that $\frac{1}{3}$ of 15 is 5 and 6 is only 1 number greater than 5.

I laughed. I enjoy when children think about something in a way I never had imagined. "Your reasoning is absolutely correct," I told Katy. "Could you also figure out what is the exact fraction that represents the blue part of the design?"

"Isn't my answer good enough?" Katy challenged me.

I answered, "It could be, depending on what the need was for figuring this out, but I'm also interested in learning as much as I can about what you know about fractions. I'm curious if you can figure out a precise answer."

Katy wasn't happy with my request, but she returned to her desk and added: *However, the exact fraction of blue diamonds is $\frac{6}{15}$.* (See Figure 12–3.)

I checked on Joey and Sarah. Together they had covered the duplicated design with

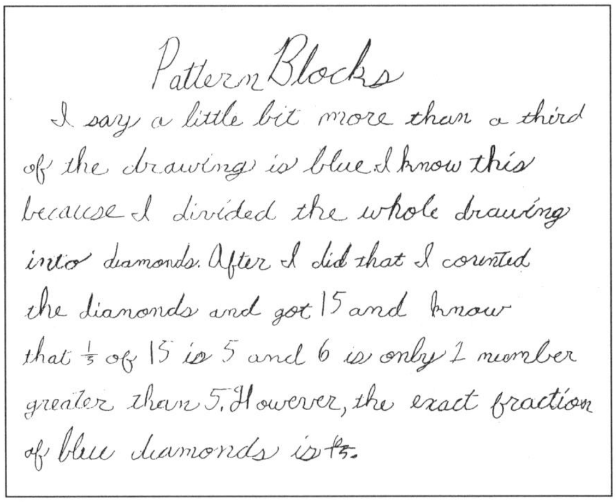

Pattern Blocks
I say a little bit more than a third of the drawing is blue. I know this because I divided the whole drawing into diamonds. After I did that I counted the diamonds and got 15 and know that $\frac{1}{3}$ of 15 is 5 and 6 is only 1 number greater than 5. However, the exact fraction of blue diamonds is $\frac{6}{15}$.

▲▲▲▲▲Figure 12–3 *Katy initially estimated the answer but then revised it to show the exact answer.*

green triangles as Sophie had. Joey watched as Sarah counted the blocks.

"There are thirty," she said to Joey. "And that would be fifteen with the blue diamonds." Sarah started covering the green triangles with blue blocks, and Joey joined in when he realized what she was doing.

"So six out of the fifteen are blue," Sarah said. "That's it." She turned to write. At the top of her paper, she wrote $\frac{6}{15}$ ths. Then she explained: *We took the picture and devided all the shapes into triangles and there were 30 and as you now 2 triangles is the same as a diamond.* She drew thirty triangles and drew circles to group them into twos to show there would be fifteen diamonds.

Joey watched for a moment and then started to write: *We took the picter and we cut them all into tiangles. We got 30 tiangels and drew them and sircled tow of them and counted the sicals [circles] and got 15.* He turned to Sarah for help about what to do next.

Just then, the resource teacher came for Joey. (Joey went to the resource room for extra help twice a week.) She stopped and looked at what Joey had written. "Can you take that with you, Joey?" she asked. "I'd like you to tell me about the problem you're working on. It looks interesting."

"Can I?" Joey asked me.

"Sure," I said. "And take a bag of pattern blocks, too."

Eli is a dreamy boy who enjoys drawing and writing poems and stories. He knows the words to many of the rock songs played on the radio and likes to write down the lyrics and discuss what they mean. On this day, Eli had trouble settling into the problem, and I stopped by his desk several times to help him refocus. Once Eli focused, however, he wouldn't leave for recess because he hadn't finished writing about his idea.

He wrote:

I believe the fraction is $\frac{1}{3}$ and a $\frac{1}{15}$. The reason I think this is because I did the work on paper. First I counted all the blues, I counted 6. Then I used only blues to make the whole *thing that time I counted 15 blues. I finally figured out it was $6\frac{1}{15}$s, but that wasn't enough.*

Eli then drew a circle and divided it into fifteen segments. He marked six of the segments and wrote next to the circle: $\frac{1}{3}$ *and a* $\frac{1}{15}$. (See Figure 12–4.)

"I'm done," he said, now eager to go outside.

"Wait just one minute," I said. "Help me understand your idea."

Impatiently, but with confidence, Eli said, "Well, five-fifteenths makes a third, okay? But there's one piece left. And that's another fifteenth. So it's one-third and one-fifteenth. Okay?" I nodded and Eli raced to the door.

DAY 2

I began class by having students volunteer to make presentations about their ideas. It was valuable, I thought, for students to hear other ways of thinking about the problem. After the presentations, I gave directions to the class.

I said, "Today you'll each make a pattern block design of your own. I have two guidelines. One is that you must use only green, blue, red, and yellow blocks, as were used in the design I showed you yesterday. The other guideline is that your design must fit

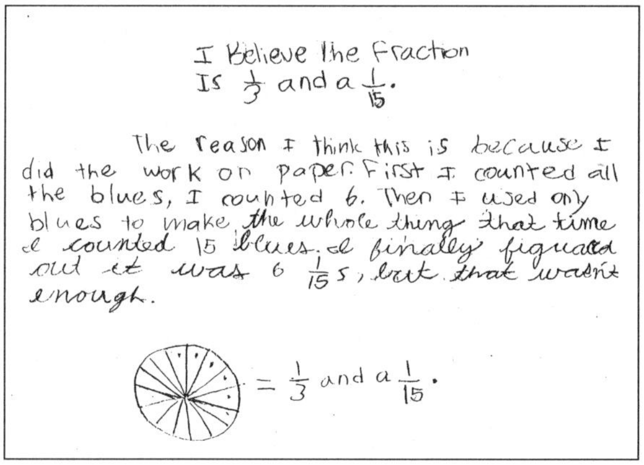

I Believe the Fraction Is $\frac{1}{3}$ and a $\frac{1}{15}$.

The reason I think this is because I did the work on paper. First I counted all the blues, I counted 6. Then I used only blues to make the whole thing, that time I counted 15 blues. I finally figured out it was $6\frac{1}{15}$s, but that wasn't enough.

◯ = $\frac{1}{3}$ and a $\frac{1}{15}$.

▲▲▲▲▲▲**Figure 12–4** *Eli explains in his paper that $\frac{6}{15}$ is the same as $\frac{1}{3}$ and $\frac{1}{15}$.*

on pattern block paper so you can reproduce it. It can't be larger than that." I held up a piece of the pattern block paper as a reminder; students were familiar with it from prior activities.

I continued with directions, "When you have recorded your design, write a problem at the top of the paper." I wrote on the board:

What fractional part of the design is _____?
(Choose one of the colors.)

"Do we have to use all four colors?" Daniel asked.

I answered, "Not necessarily."

"Can we use the orange squares and tan diamonds?" Sam wanted to know.

"No, you can't," Sophie piped up. "They don't work on the pattern block paper."

"Oh yeah," Sam remembered. Not only do the blocks not fit on the pattern block paper, but figuring their areas would be a challenge beyond the students' ability.

I gave the final instructions. "On a separate sheet, write the problem you posed, then record the answer and explain your reasoning. Before you turn in your papers, have someone try your problem to check that your answer is correct. When you check someone's paper, write your name at the bottom so that I know that the paper has been checked. Also, be sure to put your name on both your design and your answer paper." The directions seemed clear to the students and they got to work.

That night I checked their papers for accuracy. All but three were correct and I made time to talk with those students over the next two days, both the students who had created the designs and the students who had signed the papers. After all of the errors had been resolved, I put their designs into one folder and their answers in another. I showed the folders to the class.

"The problems are available as another choice activity," I explained. "You can pick any design, solve the problem, and then find the answer in the other folder. If you can't figure out the answer, or you get an answer that's different, then talk with either the person who created the design or the person who signed the answer sheet." I showed the class where I was putting the folders and added "Pattern Block Problems" to the choice list.

Questions and Discussion

▲▲

▲ *Why did you draw the design on a chart to begin the lesson instead of giving the students their own copies?*

I know posting the design made it difficult for the students to examine it and count the individual blocks, but I wanted to avoid having students begin work individually on the problem before we had had a class discussion.

▲ *Why did you ask students to think quietly first before the discussion?*

While I generally allow and encourage talking in class, there are times when I think it's valuable for students to focus on a problem by themselves. This gives them a chance to collect their thoughts. I've learned that when I teach complex topics like fractions, students may understand what others say but have difficulty explaining their thinking on their own. They need ample opportunities to formulate their own ideas.

▲ *Doesn't a class discussion give away the answer before students work on their own?*

If this were a testing situation rather than a learning opportunity, I wouldn't have the students discuss their thinking first. But I think that discussions enhance learning, which is my purpose in giving students this problem to solve. Also, students not only have to find an answer to the problem but also have to explain their reasoning. Talking and listening both help students clarify their thinking and prepare them to write. Even if students use someone else's ideas, they still have to express them in their own words.

▲ *Why do you have students write their names on the papers they check?*

Having students sign is a way for me to be sure that someone did check each paper. Also, having to sign someone else's paper seems to help students take this part of the assignment seriously. In a way, signing makes them accountable. And for papers with errors, signatures tell me which students I need to talk with about the work.

CHAPTER THIRTEEN
PUT IN ORDER

Overview

Put in Order provides students experience with comparing and ordering fractions. The class is shown fractions written on 4-by-6-inch index cards, one by one. After each is shown, a student places it on the chalkboard tray so that the fractions are in ascending order. When students place a card, they also explain their reasoning. This lesson is designed to help students become more comfortable with fractional notation, learn to order fractions according to which are larger and which are smaller, and learn to use the benchmarks of one-half and one whole when comparing fractions. Students also learn that there are various strategies to use for comparing and ordering fractions and that the choice of an effective strategy depends on the particular fractions being considered.

Materials

▲ for each lesson, a set of about 12 4-by-6-inch index cards, each with a fraction written on it, large enough for students at the back of the class to see

Sample Sets

Set 1: $\frac{1}{16}, \frac{1}{8}, \frac{3}{16}, \frac{1}{4}, \frac{3}{8}, \frac{1}{2}, \frac{5}{8}, \frac{3}{4}, \frac{15}{16}, \frac{1}{1}, \frac{9}{8}, \frac{3}{2}$

Set 2: $\frac{1}{8}, \frac{1}{6}, \frac{1}{4}, \frac{1}{3}, \frac{1}{2}, \frac{2}{3}, \frac{3}{4}, \frac{15}{16}, \frac{8}{8}, \frac{17}{16}, \frac{7}{6}, \frac{4}{3}$

Set 3: $\frac{1}{16}, \frac{1}{12}, \frac{2}{8}, \frac{3}{8}, \frac{3}{6}, \frac{3}{4}, \frac{7}{8}, \frac{11}{12}, \frac{3}{3}, \frac{17}{16}, \frac{9}{8}, \frac{5}{4}$

▲ optional: fraction kits and other materials available for students

Time

▲ one class period; lesson can be repeated multiple times throughout the year

Teaching Directions

1. Prop on the chalkboard tray one of the fraction cards. The first time, it makes sense to choose $\frac{1}{2}$ because it's a useful benchmark for students to use for comparing other fractions.

2. Explain to the class that you have written a fraction on each of the other cards you have and you are going to show them the cards one by one. For each, their job is to decide where to place the card on the chalkboard tray so that the fractions are going in order from smallest to largest. Also, when a student places a fraction, the student must give a convincing reason for the placement.

3. Show a card, allow time for thinking, and then have someone tell where it goes and why. For the first fraction, choose one that's familiar to the students, $\frac{1}{4}$ or $\frac{1}{16}$, for example. When a student explains where to place a fraction, before showing another fraction, ask if anyone has a different way to explain. This gives students the message that there are different ways to think about comparing and ordering fractions. Also, it helps students hear a variety of strategies.

4. If a student places a card incorrectly, most likely another student will offer a challenge. Give the first student a chance to rethink his or her reasoning; then give others a chance to explain their thinking. If a student places a card incorrectly and no other student challenges, continue with the activity. Usually the error will be noticed after several other fractions are placed. If no one notices, however, or there aren't any more fractions to place, tell the class that you don't agree with the placement. In this situation, asking students to discuss the fraction in small groups will often give them a chance to reason correctly.

5. Continue until all but one fraction has been placed. Use this last fraction for an individual assignment, asking each student to write about where it should be placed. This gives you an individual assessment that can guide you in your subsequent instructional choices.

6. Repeat the lesson the next day or a few days later. Use the same set of cards, but change the order in which you present them. It's still helpful to show $\frac{1}{2}$ first to reinforce its usefulness as a benchmark. Also, you may choose to change $\frac{9}{8}$ and $\frac{3}{2}$ to $1\frac{1}{8}$ and $1\frac{1}{2}$ or just write these alternate notations on the same cards. This helps students become comfortable with the notation for mixed numbers.

7. During the year, repeat the lesson with more complex fractions, being careful not to overdo the lesson so that students lose interest, but using it as a challenge from time to time.

8. Use the activity for individual assignments, either to be done during class time or for homework. Give students five fractions to order and explain their reasoning. Or give them pairs of fractions and ask them to identify at least three fractions that fit in between each pair.

Teaching Notes

Ordering fractions helps students develop understanding about equivalent and non-equivalent fractions. Prior to experiencing this lesson for the first time, the students explored fractional parts of wholes by making fraction kits with paper strips cut into halves, fourths, eighths, and sixteenths. The fraction kit activities introduced students to comparing fractions; the *Put in Order* activity extends their experience.

Students benefit from repeated experiences with *Put in Order* throughout the year. Initially, using the same set of fractions but changing the order in which they're presented is one way to change the activity sufficiently to challenge the students. Creating new sets of fractions, using some fractions from the first set and including others as well, further varies the activity. As the students continue their exploration of fractions with other activities, the complexity of the lesson can be increased by incorporating other fractions as well. It's important when choosing fractions to be careful not to include equivalent fractions in the same set of cards.

The benefit of repeating *Put in Order* is that the students are familiar with the lesson structure and understand what they are to do. I was careful, however, not to do the lesson so often that students would lose interest. From time to time, I veered from a whole-class lesson and asked students in small groups to order sets of fraction cards. And I sometimes gave students fractions to order as an individual class assignment or for homework.

The description of the lesson starts by reporting what happened the first time I introduced this activity to a class of fifth graders. This experience was typical of what I've experienced with all classes. Then I describe two different individual assignments.

As I mentioned earlier, the students had initially cut fraction kits, making halves, fourths, eighths, and sixteenths, and had played both *Cover Up* and *Uncover*. Please don't skip the fraction kit experience. It's a wonderfully effective building block for all activities that follow. You may decide, however, to try *Put in Order* either before or after students have done the fraction kit activities that follow playing the games (see Chapters 2 and 5). Also, after the students cut thirds and sixths for their fraction kits and explore fractions with pattern blocks, which also engages them in thinking about thirds and sixths, try the activity with the fractions in Set 2. Set 3 shows the fractions I used after the students had added twelfths to their fraction kits. As I repeated the lesson, I allowed students who needed the materials to use them but encouraged students to find ways to order and explain their thinking without the materials.

The Lesson

▲▲▲

To introduce the activity, I first had the students arrange their fraction kits so they could refer to them easily. On the chalkboard tray, I propped the 4-by-6-inch index card with $\frac{1}{2}$ on it, explained what we were going to do, and showed the students the card with $\frac{1}{4}$ on it. I purposely displayed $\frac{1}{2}$ first because it's a useful benchmark fraction and one that students find fairly easy to compare to other fractions. Also, I wanted to spend time at the beginning of the lesson emphasizing the importance of their explanations, and that could be more easily done if the students compared fractions that were familiar to them. I planned to follow $\frac{1}{4}$ with

$\frac{1}{16}$, then $\frac{1}{1}$, and then select the other fractions randomly.

"Where should I put one-fourth so that the fractions are in order from small to large, going up from left to right?" I asked, again explaining the activity. There were lots of volunteers.

"Remember that you also have to tell the class why you suggest putting the one-fourth where you do," I added. I noticed that Griffin, Delia, Shannon, and Jesse put down their hands after I made this last statement. But then, after a moment, Griffin and Delia raised their hands again.

I called on Lindsey. "It goes first," she said. "It's easy. One-fourth is smaller than one-half.

I can show it with the fraction pieces, see?" Lindsey held up her $\frac{1}{4}$ and $\frac{1}{2}$ pieces.

"Did anyone have a different way to explain?" I asked. Several hands went up and I called on David.

"It takes two of the one-fourth pieces to make one-half, so it has to be smaller," he said. I nodded.

"Anyone else?" I asked.

"Mine is sort of like David's but a little different," Carey said.

"Let's hear," I replied.

"One-half is twice as big as one-fourth, so one-fourth has to go first," she explained. Again, I nodded, and asked if there were any other explanations. I called on Dylan.

"Fourths are smaller pieces than halves," he said. "So one-fourth has to be smaller than one-half." I nodded and asked again for other explanations. No hands were raised for a moment, and then Jennifer's shot up.

"One-fourth is a fourth less than one-half, so it has to go first," she said.

"That's right," I affirmed. "Any other ways?"

No other students wanted to offer an explanation, so I put the $\frac{1}{4}$ in place and showed $\frac{1}{16}$. All hands shot up.

"Easy," Robert said. "It goes first. It's the smallest fraction there is."

"It's not the smallest in the world," Jack said. "What about a millionth?"

"That's not what I meant," Robert defended. "I was talking about our fraction pieces."

"Oh, okay," Jack replied.

"How else can you explain that one-sixteenth goes first?" I asked.

"The way I remember is that the bigger numbers have smaller pieces," Libby said.

"Which numbers are you talking about?" I asked.

"The numbers on the bottom," she said.

"And why does that makes sense?" I probed.

"The higher numbers mean they are smaller parts," she said.

Dylan had something to add. "The higher numbers are smaller because it takes more pieces to cover the whole. Like it takes sixteen sixteenths to cover the whole, but only four fourths, so sixteenths have to be smaller."

Maggie added, "The pieces are smaller than fourths or halves, so one of them is really little."

"It takes four sixteenths to make one fourth, so it has to go first," Dylan offered.

I continued like this, having all who volunteered give explanations for placing each fraction. Even when students have similar ideas, I encourage them to express them in their own words. They benefit from having as much practice as possible explaining their reasoning. Also, it's useful for the class to hear different ways to explain.

The next-to-last fraction was $\frac{3}{8}$, and this time I recorded on the board three students' explanations to model for the class how to record their thinking in writing.

For Shannon's explanation, I wrote:

$\frac{4}{16}$ is $\frac{1}{4}$ and $\frac{2}{16}$ is $\frac{1}{8}$ so $\frac{3}{16}$ is in between $\frac{1}{8}$ and $\frac{1}{4}$.

For Robert's explanation, I wrote:

$\frac{1}{8}$ can be $\frac{2}{16}$ and $\frac{3}{16}$ is $\frac{1}{16}$ more than $\frac{1}{8}$, and $\frac{1}{4}$ is $\frac{1}{16}$ higher than $\frac{3}{16}$.

For Carey's explanation, I wrote:

I know that $\frac{1}{8}$ is $\frac{1}{16}$ less than $\frac{3}{16}$ and $\frac{1}{4}$ is $\frac{1}{16}$ more than $\frac{3}{16}$.

After about forty minutes, we had placed eleven of the twelve fractions in the set:

$$\frac{1}{16} \quad \frac{1}{8} \quad \frac{3}{16} \quad \frac{1}{4} \quad \frac{3}{8} \quad \frac{1}{2} \quad \frac{5}{8} \quad \frac{3}{4} \quad \frac{1}{1} \quad \frac{9}{8} \quad \frac{3}{2}$$

The remaining fraction was $\frac{15}{16}$. Rather than have students give their explanations verbally about where to place $\frac{15}{16}$, I asked them to write individually about where they thought it belonged. Having students write on their own gives me information that helps me assess each student's thinking.

Students had different ways to explain. Josh, for example, wrote:

I would put $\frac{15}{16}$ between $\frac{3}{4}$ and $\frac{1}{1}$. It goes their because $\frac{3}{4}$ is $\frac{12}{16}$ and $\frac{1}{1}$ is $\frac{16}{16}$ and it is higher than $\frac{12}{16}$ and lower than $\frac{16}{16}$.

Carey used similar reasoning:

It is between $\frac{3}{4}$ and $\frac{1}{1}$. $\frac{3}{4}$ is a $\frac{1}{16}$ less than $\frac{15}{16}$ and $\frac{1}{1}$ is $\frac{1}{16}$ more. $\frac{15}{16}$ is more than $\frac{3}{4}$ because $\frac{3}{4}$ is only $\frac{12}{16}$.

Griffin and Jennifer also used the same method of changing $\frac{3}{4}$ to $\frac{12}{16}$.

When I asked each of these students how they knew that $\frac{3}{4}$ and $\frac{12}{16}$ were equivalent, Jennifer said, "One fourth is four sixteenths, so three fourths is twelve sixteenths."

"You just cut them," Carey said. "You cut each fourth into four pieces to get sixteenths and then you count them up."

Josh could explain, also, but Griffin just showed me with his fraction kit pieces and shrugged when I asked him to tell me how come that was so.

Maggie wrote:

$\frac{15}{16}$ fits in between $\frac{1}{1}$ and $\frac{3}{4}$ because $\frac{1}{1}$ is one whole and $\frac{3}{4}$ is $\frac{1}{2}$ and a $\frac{1}{4}$ so $\frac{3}{4}$ is less than $\frac{15}{16}$ is $\frac{1}{1}$ is more so that is were it goes.

She drew representations of $\frac{1}{16}$, $\frac{1}{8}$, $\frac{1}{4}$, $\frac{1}{2}$, and $\frac{1}{1}$ and then wrote an afterthought:

Because $\frac{3}{4}$ is $\frac{12}{16}$.

Robert's explanation (Figure 13–1) indicated that either he was not as clear as some of the other students or not able to express his thoughts as clearly, even though his contribution in the class discussion indicated otherwise. He wrote:

$\frac{15}{16}$ belongs under $\frac{1}{1}$ whole, $\frac{16}{16} = \frac{1}{1}$ so it has to be down there. $\frac{17}{16}$ is one over.

Daniel explained why $\frac{15}{16}$ was before $\frac{1}{1}$ but not why it was after $\frac{3}{4}$. He wrote:

I know that $\frac{16}{16}$ is one $\frac{1}{1}$ so I minus $\frac{1}{16}$ and it = $\frac{15}{16}$.

Delia's explanation (Figure 13–2) was lacking in the same way. She wrote:

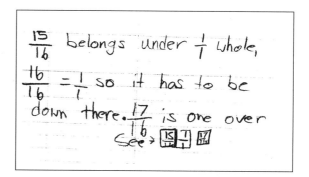

▲▲▲▲▲▲**Figure 13–1** *Robert's answer is correct but his explanation doesn't provide sufficient mathematical information to explain how he placed $\frac{15}{16}$.*

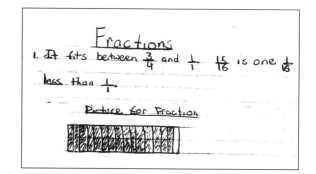
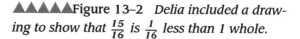

▲▲▲▲▲▲**Figure 13–2** *Delia included a drawing to show that $\frac{15}{16}$ is $\frac{1}{16}$ less than 1 whole.*

It fits between $\frac{3}{4}$ and $\frac{1}{1}$. $\frac{15}{16}$ is one $\frac{1}{16}$ less than $\frac{1}{1}$.

And Lindsey wrote:

$\frac{15}{16}$ fits in between $\frac{3}{4}$ and $\frac{1}{1}$ because $\frac{1}{1}$ is $\frac{16}{16}$ and $\frac{15}{16}$ is only one 16 under $\frac{1}{16}$.

I repeated the lesson several times again after a few days, first using the same fraction cards but presenting them in a different order, then changing a few, being sure to include mixed numbers so that the students would become familiar with that notation. In each set I included $\frac{1}{2}$ 11 and 1 to emphasize that these benchmarks are useful. Also, I started a list of strategies for comparing fractions, using the students' explanations to do so. (Read pages 29 and 137 for information about strategies I've identified from working with different classes.) Later in the year, I returned to the activity from time to time, changing the fractions to include others than halves, fourths, eighths, and sixteenths. (See Figures 13–3 and 13–4 for more student work on this lesson.)

INDIVIDUAL ASSIGNMENTS

In a fourth-grade class, after two experiences with *Put in Order*, I asked the students to order five fractions—$\frac{5}{8}$, $\frac{1}{8}$, $\frac{1}{16}$, $\frac{2}{4}$, $\frac{15}{16}$—and explain their reasoning in writing. They were beginning to learn about fractions and had just cut their fraction kits and played *Cover Up* and *Uncover.* Their papers helped me see who needed more concrete experiences and who was able to think abstractly about fractions. Also, their papers reminded me that partial understanding and confusion are natural to the learning process. I know that learning about fractions is hard for some students, and I'm careful not to make children feel deficient for an incorrect notion. Instead I try to understand their thinking and give them a way to reconsider the notions they've formed.

For example, on this assignment, Penny explained why $\frac{5}{8}$ was in between $\frac{2}{4}$ and $\frac{15}{16}$:

I knew that $\frac{5}{8}$ came next because 5 is lower than 15 and higher than 2 so it would go between 2 and 15. And the only one left is $\frac{15}{16}$ and 15 is higher than all the other top numbers, so it goes at the top.

While Penny had ordered the fractions correctly—$\frac{1}{16}$, $\frac{1}{8}$, $\frac{2}{4}$, $\frac{5}{8}$, $\frac{15}{16}$—she was relying only on looking at the numerators. (See Figure 13–5.)

To help her rethink this idea, the next day in class I found time to talk with her. "You ordered the fractions correctly on your paper, but I'm not clear about your reasoning," I began. "Can you tell me how you would order these two fractions?" I wrote $\frac{2}{4}$ and $\frac{5}{100}$ on a piece of paper.

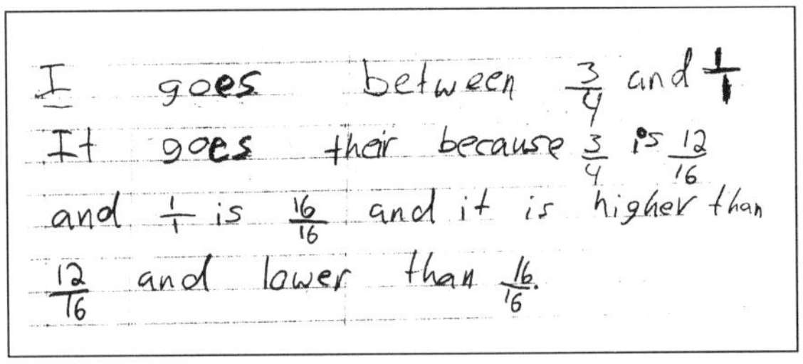

> I goes between $\frac{3}{4}$ and $\frac{1}{1}$
> It goes thair because $\frac{3}{4}$ is $\frac{12}{16}$ and $\frac{1}{1}$ is $\frac{16}{16}$ and it is higher than $\frac{12}{16}$ and lower than $\frac{16}{16}$.

▲▲▲▲▲▲**Figure 13–3** *Josh explained by converting $\frac{3}{4}$ to $\frac{12}{16}$ and $\frac{1}{1}$ to $\frac{16}{16}$.*

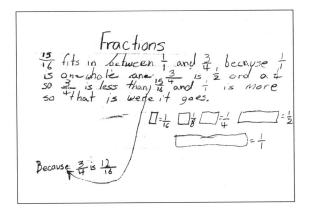

Fractions
$\frac{15}{16}$ fits in between $\frac{1}{1}$ and $\frac{3}{4}$, becayse $\frac{1}{1}$ is one whole ane $\frac{15}{16}$ is $\frac{3}{4}$ ord a $\frac{4}{4}$ so $\frac{3}{4}$ is less than $\frac{15}{16}$ and $\frac{1}{1}$ is more so that is were it goes.

$\square = \frac{1}{16}$ $\square = \frac{1}{8}$ $\square = \frac{1}{4}$ $\square = \frac{1}{2}$
$\square = \frac{1}{1}$

Because $\frac{3}{4}$ is $\frac{12}{16}$

▲▲▲▲▲▲**Figure 13–4** *Maggie's paper shows that she understands the relative sizes of $\frac{1}{16}$, $\frac{1}{8}$, $\frac{1}{4}$, $\frac{1}{2}$, and $\frac{1}{1}$ and knows where $\frac{15}{16}$ fits.*

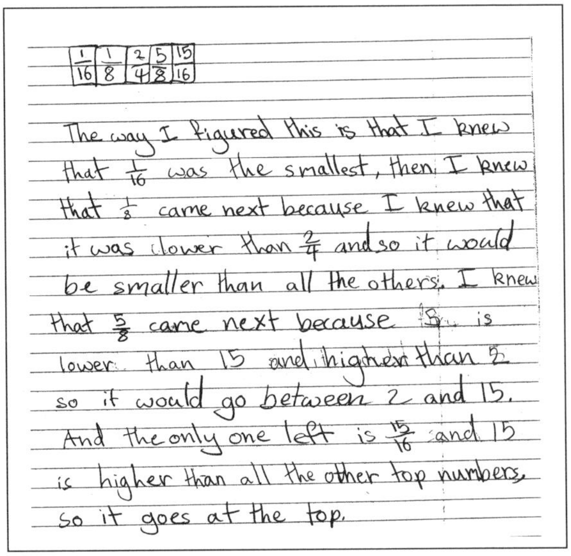

> | $\frac{1}{16}$ | $\frac{1}{8}$ | $\frac{2}{4}$ | $\frac{5}{8}$ | $\frac{15}{16}$ |
>
> The way I figured this is that I knew that $\frac{1}{16}$ was the smallest, then I knew that $\frac{1}{8}$ came next because I knew that it was lower than $\frac{2}{4}$ and so it would be smaller than all the others. I knew that $\frac{5}{8}$ came next because $\frac{5}{8}$ is lower than 15 and highen than 2. so it would go between 2 and 15. And the only one left is $\frac{15}{16}$ and 15 is higher than all the other top numbers. so it goes at the top.

▲▲▲▲▲▲**Figure 13–5** *Penny's explanation for placing $\frac{5}{8}$ and $\frac{15}{16}$ shows her partial understanding.*

Penny giggled and answered, correctly, "That's easy. Two-fourths is more. It's the same as one-half and five-hundredths is much less."

"But five is more than two, and the reason you gave on your paper to explain why five-eighths was larger than two-fourths was because five is higher than two."

"Let me see," Penny said, reaching for her paper.

"Your answer was correct," I said again to reassure Penny. "But your reasoning didn't make sense. Is there another way to explain why five-eighths is greater than two-fourths?"

Penny thought for a moment and then said, "Two-fourths is the same as one-half, and so is four-eighths, so five-eighths is bigger." Then she added, "And I know that fifteen-sixteenths is almost a whole."

"Those reasons make good sense to me," I said.

"Do I have to do it over?" Penny asked, referring to the assignment. This is one of those moments that call for making a judgment. I decided that it wasn't necessary, that Penny would have lots of opportunities to express her reasoning about fractions.

"No, that's not necessary," I told her. "I feel satisfied that you have another way to explain. You don't have to change this paper."

I then talked with Hannah about her paper. She had also ordered the fractions correctly, though she had miscopied $\frac{15}{16}$ and written $\frac{15}{11}$ instead—$\frac{1}{16}, \frac{1}{8}, \frac{2}{4}, \frac{5}{8}, \frac{15}{11}$. She explained why she thought $\frac{1}{16}$ was the smallest fraction: *because this one has the biggest amount of numbers between it.* She correctly placed $\frac{1}{8}$ next and wrote: *this has the second amount of numbers between it.* It took me a moment to realize that she was comparing the differences between the numerators and denominators. The difference between 1 and 16 was the largest of the five fractions, and the difference between 1 and 8 was the next largest. (See Figure 13–6.)

I began my conversation with Hannah as I had done with Penny. I said, "You ordered the fractions correctly on your paper, but I'm not clear about your reasoning. What did you mean by the biggest amount of numbers between it?" I pointed to $\frac{1}{16}$ on her paper.

"I did sixteen minus one," she said.

"Oh, that's what I figured," I said. "So the difference between one and eight is seven, and that's why you put that fraction next." I changed the terminology that Hannah had used but she understood what I said and nodded.

"Then for two-fourths, the difference between the two and the four is two?" I asked. Again, Hannah nodded.

I continued, "Now I'm confused. For five-eighths, the difference is three, but you put five-eighths after two-fourths, not before as you did when looking at the differences for the other fractions."

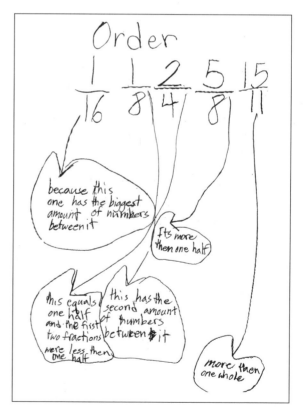

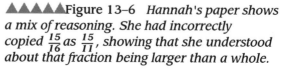Figure 13–6 *Hannah's paper shows a mix of reasoning. She had incorrectly copied $\frac{15}{16}$ as $\frac{15}{11}$, showing that she understood about that fraction being larger than a whole.*

Hannah thought and then replied, "Oh, that's because I know that five-eighths is more than one-half." After a moment, she added, "My rule is for fractions that are littler than one-half."

I was stumped for a moment as I searched for how to respond. I wanted to find an example that would present Hannah with a contradiction to her thinking so that she might reconsider her idea. "What about three-sixteenths and one-half?" I asked, writing $\frac{3}{16}$ and $\frac{1}{2}$ on a piece of paper. "Which is smaller?"

"Three-sixteenths," Hannah responded with confidence.

"How many numbers between three and sixteen?" I asked, using her wording this time.

"Thirteen," Hannah answered.

"Where would you put it with the other fractions?" I pressed. Hannah looked at the fractions, pointed at the space between $\frac{1}{16}$ and $\frac{1}{8}$, then pulled back her finger. "Hey," she said. "That's not right."

"What are you thinking?" I asked.

"I know that one-eighth is the same as two-sixteenths, so three-sixteenths has to be more," she said. Her former confidence left and she looked at me and asked, "Is my paper wrong?"

"You have the fractions in the right order, but your explanation doesn't make sense," I replied. "You can't use a rule that works for some fractions but not for others. Can you think of another way to explain why one-sixteenth and one-eighth go first?"

Hannah seemed stumped. I asked her to talk with Janelle. Janelle was sitting next to Hannah and had both ordered the fractions and reasoned correctly on her paper.

Giving students other ways to think about their ideas calls for not only understanding their thinking but also analyzing the math underlying the correct answer. Papers like these reminded me why

answers by themselves, without insights into how students arrived at them, can mislead us about what children really know. (Figure 13–7 shows how another student thought.)

In a fifth-grade class, just after the middle of the year, I gave a different assignment related to *Put in Order*. I listed four pairs of fractions with the first smaller than the second. I asked the students to find three fractions that fit in between each pair, that is, that were larger than the first fraction and smaller than the second.

$$\frac{1}{8} \quad \frac{1}{2}$$
$$\frac{9}{16} \quad 1$$
$$\frac{1}{2} \quad \frac{3}{4}$$
$$\frac{1}{2} \quad \frac{2}{3}$$

The fifth graders had played *Put in Order* on and off during the first half of the year, interspersed with activities that expanded their experience with fractions beyond those introduced in the fraction kit. After we

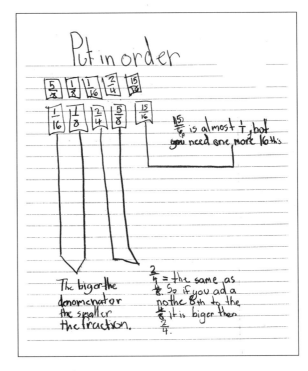

▲▲▲▲▲▲**Figure 13–7** *Xavier ordered the fractions correctly.*

had completed ordering a set of cards, about ten minutes remained in the class period. I wrote the four pairs of fractions on the board and asked the students to find three fractions in between each pair. In this particular case, I didn't ask students to explain their reasoning. Not much time was left and I wanted to use the papers as a quick assessment of how they were doing. Also, I didn't say that the fractions they wrote in between had to be in ascending order; some students chose to do so while others didn't.

Their papers were useful for a follow-up experience. To begin class the next day, I asked students to compare their papers with partners and discuss the particular fractions they had chosen. Afterward, I led a class discussion in which students reported how they had reasoned. Most agreed that the fourth pair of fractions—$\frac{1}{2}$ and $\frac{2}{3}$—was the most difficult. (Figures 13–8 through 13–10 show how three students completed this assignment.)

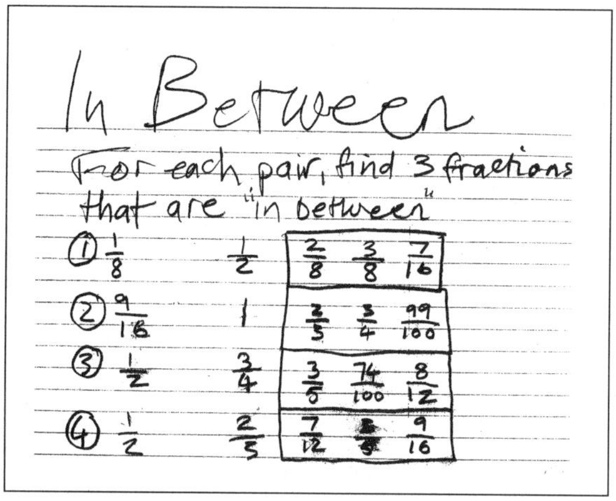

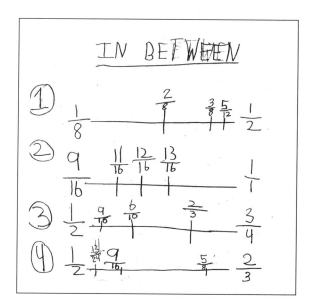

▲▲▲▲▲▲Figure 13–9 *John found hundredths to be useful for finding "in between" fractions.*

▲▲▲▲▲▲Figure 13–8 *Kent tried to place the fractions as they might be placed on a number line.*

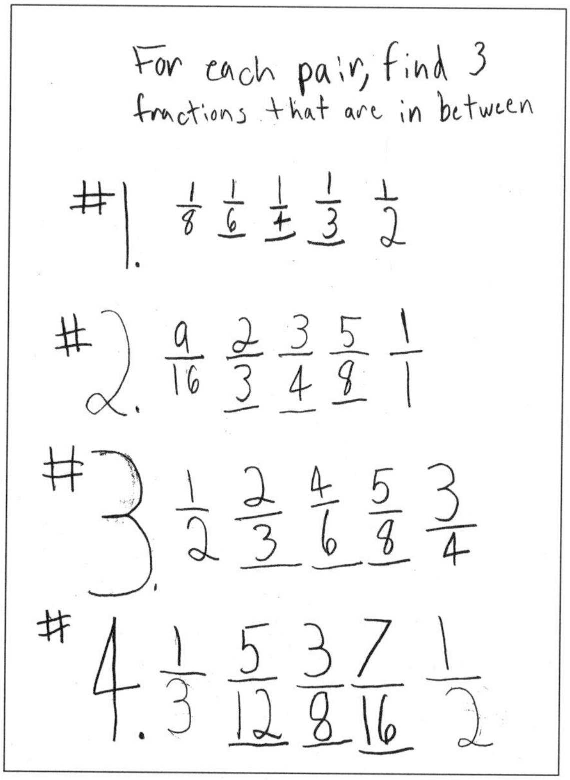

▲▲▲▲▲▲Figure 13–10 *Lela commented that she found the last pair to be hard; others agreed.*

EXTENSION

To give the activity an extra challenge, when you show students a fraction card, instead of having them place the card on the chalkboard tray, ask them to indicate where the fraction would fall on a number line. Draw a number line on the board with the numbers 0, 1, and 2 on it; leave at least 12 inches between each number. Remember to ask students to explain their reasoning. Also, after a student places a fraction, ask the class if anyone thinks that adjustments should be made to any of the fractions placed.

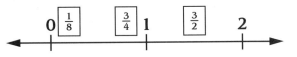

Questions and Discussion

▲▲

▲ How did you decide which fractions to put in each of the sets you made?

The fractions I chose for Set 1 all had denominators of 2, 4, 8, or 16, allowing the children to use their fraction kits as a reference. I included in the set unit fractions, those with a 1 in the numerator ($\frac{1}{2}$, $\frac{1}{4}$, $\frac{1}{8}$, and $\frac{1}{16}$), fractions that were a unit fraction away from 1 whole ($\frac{3}{4}$, $\frac{15}{16}$, $\frac{9}{8}$, and $\frac{3}{2}$), and fractions that were a unit fraction away from $\frac{1}{2}$ ($\frac{3}{8}$ and $\frac{5}{8}$). I realized that $\frac{3}{4}$ fit both of these last categories since it is $\frac{1}{4}$ away from both $\frac{1}{2}$ and 1 whole. I also included 1 whole in this set, representing it as $\frac{1}{1}$ so that children would become familiar with this notation. And I included $\frac{3}{16}$ to test the waters and see how students would make a decision about what to do next.

I constructed Set 2 with the same guidelines, including thirds and sixths. For Set 3, I didn't include the familiar benchmark of $\frac{1}{2}$, substituting $\frac{3}{6}$ instead. Also, I purposely included $\frac{3}{8}$, $\frac{3}{6}$, $\frac{3}{4}$, and $\frac{3}{3}$ so that I could point out for the students, if they didn't notice, that common numerators were useful for comparing the relative sizes of fractions.

While I chose these fractions carefully and deliberately, you may want to make other choices for your class. Also, I don't want to imply that students' understanding necessarily progresses from knowing how halves, fourths, eighths, and sixteenths work to being able to incorporate thirds, sixths, twelfths, and so on. Learning isn't that tidy. Students come to generalizations about fractions in different and unique ways, and I'm careful to remember that my instructional choices may or may not match each child's path for making sense of fractions. That's why I have to keep the mix of activities varied and make many different paths available for students to construct their understanding.

▲ How did you decide on the order in which to present the fractions to the class?

As I explained in the vignette, the first time I introduced the activity, I chose initial fractions that I thought would be most accessible to the students so that as many students as possible would enter into the conversation. For later repeats I would just shuffle the cards and take them in random order. If a fraction was too difficult for the students or there was disagreement about where it should go, rather than resolve the situation, I'd set the card aside on the chalkboard tray for later consideration. Eventually it became clear to students where it should go.

▲ *You seem to get explanations from so many students. How do you do this? What if my students don't give explanations like your students do?*

My method is to be consistent. After each student explains, I ask, "Does anyone have another idea?" Asking this question gives students the message that I'm interested in hearing other ideas. Also, after asking the question, it's helpful to give students sufficient time to think about their answers; this is especially important for students who think more slowly.

▲ *What do you do about students who don't ever volunteer?*

There are some students who aren't comfortable talking with the entire class as an audience. I respect this. This is one reason that I sometimes ask students to talk with partners. Also, sometimes I use the lesson as a small-group activity, giving each group a stack of fraction cards to turn over one by one and order. When they're done, they record the order. Students are more likely to offer their ideas in this setting.

▲ *If students use their fractions kits, aren't they just relying on the pieces and not really thinking about the fractions?*

When students are learning, it's fine for them to rely on the fraction pieces, pattern blocks, or any other materials. The materials support their reasoning and help students build their own mental models on which they rely later. They stop referring to the materials when they're ready, which comes after they've had sufficient experience hearing others' ideas, thinking for themselves in different ways, and having opportunities to explain their thinking.

▲ *What do you do when a student answers incorrectly and suggests placing a fraction in the wrong location?*

Typically, another student will challenge the placement. If no one does, I sometimes do nothing and wait until placing a later fraction causes someone to notice. Of course, if no one notices, then I'll point it out. And if confusion still exists, this gives me important information that guides my subsequent lesson plans.

CHAPTER FOURTEEN
NICHOLAS'S GAME

Overview

Students benefit from many opportunities to compare fractions and explain their reasoning. This activity asks students to identify fractions that are less than, equal to, and greater than a particular starting fraction. The activity doesn't rely on any contextual setting or use of concrete material but rather draws on students' reasoning abilities. It also provides students experience thinking about fractions that are greater than one whole. After a whole-class introduction, students then engage with the activity as an individual assignment.

Materials

▲ optional: *Nicholas's Game* worksheet (see Blackline Masters)
▲ dice, one per student

Time

▲ one class period plus part of the next day's class; lesson can be repeated multiple times

Teaching Directions

1. Write a fraction on the board—$\frac{1}{2}$ for classes just beginning to study fractions or $\frac{3}{4}$ for classes that have had more experience. Ask: "Who can think of a fraction that has a numerator larger than the numerator of this 'starting fraction' and a denominator larger than its denominator?"

2. List on the board the fractions the students suggest. If a student suggests a fraction that doesn't meet the criteria you stated, point out the error. For example, if a student suggests one-fifth, say: "The denominator is fine because it's greater than four, but the numerator must be larger than three."

3. Ask students: "How many fractions do you think there are that follow the rule?" Have students share their reasoning about why there are an infinite number of possibilities.

4. Draw three columns on the board and label them <, =, and >. Ask for a fraction that follows the rule and belongs in the "is greater than" column. Ask the student to explain his or her reasoning. Then ask for fractions for each of the other columns. Continue until you have five fractions in each column.

$$\boxed{\dfrac{1}{2}}$$

<	=	>
$\dfrac{2}{6}$	$\dfrac{4}{8}$	$\dfrac{3}{4}$
$\dfrac{3}{8}$	$\dfrac{5}{10}$	$\dfrac{2}{3}$
$\dfrac{3}{10}$	$\dfrac{6}{12}$	$\dfrac{5}{6}$
$\dfrac{2}{5}$	$\dfrac{2}{4}$	$\dfrac{8}{8}$
$\dfrac{4}{9}$	$\dfrac{3}{6}$	$\dfrac{7}{8}$

5. Give directions for an individual assignment. Write the directions on the board or, if you'd prefer, duplicate and distribute them.

Nicholas's Game

1. Rule three columns and label them <, =, and >. Above the columns draw boxes for the numerator and denominator of the starting fraction.

2. To find the starting fraction, roll a die twice. Use the smaller number for the numerator and the larger number for the denominator. (If both numbers you roll are the same, roll again so that the numerator and denominator of your starting fraction are different.)

3. Write at least five fractions in each column. The numerator and denominator in each fraction you write must be greater than the numerator and denominator in the starting fraction.

4. Choose one fraction from each column and explain how you know it belongs there. For example, write: I know that $\frac{3}{4}$ is greater than $\frac{2}{3}$ because _____.

5. You may use only one fraction that is equivalent to 1 whole such as $\frac{5}{5}$ or $\frac{11}{11}$ or any fraction with the same numerator and denominator.

6. If you think of a fraction that follows the rule, but you're not sure in which column it belongs, write it to the side and bring it to class for a discussion of "hard" fractions.

Teaching Notes

While talking about fractions in real-world contexts and providing students experiences exploring fractions with concrete materials are both valuable for students' learning, it's also beneficial for them to think about fractions presented only symbolically. Students then have to bring meaning to the fractions by forming mental models of their own. Some students visualize concrete materials, others think about geometric representations, and others reason numerically. By focusing class discussions on how children reason, not only do you receive information about how individual students think, but students have the opportunity to learn from one another.

I first learned about this activity when Nicholas Branca, a mathematics professor at San Diego State University, visited the fifth-grade class I was teaching. He observed part of a fraction lesson and then offered to try an activity with the class. I found the activity he presented engaged the students' interest as well as gave me information for learning about how students reasoned about fractions. Since then, I've tried the activity with other classes. When using Nicholas's activity with classes just beginning to learn about fractions, I introduce the activity with the starting fraction of one-half; with classes that are more advanced, I start with other fractions, such as two-thirds or three-fourths. The vignette that follows is from a fifth-grade class that had been studying fractions for about a month.

Depending on the numbers that come up when students roll the dice, the individual assignment can provide students experience thinking about fractions that are greater than one. This helps avoid a misconception students sometimes have that fractions are always less than one. Also, because there are an infinite number of possible fractions for each column, when doing the assignment, students tend to choose fractions that they can interpret and avoid those about which they're not certain. Talking with students about the fractions they avoid can help build their understanding and comfort with fractions.

The Lesson

▲▲

DAY 1

I wrote $\frac{3}{4}$ on the board and asked the class, "Who can think of a fraction that has a numerator that's greater than the numerator of the fraction I wrote on the board and also a denominator that's greater than the denominator on the board?"

A few hands sprung up. I waited a bit, but no one else volunteered. I suspected that some hadn't heard or didn't understand my directions, so I repeated them to get more students involved. I pointed at the fraction I had written on the board and said, "You're trying to think of a fraction with a numerator larger than three and a denominator larger than four. Raise your hand when you have a fraction in mind." About half a dozen more hands were raised. I called on Josh.

"Four-fifths," he said. I wrote $\frac{4}{5}$ on the board.

"Yes, this follows my rule because the four is greater than three and five is greater than four," I said. I called on several other students and recorded the fractions as they offered them.

"Six-eighths," Mariah offered.

"Fifteen-sixteenths," Lily said.

"Sixteen-sixteenths," Pamela said.

"Oh, I get it now," Claire said and raised her hand to volunteer. "Eight-eighths," she said.

"Six-sixths," Jeremy said, following the pattern Pamela and Claire had set.

"Five-fifths," Michael offered, grinning.

"Four-fourths," Martin then offered.

When I wrote $\frac{4}{4}$ on the board, I didn't have to correct him because Josh complained, "That doesn't work. You can't have a four on the bottom."

Martin's face reddened. "Can I change it?" he asked me. I reminded him that everyone could change his mind at any time in math class, as long as he had a reason.

Martin said, "Well, I need a bigger number on the bottom. I'll say four-eighths." I recorded this on the board.

By now everyone had a hand up. Instead of taking more fractions, I asked, "How many fractions do you think there are that follow the rule?"

"Lots," Rebecca said.

"Really a lot!" Jack exclaimed.

"There's an infinite amount," Andrew added.

"How do you know that there are an infinite number of possible fractions?" I asked Andrew.

He explained, "Because you can always think of bigger numbers, and you can pair different numbers together. There are jillions."

I then drew three columns on the board and labeled them <, =, and >. I reviewed the signs and then pointed to the last column labeled with the "greater than" sign. I asked, "Who knows a fraction that follows the rule and also belongs in this column?" I waited until about half the students had raised their hands.

"My fraction, sixteen-sixteenths, works," Pamela said.

"Explain why," I said.

"It's the same as one, and three-fourths is less than one," she said with confidence. Several other students raised their hands, seeming to be inspired by Pamela.

"Mine works, too," Jeremy said. "Sixth-sixths is one."

"Mine, too, five-fifths," Michael said.

"Who can think of a fraction for the 'greater than' column that's not equivalent to one?" I asked.

Sam raised a hand. "Seven-eighths works," he said. "I know that because three-fourths is the same as six-eighths, so seven-eighths has to be more."

I continued by asking the class for fractions for the other two columns, each time having the student explain her reasoning for the fraction she identified. Then I repeated the activity using three-eighths and then one-fourth as starting fractions. I continued the lesson until only ten minutes remained in the period. Then I stopped to give the homework assignment.

To avoid confusion when they were at home, I duplicated the directions for the homework (see Blackline Masters).' I distributed them and explained to the students what they were to do. I emphasized the fifth rule. "This is so you'll have the chance to stretch your thinking beyond fractions that are equivalent to one," I said.

DAY 2

The next day, I had students report about what they had learned from the assignment.

"Getting fractions that are bigger is easy," Sam said. "You just have to use fractions that have a bigger numerator. Then it's more than one, so you're sure it works."

"I rolled four-fifths," Lily said. "But I thought it was too hard so I rolled again."

"I thought it would be hard, but it wasn't. You kind of got into the swing after doing it a bit," Rebecca said.

"Did anyone think of a fraction that was too hard to place in one of the columns?" I asked. No one reported having this problem.

"Let's try the activity for one of your fractions," I then said. "Raise your hand if you think that the fraction you rolled would be particularly interesting for the class." Josh suggested three-fifths. I ruled columns and

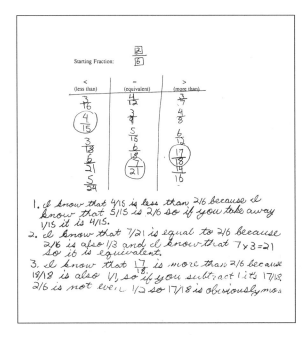

Starting Fraction: $\frac{\boxed{2}}{\boxed{6}}$

< (less than)	= (equivalent)	> (more than)
$\frac{3}{16}$	$\frac{4}{12}$	$\frac{3}{7}$
$\frac{4}{15}$	$\frac{3}{9}$	$\frac{4}{8}$
$\frac{3}{18}$	$\frac{5}{15}$	$\frac{6}{12}$
$\frac{6}{21}$	$\frac{6}{18}$	$\frac{17}{18}$
$\frac{5}{24}$	$\frac{7}{21}$	$\frac{14}{16}$

1. I know that 4/15 is less than 2/6 because I know that 5/15 is 2/6 so if you take away 1/15 it is 4/15.
2. I know that 7/21 is equal to 2/6 because 2/6 is also 1/3 and I know that 7 x 3 = 21 so it is equivalent.
3. I know that 17/18 is more than 2/6 because 18/18 is also 1/1, so if you subtract 1 it's 17/18. 2/6 is not even 1/2 so 17/18 is obviously more.

▲▲▲▲▲▲Figure 14–1 *Delia's explanations are clear and correct.*

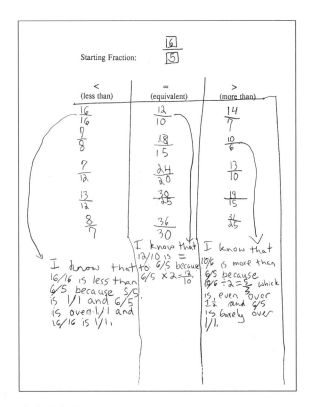

Starting Fraction: $\frac{\boxed{6}}{\boxed{5}}$

< (less than)	= (equivalent)	> (more than)
$\frac{16}{16}$	$\frac{12}{10}$	$\frac{14}{7}$
$\frac{9}{8}$	$\frac{18}{15}$	$\frac{10}{6}$
$\frac{9}{12}$	$\frac{24}{20}$	$\frac{13}{10}$
$\frac{13}{12}$	$\frac{30}{25}$	$\frac{19}{15}$
$\frac{8}{7}$	$\frac{36}{30}$	$\frac{31}{25}$

I know that 16/16 is less than 6/5 because 5/5 is 1/1 and 6/5 is over 1/1 and 16/16 is 1/1.

I know that 12/10 is = to 6/5 because 6/5 x 2 = 12/10.

I know that 10/6 is more than 6/5 because 10/6 ÷ 2 = 5/3 which is even over 1½ and 6/5 is barely over 1/1.

▲▲▲▲▲▲Figure 14–2 *As Libby's paper shows, the game can provide experience with fractions greater than 1.*

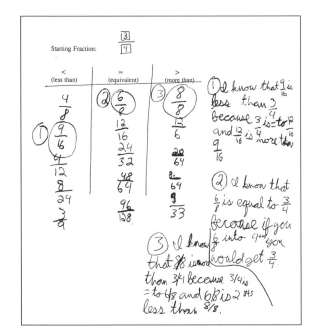

Starting Fraction: $\frac{\boxed{3}}{\boxed{4}}$

< (less than)	= (equivalent)	> (more than)
$\frac{4}{8}$	$\frac{6}{8}$	$\frac{8}{8}$
$\frac{9}{16}$	$\frac{12}{16}$	$\frac{8}{6}$
$\frac{6}{12}$	$\frac{24}{32}$	$\frac{20}{64}$
$\frac{8}{24}$	$\frac{48}{64}$	$\frac{8}{64}$
$\frac{3}{9}$	$\frac{96}{128}$	$\frac{9}{33}$

1. I know that 9/16 is less than 3/4 because 3/4 is = to 12/16 and 12/16 is 3/4 more than 9/16.

2. I know that 6/8 is equal to 3/4 because if you 6 into 9ths you would get 3/4.

3. I know that 8/8 is more than 3/4 because 3/4 is = to 6/8 and 6/8 is 2 8ths less than 8/8.

▲▲▲▲▲▲Figure 14–3 *From his paper, Josh's understanding of equivalence seems strong.*

started the activity. We continued for about fifteen minutes. (See Figures 14–1 through 14–3 for three students' homework assignments.) I then added *Nicholas's Game* to our choice list and switched to another activity.

EXTENDING THE ACTIVITY

From time to time over the next several weeks, I'd initiate the activity in class. It was a good filler when we had ten or fifteen spare minutes, and the children became more adept at identifying fractions. Also, I assigned *Nicholas's Game* for homework several more times. For one assignment, I asked students to introduce the activity to someone at home and report back about the experience. For another assignment, I asked students to do the activity twice, choosing their own starting fractions each time. I told them, "For the first one, choose a starting fraction that you think will be particularly easy. For the other, choose a starting fraction that you think will be really hard and give you a challenge."

"Do we have to use the numbers on the dice?" Jeremy asked.

"No," I responded. "You can use any numbers you'd like."

For "hard" fractions, students chose a variety, some with large numbers for the numerators and denominators, others that were larger than one. We used some of these "hard" starting fractions for follow-up lessons. It turned out that no fraction was really hard, a realization that contributed to the students feeling good about their learning.

Questions and Discussion

▲▲▲

▲ *You gave the homework assignment of asking students to teach the activity to someone at home. Why did you do this?*

Having children involve someone at home with math homework helps communicate to families about the kind of math thinking and learning that is going on in school. In this way, the students become emissaries for your math program. Also, it can give children new status at home by giving them the chance to demonstrate their expertise and teach others. I avoid confusion at home by being careful to choose assignments with which the students are clear about what to do and understand the mathematics.

▲ *How do you handle students like Lily, who change a starting fraction because they think it's too hard?*

I don't worry about this at all. My goal is for children to be meaningfully engaged with the mathematics, and that can happen with any fraction. Lily was more comfortable working with a starting fraction other than four-fifths, and that was fine with me. Of course, my goal is to help her become comfortable thinking about all fractions and build her understanding and confidence. I move toward that goal in follow-up lessons, using four-fifths, for example, for a class discussion.

▲ *Wouldn't it be a good idea for a follow-up class discussion to have the students all use the same starting fraction for a homework assignment?*

This is a fine idea that gives you the option of choosing a particular starting fraction as the focus for the entire class and then having students compare and discuss how they completed the assignment. Learning is supported when students have the opportunity to talk among themselves as well as in whole-class discussions, and having students compare homework assignments in pairs or small groups is a way to structure these conversations.

▲ *You put this activity on the class choice list. How do you use this list and how do you decide which activities to put on it?*

There are always times when some students finish an assignment more quickly than others or when I complete a lesson with the entire class and time still remains in the period. In both situations, when students select an activity from the list of choices, they will continue to be engaged with thinking about fractions. Also, when students are working independently on choices, I have the chance to meet with those who need special help.

For the choice list, I select activities that children can do successfully on their own and that help develop, cement, or extend their understanding. All of the activities on the list essentially deal with the same concepts and skills, but the variety is interesting to students. Also, I've found that giving students choices supports their involvement in their own learning process.

CHAPTER FIFTEEN
ONLY ONE
FRACTION KIT ACTIVITIES

Overview

This lesson describes four activities that help promote students' understanding of equivalence and combining fractions—*Pick Two, Pick Three, Roll Five,* and *Make a Whole.* The students rely on their fraction kit pieces to help them reason. For the first three activities, they build trains of fraction kit pieces and then figure out, using only one fraction, how to represent their lengths. For *Make a Whole,* the students figure out how much more they need to add on to make one whole. Also, *Roll Five* provides students experience with mixed numbers.

Materials

▲ fraction kits, 1 per student
▲ fraction dice as for *The Fraction Kit* lesson (see page 10), 1 per pair of students
▲ *Pick Two, Pick Three,* and *Roll Five* worksheets, 1 of each per student (see Blackline Masters)
▲ to extend the activities: 3 additional colors of 12-by-18-inch construction paper cut into 3-by-18-inch strips, 1 set of strips per student, 1 set for you, and several extra sets for possible mishaps

Time

▲ three class periods

Teaching Directions

1. Review with the students the *Cover the Whole* activity they did earlier, reminding them how to write mathematical sentences to record trains and then shorten the sentences by combining fractions with like denominators.

2. Tell the students that for the *Only One* activities, they will also represent trains they build, but the trains won't be exactly as long as one whole. For each train, they have to figure out how to represent it using only one fraction. Model this with an example, using the fraction kit and having students gather around so that they can see the pieces. On the whole strip, build a train using two one-eighth pieces and one one-half piece.

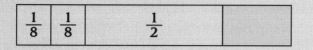

Record: $\frac{1}{8} + \frac{1}{8} + \frac{1}{2}$. Then ask students: "How can I shorten what I've recorded?"

Record: $\frac{2}{8} + \frac{1}{2}$. Then ask: "What color piece can I use to build a train that's the same length but uses pieces of only one color?" Whichever they suggest, use that color to build a train next to the one you've already built. Students typically suggest either one-eighth pieces or one-fourth pieces. In either case, after you've built a train and verified that the two are the same length, record: $\frac{1}{8} + \frac{1}{8} + \frac{1}{2} = \frac{3}{4}$. Then ask for another color to use, try it, and record again. Continue until you've used all possibilities.

$\frac{1}{8}$	$\frac{1}{8}$	$\frac{1}{2}$				

$\frac{1}{4}$	$\frac{1}{4}$	$\frac{1}{4}$

$\frac{1}{8}$	$\frac{1}{8}$	$\frac{1}{8}$	$\frac{1}{8}$	$\frac{1}{8}$	$\frac{1}{8}$

$\frac{1}{16}$	$\frac{1}{16}$	$\frac{1}{16}$	$\frac{1}{16}$	$\frac{1}{16}$	$\frac{1}{16}$	$\frac{1}{16}$	$\frac{1}{16}$	$\frac{1}{16}$	$\frac{1}{16}$	$\frac{1}{16}$	$\frac{1}{16}$

$$\frac{1}{8} + \frac{1}{8} + \frac{1}{2} = \frac{3}{4} = \frac{6}{8} = \frac{12}{16}$$

3. Repeat for another train, again building, recording, then building another train using pieces of only one color, and finally recording the length of the train with only one fraction.

4. Give the directions for *Pick Two* and *Pick Three* (see Blackline Masters) and have the students work on the activities for the rest of the period. You may wish to duplicate the directions and give them to the students for their reference. Circulate to assist students as needed. Collect their papers at the end of the period or ask students to take incomplete papers home for homework.

5. Begin the next day by discussing *Pick Two* and *Pick Three* and then introducing *Roll Five.* This activity is essentially the same but has the added feature that students must roll the fraction die five times and use the fractions they roll to build their trains. Again, they shorten and record the length of the train with only one fraction. Model this for the class by building and recording a train that is longer than one whole, for example: $\frac{1}{2} + \frac{1}{2} + \frac{1}{8} + \frac{1}{8} + \frac{1}{8}$. Ask for suggestions for how to build an equivalent train with pieces of only one color. Show students how to record with a fraction—$\frac{11}{8}$—and with a mixed number—$1\frac{3}{8}$. Have students return to work on *Pick Two* and *Pick Three*, if they didn't finish them for homework, and also work on *Roll Five*. Because *Roll Five* usually requires more pieces, you might want students to work together; however, it's good practice for them to record individually.

6. Begin the third day by introducing the last activity, *Make a Whole*. Students roll the fraction die twice, build a train using the fractions that come up, and then figure out how much more to add on to the train to make one whole. They have to represent the amount with only one fraction. Model this and show them how to record their original sentence. For example, if the original train was made from one-sixteenth and one-fourth, then record: $\frac{1}{16} + \frac{1}{4} + ? = 1$. You may prefer to use a letter or a box as the variable instead of a question mark. Have students work on the activities.

7. Have students add thirds, sixths, and twelfths to their kits by cutting additional strips. Repeat the *Only One* activities using all of the pieces. Instead of using the fraction die for *Roll Five* and *Make One Whole*, ask students to choose pieces for them that give them practice mixing thirds, sixths, and twelfths with their original pieces.

Teaching Notes

Prior to introducing these activities, make sure the students have had ample experience with fraction kits. You'll know that they are familiar enough with them when they can identify, without referring to their kits, the color for each fractional part and are comfortable with relationships among fractional parts, such as eight-sixteenths being equal to one-half. Also, aside from playing the games of *Cover Up* and *Uncover*, students should have completed the activities *Cover the Whole*, *Comparing Pairs*, and *What's Missing?* (See pages 10–29.)

In the activity *Cover the Whole*, students learned to shorten the mathematical sentences they recorded for covering the whole strip. For example, a student might have covered the whole strip with three one-fourth pieces and two one-eighth pieces and then recorded $\frac{1}{4} + \frac{1}{4} + \frac{1}{4} + \frac{1}{8} + \frac{1}{8} = 1$. This sentence could then be shortened to $\frac{3}{4} + \frac{2}{8} = 1$. For the *Only One* activities, students again shorten the mathematical sentences they write, this time finding only one fraction to represent the train of pieces. Also, students build trains of pieces that don't add up to one whole. For example, a student building a train with two one-fourth pieces and one one-eighth piece would first record $\frac{1}{4} + \frac{1}{4} + \frac{1}{8}$. This could be shortened to $\frac{2}{4} + \frac{1}{8}$. And this could be further shortened, by building an equivalent train using pieces of only one color, to either $\frac{5}{8}$ or $\frac{10}{16}$.

After students have had sufficient experience using the fraction kits, they will begin to figure sums mentally without using their fraction pieces. However, students should still have fraction kits available to verify their mental calculations. Also, it's important to remember that the time required for "sufficient experience" with the kits varies from student to student.

The last activity, *Roll Five*, results in producing trains that are sometimes longer than a whole. This activity gives students experience with thinking about and representing fractions greater than one and gives you a context in which to introduce the notation used for mixed numbers.

The Lesson

▲▲

DAY 1

The students hadn't worked with their fraction kits for a while and were interested when I told them that I was going to introduce them to four new activities with them. I listed the activities on the board:

Pick Two
Pick Three
Roll Five
Make a Whole

"Are they games?" Tom asked.

"No," I responded. "They're explorations that will give you practice thinking about fractions in different ways. I'm going to introduce two of the activities today and you can get started on them. Then I'll explain the third one tomorrow and the fourth the next day."

I modeled an example for *Pick Three*. I gathered the students around so that they could see both the chalkboard and what I was building with my fraction kit. "For *Pick Three,* you put any three of your fraction pieces on your whole strip. The only rule is that the pieces can't all be the same color," I said. On the whole strip, I built a train using two one-eighth pieces and one one-half piece.

$\frac{1}{8}$	$\frac{1}{8}$	$\frac{1}{2}$	

I then recorded on the board:

$\frac{1}{8} + \frac{1}{8} + \frac{1}{2}$.

"How can I shorten what I've recorded the way you shortened your sentences for the *Cover the Whole* activity?" I asked the students. I called on Mariah and recorded what she said:

$\frac{2}{8} + \frac{1}{2}$

I then asked, "What color piece can I use to build a train that's the same length but uses pieces of only one color?"

"Use the one-eighth pieces," Lily suggested.

"Why do you think that will work?" I asked.

"Because you've already got some and I know that it takes four one-eighth pieces to make one-half," she answered. I built a train with one-eighth pieces adjacent to the original train.

$\frac{1}{8}$	$\frac{1}{8}$		$\frac{1}{2}$		
$\frac{1}{8}$	$\frac{1}{8}$	$\frac{1}{8}$	$\frac{1}{8}$	$\frac{1}{8}$	$\frac{1}{8}$

"How long is this train?" I asked. I called on Jeremy.

"Six-eighths," he said.

"So that's how I can record my original train with only one fraction," I said and recorded:

$\frac{1}{8} + \frac{1}{8} + \frac{1}{2} = \frac{6}{8}$

"What other fraction piece could we use instead of the one-eighth pieces to build a train the same length?" I asked.

"The one-fourth pieces will work," Sam said. "You'll use just three of them." I did this.

$\frac{1}{8}$	$\frac{1}{8}$		$\frac{1}{2}$		
$\frac{1}{8}$	$\frac{1}{8}$	$\frac{1}{8}$	$\frac{1}{8}$	$\frac{1}{8}$	$\frac{1}{8}$
$\frac{1}{4}$		$\frac{1}{4}$		$\frac{1}{4}$	

I then added to what I had recorded:

$\frac{1}{8} + \frac{1}{8} + \frac{1}{2} = \frac{6}{8} = \frac{3}{4}$

"You could use the sixteenths, too," Claire said.

"How many do you think I'll need?" I asked. Claire thought for a moment and then said, tentatively, "Maybe ten?"

"What makes you think ten?" I probed. Claire just shrugged.

"Oh, I know," Delia said. "It has to be twelve because two-sixteenths is the same as one-eighth."

"Let's try it and see," I said, beginning to build another train using all one-sixteenth pieces. A benefit of the fraction pieces is that children can use them to test predictions and verify relationships. After building the train, I again added to what I had recorded:

$$\frac{1}{8} + \frac{1}{8} + \frac{1}{2} = \frac{6}{8} = \frac{3}{4} = \frac{12}{16}$$

I then said, "All of the fractions I've recorded to describe the train are worth the same. We call them equivalent fractions. If you wanted to use the fewest pieces, then you would use just three of the one-fourth pieces. But all of the ways are correct." I used the word *equivalent* to help build students' familiarity with it.

"So you'll try and find all the possible equivalent fractions to represent each train you build. What other pieces will work for this example?" I asked. I knew that there were no other possibilities, but I asked the question anyway. Students' mathematical thinking can be strengthened by thinking about questions for which there might not be a solution. The students agreed that there were no other ways to build a train using pieces of just one color.

"For *Pick Three,* you'll do just what I did. You'll build a train with three pieces that aren't all the same color and record what you built. Then you have to figure out how to build another train next to it that's the same length, but using pieces that are all the same color so you can record the length of your train with only one fraction. And then you should see if you can build the

train with any other color pieces. You have to do this for five different trains."

Andrew had a comment. "If I pick the two one-half pieces and one more, then I'm over the whole."

"That's all right," I said. "But it may make the problem harder for you. Try it and then you can decide if you'd rather choose other pieces."

I then pointed to the list of the four activities and asked the students, "Who thinks he knows what to do for *Pick Two?*"

"It's probably the same as *Pick Three,* but you pick two instead," Josh said.

"That's right," I said. "Let's try one." I built a train using a one-half piece and a one-sixteenth piece.

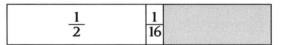

I recorded:

$$\frac{1}{2} + \frac{1}{16}$$

"Now what?" I asked. I called on Claudia.

"Well, you can't make it any shorter, so you build another train," she said. "I think you have to use sixteenths. I think you'll need nine of them."

"How did you figure that out?" I asked.

"It's easy," she said. "You need eight of them to match one-half and the extra one makes nine." I built this to verify Claudia's idea:

$\frac{1}{2}$			$\frac{1}{16}$	

$\frac{1}{16}$	$\frac{1}{16}$	$\frac{1}{16}$	$\frac{1}{16}$	$\frac{1}{16}$	$\frac{1}{16}$	$\frac{1}{16}$	$\frac{1}{16}$	$\frac{1}{16}$

"So it's nine-sixteenths," Joey said. I agreed and recorded:

$$\frac{1}{2} + \frac{1}{16} = \frac{9}{16}$$

"What other train could we build using the same color pieces that's the same length?" I asked.

"I think eighths will work," Martin said.

"No, they won't," Andrew said.

"Let's try it," I said. "That's what the fraction pieces are for—to help you test your ideas." I built a train using eighths so Martin could see that it wasn't possible to match the other trains.

$\frac{1}{2}$				$\frac{1}{16}$	

$\frac{1}{16}$	$\frac{1}{16}$	$\frac{1}{16}$	$\frac{1}{16}$	$\frac{1}{16}$	$\frac{1}{16}$	$\frac{1}{16}$	$\frac{1}{16}$	$\frac{1}{16}$

$\frac{1}{8}$	$\frac{1}{8}$	$\frac{1}{8}$	$\frac{1}{8}$	$\frac{1}{8}$

I reminded the students that they had to do five examples for each activity. They then got to work. I circulated, giving help as needed. At times I made informal assessments, asking students to predict how many of a piece they'd need to build a train. (Figures 15–1 through 15–3 show how some students completed this activity.)

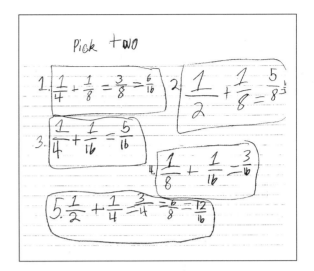

▲▲▲▲▲▲Figure 15–2 *Cynthia showed equivalent fractions whenever possible for each answer.*

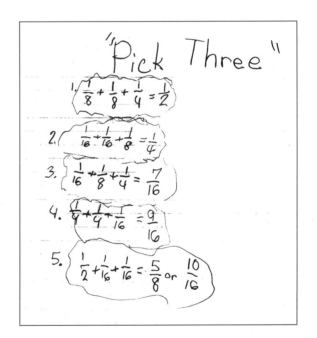

▲▲▲▲▲▲Figure 15–3 *It wasn't until the last Pick Three problem that Sally caught on to the different possible fractions.*

DAY 2

To begin class, I asked if anyone had questions about either *Pick Two* or *Pick Three*. No one did. "Before you get back to work, I want to explain what you have to do for *Roll*

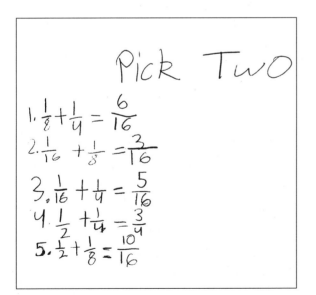

▲▲▲▲▲▲Figure 15–1 *Drew recorded only one fraction for each problem, using sixteenths for all but one of them. "They always work," he told me.*

Five," I said. "Then you can work on the three activities."

I got out a fraction kit and a fraction die and again had the students gather around. *"Roll Five* is like *Pick Three,* but you don't get to choose the pieces," I said. "Instead, you roll the fraction die five times and build a train with the pieces that match the fractions that come up. Then you figure out how to cover your train with pieces of one color and write one fraction that represents the train's length."

The reason I included this activity was to give the students experience thinking about and recording fractional quantities that were greater than one. I chose fractions to model this. "Let's suppose I rolled these fractions," I said, and wrote on the board:

$$\frac{1}{2} \quad \frac{1}{4} \quad \frac{1}{4} \quad \frac{1}{2} \quad \frac{1}{8}$$

"What do you think about the train these pieces will make?" I asked.

"It's really long," Tom said.

"It's longer than the whole strip," Jennifer said. "The two halves make the whole and then you have the others."

"Do you think it's longer than two whole strips?" I asked. I heard several responses. "Yeah, maybe." "I don't think so." "It could be." "No way."

Then Claudia's hand shot up. "It's a whole strip and half more," she said. "Look, the two halves make a whole, like Jennifer said, then the two fourths make a half. No, wait, so it's a whole and a half and an eighth more."

This went too fast for most of the class, so I built the train.

$\frac{1}{2}$	$\frac{1}{4}$	$\frac{1}{4}$	$\frac{1}{2}$	$\frac{1}{8}$

I recorded:

$$\frac{1}{2} + \frac{1}{4} + \frac{1}{4} + \frac{1}{2} + \frac{1}{8}$$

"I know how to shorten it," David said. "You write two-halves plus two-fourths plus one-eighth." I recorded:

$$\frac{2}{2} + \frac{2}{4} + \frac{1}{8}$$

"You can cover it with halves, but you don't have enough," Sarah said. "You need three of them."

"I'll have to use one from another kit," I said. "When you do this activity, team up with a partner so you'll have enough pieces. But you'll each have to do your own recording."

"Look, the halves don't work," Joey said.

"I could have told you that," Claudia said. "Use eighths."

"How many?" I asked.

Andrew piped up, "You need thirteen, eight for the whole, then four, and then one more." I built a train with eighths and verified that Andrew was correct.

$\frac{1}{2}$		$\frac{1}{4}$	$\frac{1}{4}$	$\frac{1}{2}$		$\frac{1}{8}$

$\frac{1}{8}$	$\frac{1}{8}$	$\frac{1}{8}$	$\frac{1}{8}$	$\frac{1}{8}$	$\frac{1}{8}$	$\frac{1}{8}$	$\frac{1}{8}$	$\frac{1}{8}$	$\frac{1}{8}$	$\frac{1}{8}$	$\frac{1}{8}$	$\frac{1}{8}$

"But what can you write?" Delia asked. "It's not a fraction."

"How many eighths did we use?" I asked.

"Thirteen," Delia said.

"So I can write thirteen-eighths," I said and recorded:

$$\frac{2}{2} + \frac{2}{4} + \frac{1}{8} = \frac{13}{8}$$

"Oh, I get it," she said.

"There's another way to write thirteen-eighths," I said. "It's called a mixed number because you mix together a whole number and a fraction." I covered eight of the eighths in the train with a whole strip:

$\frac{1}{2}$		$\frac{1}{4}$	$\frac{1}{4}$	$\frac{1}{2}$			$\frac{1}{8}$
1				$\frac{1}{8}$	$\frac{1}{8}$	$\frac{1}{8}$	$\frac{1}{8}$ $\frac{1}{8}$

"This way it's one whole and five-eighths," I said. "Look at how I write this." I recorded:

$$\frac{2}{2} + \frac{2}{4} + \frac{1}{8} = \frac{13}{8} = 1\frac{5}{8}$$

"See how I wrote the one larger than the numbers in the numerator and denominator and then the five-eighths next to it?" I pointed out. The way we write mixed numbers is one of the social conventions of mathematics, not an idea that students should be expected to discover or figure out. As a convention, the representation isn't rooted in logic, and it's appropriate to teach it by telling.

The students then began to work. The lure of the fraction die pulled most of them to start with *Roll Five*. The room had the feeling of purposeful activity. Because this was the second day with these activities, the students were more sure about what to do and the period went smoothly. The incidental conversations and comments about what they were doing showed that many of them were becoming comfortable with the relationships among pieces. (Figures 15–4 and 15–5 show how two students completed the *Roll Five* activity.)

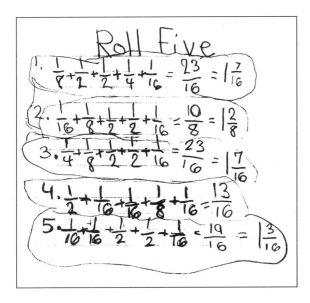

▲▲▲▲▲▲Figure 15–4 *Marlo's Roll Five paper shows her ability to record mixed numbers when possible.*

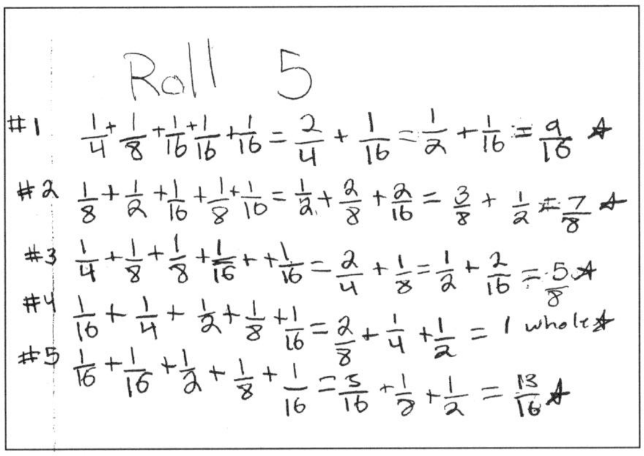

[Figure 15–5 handwritten:]

Roll 5

#1 $\frac{1}{4} + \frac{1}{8} + \frac{1}{16} + \frac{1}{16} + \frac{1}{16} = \frac{2}{4} + \frac{1}{16} = \frac{1}{2} + \frac{1}{16} = \frac{9}{16}$ ✗

#2 $\frac{1}{8} + \frac{1}{2} + \frac{1}{16} + \frac{1}{8} + \frac{1}{16} = \frac{1}{2} + \frac{2}{8} + \frac{2}{16} = \frac{3}{8} + \frac{1}{2} \neq \frac{7}{8}$ ✗

#3 $\frac{1}{4} + \frac{1}{8} + \frac{1}{8} + \frac{1}{16} + \frac{1}{16} = \frac{2}{4} + \frac{1}{8} = \frac{1}{2} + \frac{2}{16} = \frac{5}{8}$ ✗

#4 $\frac{1}{16} + \frac{1}{4} + \frac{1}{2} + \frac{1}{8} + \frac{1}{16} = \frac{2}{8} + \frac{1}{4} + \frac{1}{2} = 1$ whole ✗

#5 $\frac{1}{16} + \frac{1}{16} + \frac{1}{2} + \frac{1}{8} + \frac{1}{16} = \frac{5}{16} + \frac{1}{2} + \frac{1}{2} = \frac{13}{16}$ ✗

▲▲▲▲▲▲Figure 15–5 *Penny was able to do most of the problems without relying on the fraction pieces. She was surprised when #4 came out to be exactly 1 whole.*

DAY 3

I began class by introducing *Make a Whole.* "Let me explain this last activity," I said. "Then you can complete work on them all. For this activity, you roll the fraction die twice and record the fractions that come up. Then you have to figure out how to write one fraction to add on to these two to make exactly one whole. You can use your fraction kit to help by putting on the pieces from your two rolls and then figuring out what else you need to put on. Remember to use pieces of all the same color for completing the whole so you can write your answer as only one fraction."

I demonstrated by having Sarah roll a fraction die twice. She came up with $\frac{1}{8}$ both times. I wrote:

$$\frac{1}{8} + \frac{1}{8} + ? = 1$$

After I made a train on the whole strip with two one-eighth pieces, Sam said, "It's easy. You need three-fourths."

"That's what I think," Claudia added.

"I don't get it," Tom said. I gave a little time for the students to talk among themselves before asking for their attention.

"I agree with Sam and Claudia that three-fourths works, but you could cover the rest with more eighths," Sarah said. "You need six of them, so I think that you can write six-eighths where the question mark is." I recorded both ideas:

$$\frac{1}{8} + \frac{1}{8} + \frac{3}{4} = 1$$

$$\frac{1}{8} + \frac{1}{8} + \frac{6}{8} = 1$$

"Where does the three-fourths come from?" Martin wanted to know.

"Can I show?" Sam asked. I agreed and he showed how three of the one-fourth pieces covered the six one-eighth pieces. Martin seemed satisfied.

There were no other suggestions, so I said, "I know of another way." I waited. No one had an idea and then Joey shouted, "You can use twelve sixteenths!" I did this with fraction pieces and recorded:

$$\frac{1}{8} + \frac{1}{8} + \frac{12}{16} = 1$$

"As with the other activities, you'll do this five times," I said.

"What if you roll one-half and then one-half again?" Josh asked.

"How many pieces would you then need to make a whole?" I asked.

"Zero," Josh said, grinning. I showed him how he would record in this situation:

$$\frac{1}{2} + \frac{1}{2} + 0 = 1$$

Before the students got to work, I offered them two alternatives for representing the missing fraction. "I used a question mark, but when there's something unknown in a mathematical sentence like this, we can use other symbols to represent it." I explained that we could use a box in which a number could be written or a letter that could be replaced by a number. I demonstrated by writing on the board:

$$\frac{1}{8} + \frac{1}{8} + \quad = 1$$

$$\frac{1}{8} + \frac{1}{8} + x = 1$$

There were no more questions and the students got to work. (See Figures 15–6 and 15–7 for two students' work with *Make a Whole*.)

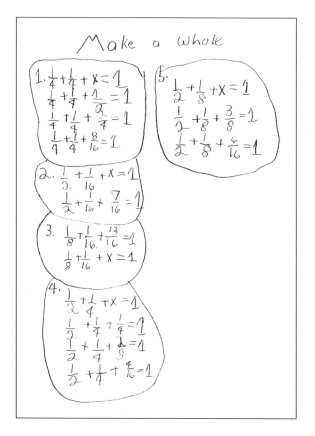

▲▲▲▲▲▲**Figure 15–6** *Drew found several solutions when possible for the Make a Whole problems.*

EXTENSIONS

For students who want more of a challenge, suggest that for *Roll Five,* for each fraction that comes up they take two of those pieces. This increases the lengths of their trains so they are sometimes longer than two wholes.

Also, after students have had experience with the four activities, ask them to try solving *Only One* problems without using their fraction kits. (See Figures 15–8 through 15–11.) Begin with problems that involve the fractions that students are most comfortable with from the fraction kit activities—halves, fourths, eighths, and sixteenths. When students are more confident, pose problems with thirds, sixths, and twelfths, and finally problems involving fractions with other denominators. Most likely, some students will be ready for this challenge and others won't be yet. Allow

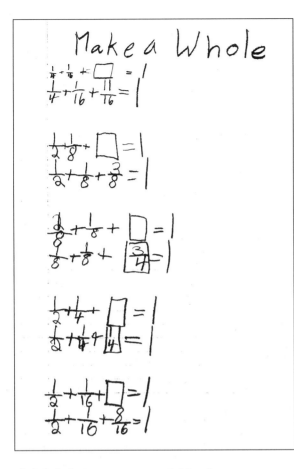

Make a Whole

$$\frac{1}{4} + \frac{1}{16} + \boxed{} = 1$$
$$\frac{1}{4} + \frac{1}{16} + \frac{11}{16} = 1$$

$$\frac{1}{2} + \frac{1}{8} + \boxed{} = 1$$
$$\frac{1}{2} + \frac{1}{8} + \frac{3}{8} = 1$$

$$\frac{1}{8} + \frac{1}{8} + \boxed{} = 1$$
$$\frac{1}{8} + \frac{1}{8} + \boxed{\frac{3}{4}} = 1$$

$$\frac{1}{2} + \frac{1}{4} + \boxed{} = 1$$
$$\frac{1}{2} + \frac{1}{4} + \boxed{\frac{1}{4}} = 1$$

$$\frac{1}{2} + \frac{1}{16} + \boxed{} = 1$$
$$\frac{1}{2} + \frac{1}{16} + \frac{8}{16} = 1$$

▲▲▲▲▲▲**Figure 15–7** *Nickie chose to use a box for the variable in the Make a Whole problems.*

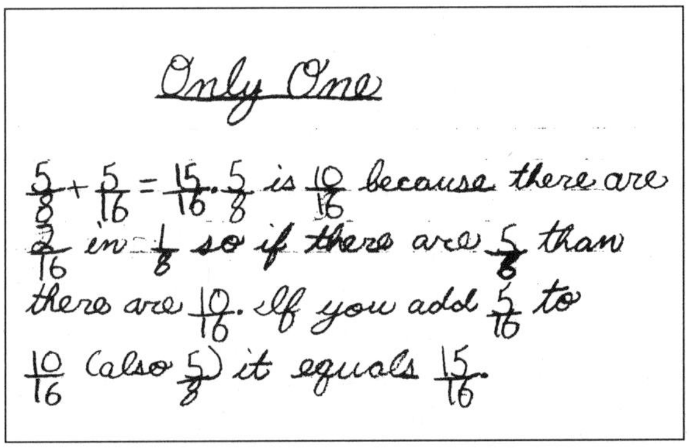

Only One

$$\frac{5}{8} + \frac{5}{16} = \frac{15}{16}.$$ 5 is 10 because there are 2 in $\frac{1}{8}$ so if there are 5 than there are 10. If you add $\frac{5}{16}$ to $\frac{10}{16}$ (also $\frac{5}{8}$) it equals $\frac{15}{16}$.

▲▲▲▲▲▲**Figure 15–8** *Delia added $\frac{5}{8}$ and $\frac{5}{16}$ by converting the problem to $\frac{10}{16} + \frac{5}{16}$.*

students who still need the support of the fraction pieces to use them, and also encourage them to listen to the strategies used by classmates who solve problems without the kits.

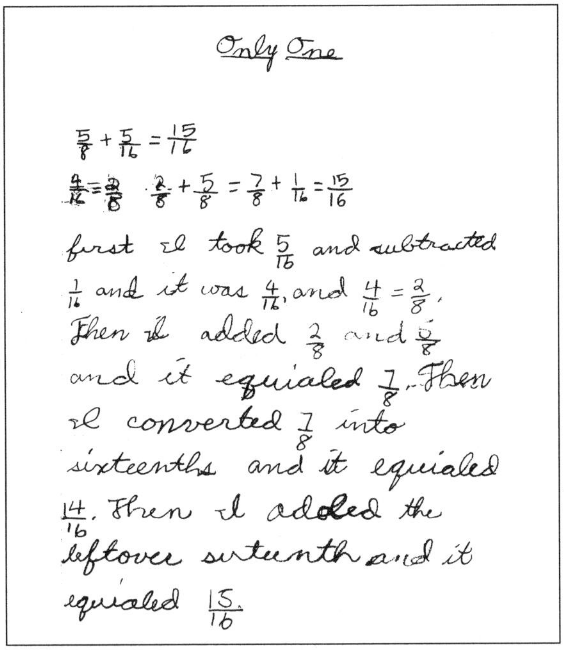

Only One

$$\frac{5}{8} + \frac{5}{16} = \frac{15}{16}$$
$$\frac{4}{16} = \frac{2}{8} \quad \frac{2}{8} + \frac{5}{8} = \frac{7}{8} + \frac{1}{16} = \frac{15}{16}$$

first I took $\frac{5}{16}$ and subtracted $\frac{1}{16}$ and it was $\frac{4}{16}$, and $\frac{4}{16} = \frac{2}{8}$. Then I added $\frac{2}{8}$ and $\frac{5}{8}$ and it equaled $\frac{7}{8}$. Then I converted $\frac{7}{8}$ into sixteenths and it equaled $\frac{14}{16}$. Then I added the leftover sixteenth and it equaled $\frac{15}{16}$.

▲▲▲▲▲▲**Figure 15–9** *Claudia's unique approach of initially using eighths and then converting to sixteenths shows her comfort with reasoning with fractions.*

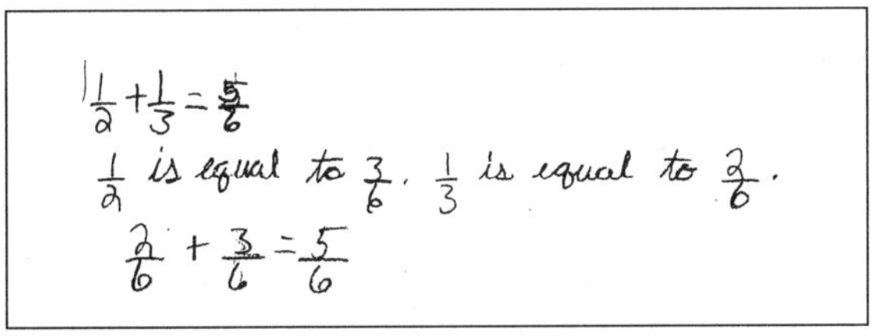

$$\frac{1}{2} + \frac{1}{3} = \frac{5}{6}$$
$\frac{1}{2}$ is equal to $\frac{3}{6}$. $\frac{1}{3}$ is equal to $\frac{2}{6}$.
$$\frac{2}{6} + \frac{3}{6} = \frac{5}{6}$$

▲▲▲▲▲▲**Figure 15–10** *Jennifer presented a straightforward approach to find the answer to $\frac{1}{2} + \frac{1}{3}$.*

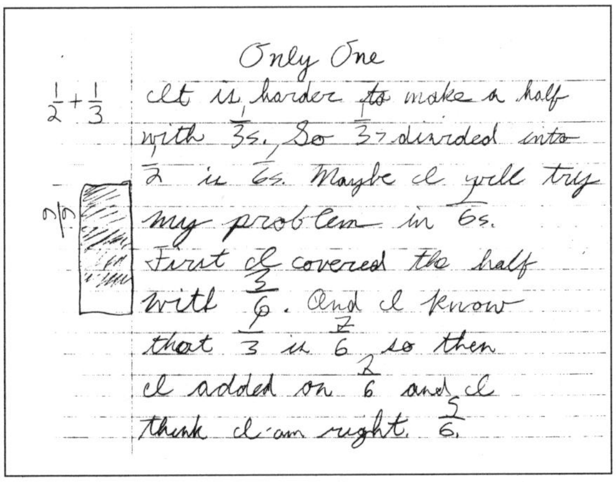

Only One

$\frac{1}{2} + \frac{1}{3}$ It is harder to make a half with 3s. So 3 divided into $\frac{1}{2}$ is 6s. Maybe I will try my problem in 6s. First I covered the half with $\frac{3}{6}$. And I know that $\frac{1}{3}$ is $\frac{2}{6}$ so then I added on $\frac{2}{6}$ and I think I am right. $\frac{5}{6}$

▲▲▲▲▲▲**Figure 15–11** *Libby's solution for $\frac{1}{2} + \frac{1}{3}$ shows her need for the support of the fraction pieces.*

Questions and Discussion

▲▲▲

▲ *What about students who don't seem to be giving up the fraction kits but continue to rely on them to solve the problems?*

Students rely on the fraction kits when they don't have either the understanding or the confidence to reason without them. You may want to think first before letting them reach for their kits, but my advice is to do so gently. Also, students should always have the fraction kit pieces available to them to verify their thinking. To help build students' understanding, have frequent and ongoing class discussions about problems in which students share their thinking. Students' understanding develops both from having opportunities to explain their thinking and from hearing others' ideas.

▲ *Pick Two, Pick Three, and Roll Five are all really the same. Why do you present them as different activities?*

The fact that they are the same is one of the benefits of using all three activities. Students are confident with what to do, but there's enough variety to keep them interested and, therefore, learning.

▲ *These problems are fine for halves, fourths, eighths, and sixteenths. But what about other fractions?*

It's very beneficial to give the students each three more strips of paper in different colors and have them cut thirds, sixths, and twelfths. Folding doesn't produce particularly accurate pieces. Instead, give students the problem of figuring out the length of each of these parts, knowing the whole strip is 18 inches long. This is a fine measurement problem for them to solve. Once they have made these strips, model *Pick Three* using two of the "old" strips and one of the strips they just cut. Then have them do five problems for each of *Pick Two* and *Pick Three.* If you'd like them to have experience combining five addends, as they did with *Roll Five,* then change it to *Pick Five* so that you don't have to create new fraction dice.

ASSESSMENTS

This section suggests ten assessments that are useful for assessing students' progress as they study fractions. *Pizza Sharing* relates fractions to a real-world problem and can be used either before beginning fraction instruction or after the students have experienced some of the lessons. *Closest to 0, $\frac{1}{2}$, or 1?*, *Put in Order*, and *Where Does _____ Fit?* are appropriate after students have had experience with fraction kits (see Chapter 2) and the *Put in Order* lesson (see Chapter 13). *Which Is Larger?* and *Who Ate More?* monitor students' ability to compare fractions, one abstractly and the other in a real-world context. *Write Three Statements* provides insights into students' understanding of specific fractions. *How Many Inches Wide Is $\frac{1}{12}$*, *The Y Problem*, and *The Birthday Cake Problem* measure students' ability to apply fractions to problem-solving situations.

Teaching Notes

In all of the lessons suggested in this book, students have opportunities to collaborate on problems, present their thinking, and consider the ideas of others, thus experiencing interaction that supports the development of their understanding of fractions. However, it's also important for students to tackle problems individually and learn to think on their own, both by taking on new challenges and practicing what they've already learned. Students' individual work is key for assessing their learning progress.

When I was an elementary student, most of the individual assignments I did when learning fractions called for solving either computational exercises or word problems. The emphasis was on getting right answers, and assignments typically presented ten or more problems to provide us adequate practice. The assessments suggested in this chapter are different from those I was given. Each of these presents only one or just a few problems, and while correct answers are important, equal emphasis is put on students explaining their reasoning.

I've tried all of these assessments with several classes of students and I've included student work to serve as examples of how students have responded. Many of the papers offer examples of what I consider to be acceptable work; others show erroneous or fragile thinking that was useful to me for planning further instruction. I've found that reading students' papers carefully to figure out how they reasoned is good preparation for offering individuals the help they need. Also, I've found it useful at times to use students' papers to initiate whole-class discussions.

You'll notice that this section doesn't follow the format of the other chapters in the book. There aren't any teaching directions, vignettes, or question-and-answer reflections included. Instead, for each assessment I've included the prompt I gave to the students, some comments about the activity, and samples of student work.

Pizza Sharing

PROMPT

Share two pizzas among three people. Explain with words, numbers, and pictures.

I've used this assessment in a variety of ways. At times, I've given it even before beginning fraction instruction; at other times, I've assigned it after fraction kit activities to extend the students' experiences to include thirds. The problem is similar to what students do in the *Sharing Cookies* problems (see Chapter 11), and it's particularly useful for discussing with the class the importance of clearly identifying the whole when you describe fractional parts. The papers shown in Figures 1 through 4 were done just two days after the same class had worked on the assignment *Closest to 0, $\frac{1}{2}$, or 1?*, and before they experienced the lesson on sharing cookies.

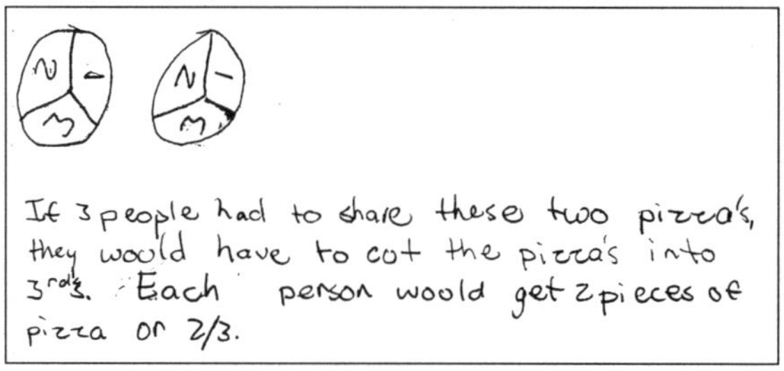

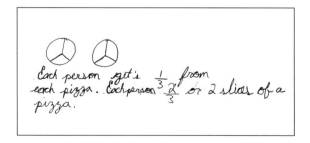

▲▲▲▲▲▲**Figure 1**   *Delia's explanation is clear and correct.*

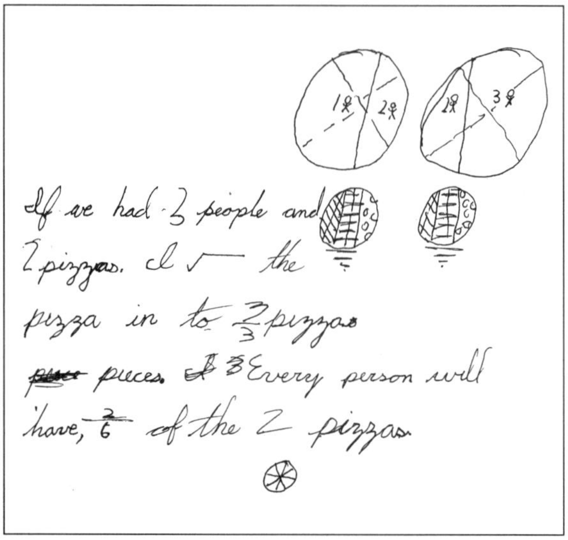

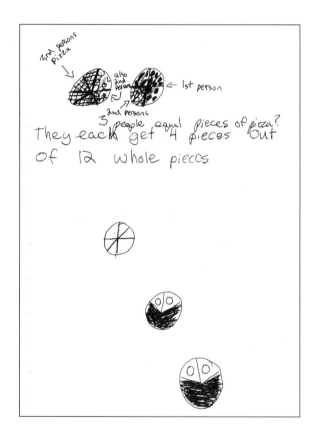

▲▲▲▲▲▲**Figure 3**   *Maggie's paper shows her difficulty in dividing a circle correctly into thirds. Her answer is different from what most other students wrote, but it's correct.*

▲▲▲▲▲▲**Figure 2**   *Jennifer used both $\frac{1}{3}$ and $\frac{2}{3}$ in her answer.*

▲▲▲▲▲▲**Figure 4**   *Libby divided each pizza into sixths, but her paper shows her difficulty dividing circles into equal-size segments. While Libby correctly figured out that each person gets 4 out of 12 pieces, she did not include a fraction in her answer.*

Closest to 0, $\frac{1}{2}$, or 1?

PROMPT

Decide if each fraction is closest to 0, $\frac{1}{2}$, or 1.
Explain your reasoning.

$$\frac{3}{4} \quad \frac{3}{8} \quad \frac{11}{16} \quad \frac{1}{4} \quad \frac{1}{16}$$

This assessment is appropriate after students have cut fraction kits and played the initial games (see Chapter 2) and also have been involved in discussions about one-half (see Chapters 6 and 7). I repeat this assessment from time to time, changing the fractions to make it more challenging as the year goes on. I typically include three to five fractions in an assessment and ask students to decide for each fraction whether it is closest to zero, one half, or one. For beginning experiences, I include fractions that are halfway between zero and one half or one half and one. The student work shown in Figures 5 and 6 is from the fall of a year when students had recently begun studying fractions.

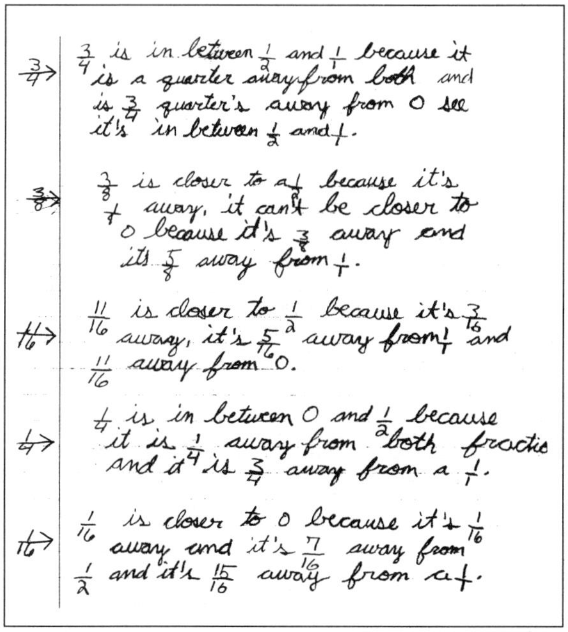

▲▲▲▲▲▲**Figure 5** *Jennifer explained her thinking clearly for each fraction.*

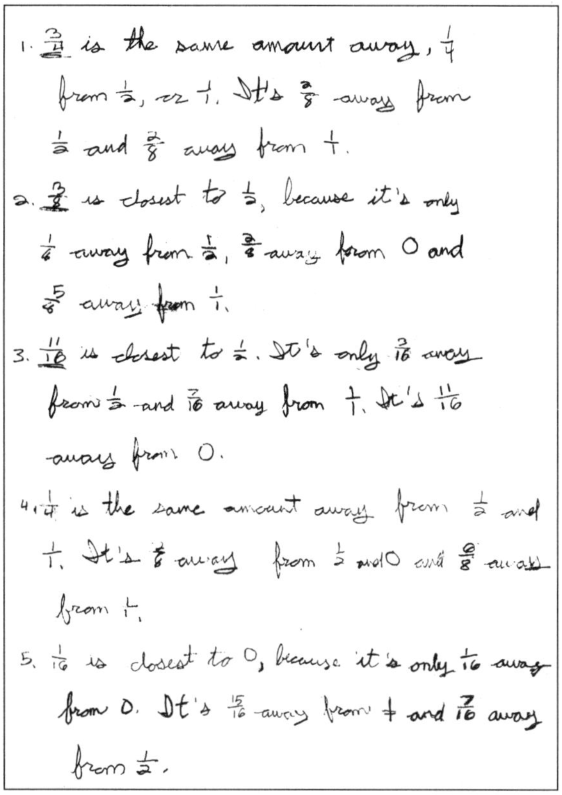

▲▲▲▲▲▲**Figure 6** *Aside from presenting correct reasoning, Shannon's paper also shows her understanding of relationships among the fractions.*

Put in Order

PROMPT

Put each set of fractions in order from smallest to largest. Explain your reasoning.

$$\frac{1}{2} \quad \frac{3}{8} \quad \frac{7}{16}$$

$$\frac{7}{16} \quad \frac{5}{8} \quad \frac{1}{2}$$

$$\frac{1}{4} \quad \frac{1}{8} \quad \frac{3}{16}$$

$$\frac{5}{16} \quad \frac{5}{8} \quad \frac{5}{4}$$

$$\frac{4}{8} \quad \frac{1}{4} \quad \frac{3}{16}$$

This assessment gives students the same sort of problem they experience in the *Put in Order* lesson (see Chapter 13). At first, I choose fractions that relate to the students' fraction kit pieces and give students only three fractions to order. Later, I include fractions other than halves, fourths, eighths,

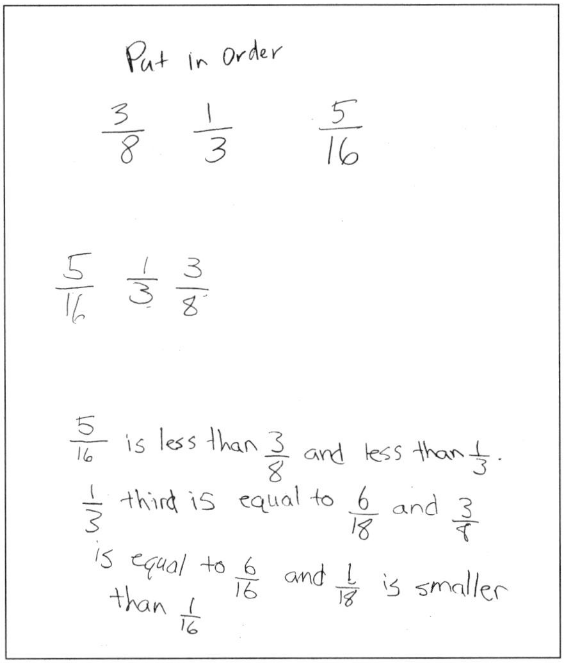

Put In Order

$\frac{3}{8}$ $\frac{1}{3}$ $\frac{5}{16}$

$\frac{5}{16}$ $\frac{1}{3}$ $\frac{3}{8}$

$\frac{5}{16}$ is less than $\frac{3}{8}$ and less than $\frac{1}{3}$.
$\frac{1}{3}$ third is equal to $\frac{6}{18}$ and $\frac{3}{8}$
is equal to $\frac{6}{16}$ and $\frac{1}{18}$ is smaller than $\frac{1}{16}$

▲▲▲▲▲▲**Figure 7** *Claudia was able to order* $\frac{3}{8}$, $\frac{1}{3}$, *and* $\frac{5}{16}$ *correctly.*

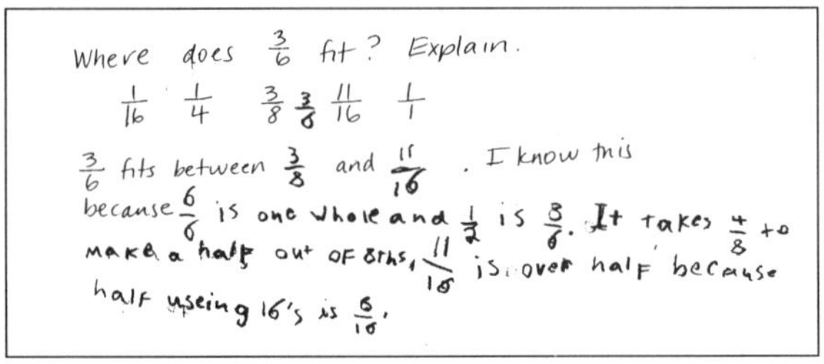

Where does $\frac{3}{6}$ fit? Explain.
$\frac{1}{16}$ $\frac{1}{4}$ $\frac{3}{8}$ $\frac{3}{6}$ $\frac{11}{16}$ $\frac{1}{1}$

$\frac{3}{6}$ fits between $\frac{3}{8}$ and $\frac{11}{16}$. I know this because $\frac{6}{6}$ is one whole and $\frac{3}{8}$ is $\frac{3}{8}$. It takes $\frac{4}{8}$ to make a half out of 8ths, $\frac{11}{16}$ is over half because half useing 16's is $\frac{8}{16}$.

▲▲▲▲▲▲**Figure 8** *Sean explains why* $\frac{3}{6}$ *fits in between* $\frac{3}{8}$ *and* $\frac{11}{16}$.

Where does $\frac{3}{6}$ fit? Explain.
$\frac{1}{16}$ $\frac{1}{4}$ $\frac{3}{8}$ $\frac{3}{6}$ $\frac{11}{16}$ $\frac{1}{1}$

$\frac{3}{6}$ fits between $\frac{3}{8}$ and $\frac{11}{16}$. I know this because $\frac{3}{8}$ is $\frac{1}{8}$ less then $\frac{1}{2}$ and $\frac{3}{6} = \frac{1}{2}$, and $\frac{11}{16}$ is $\frac{3}{16}$ over a $\frac{1}{2}$.

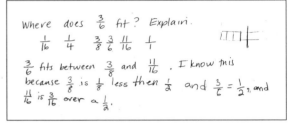

▲▲▲▲▲▲**Figure 9** *Claudia's explanation is clear, correct, and concise.*

and sixteenths, and I also increase the number of fractions in each set. The example shown in Figure 7 was done after the student had completed ordering the sets of fractions listed previously.

Where Does ____ Fit?

PROMPT

Where does $\frac{3}{6}$ *fit? Explain your reasoning.*

$\frac{1}{16}$ $\frac{1}{4}$ $\frac{3}{8}$ $\frac{11}{16}$ $\frac{1}{1}$

This assessment is another variation on the *Put in Order* lesson (see Chapter 13). Changing the fractions makes the assessment appropriate for repeat experiences. I used this particular example as part of an assessment after the students had had introductory experiences with fraction kits (see Chapter 2). The problem was one of three that the students were asked to solve. (Figures 8 and 9 show how two students solved this problem.)

How Many Inches Wide Is $\frac{1}{12}$?

PROMPT

The whole fraction strip is 18 inches long. If we cut a strip into 12ths, how many inches wide will each strip be?

An appropriate time to use this assessment is before students extend their fraction kits by cutting three additional whole strips into thirds, sixths, and twelfths. Sometimes I've given classes the easier problem of figuring the width of thirds or sixths instead of twelfths. Twelfths offer an additional challenge because eighteen is not a multiple of twelve, resulting in pieces that are each $1\frac{1}{2}$ inches wide. In this instance, I felt that this class was capable of the harder problem, although it was difficult for some. After I had reviewed the students' work, I initiated a class discussion that resulted in a lively exchange of students' ideas. (See Figures 10 through 12 for examples of how students responded to this problem.)

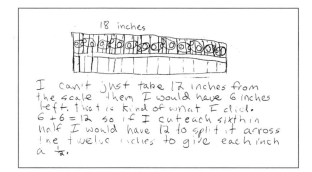

▲▲▲▲▲▲Figure 10 *Libby divided a whole strip into eighteenths and then figured out she would get 12 equal-size pieces, each $\frac{1}{18}$ plus $\frac{1}{2}$ of $\frac{1}{18}$. This worked, but she couldn't explain clearly what she had done.*

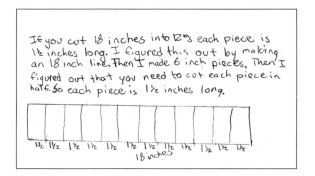

▲▲▲▲▲▲Figure 11 *Delia's approach was the same as Libby's, but she was able to explain it more clearly. Libby was helped by hearing what Delia had written.*

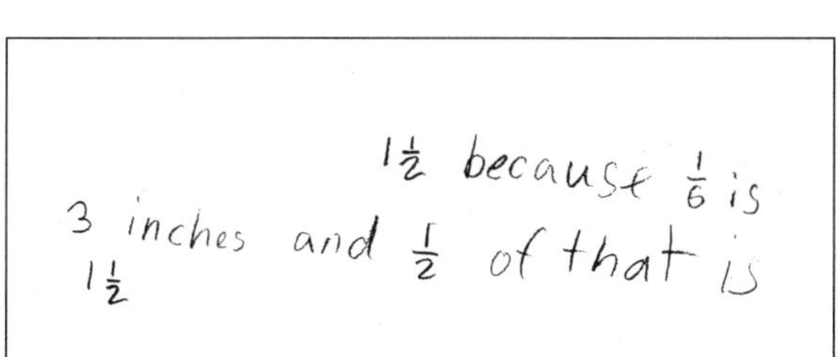

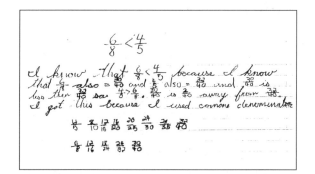

▲▲▲▲▲▲Figure 12 *Dan didn't feel he needed to include a drawing. He based his explanation on his understanding that $\frac{1}{2}$ of $\frac{1}{6}$ is equal to $\frac{1}{12}$.*

Which Is Larger?

PROMPT

Which is larger, $\frac{6}{8}$ or $\frac{4}{5}$? Explain your reasoning.

I ask children to compare fractions in this way many times during the course of the year. At first I ask them to compare unit fractions such as one half and one third. Then I choose other fractions that relate to fraction kits—two eighths and five sixteenths, for example, and later two thirds and three fourths. Sometimes I include fractions with common numerators such as three fourths and three fifths. I vary the fractions throughout the year. I assigned this particular version of the problem later in the year when students were able to think about fractions more abstractly. Their papers revealed that they drew on different aspects of their previous experiences. On some of these assessments, I ask children to explain in more than one way. We then compile a class list of all the strategies they used and apply these strategies to comparing other pairs of fractions. (Figures 13 through 17 show how five students worked on this problem.)

▲▲▲▲▲▲Figure 13 *Maggie described how she converted the fractions so they had common denominators. The method she used was one she invented—writing equivalent fractions for each until she came up with a match for the denominators.*

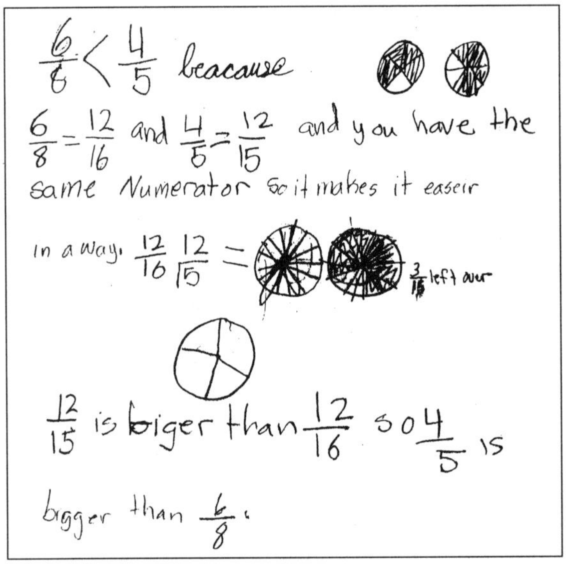

$\frac{6}{8} < \frac{4}{5}$ beacause   ⊘ ⊘

$\frac{6}{8} = \frac{12}{16}$ and $\frac{4}{5} = \frac{12}{15}$ and you have the same Numerator So it makes it easeir

in a way. $\frac{12}{16}$ $\frac{12}{15}$ = ⊛ ⊛ $\frac{3}{16}$ left over

⊕

$\frac{12}{15}$ is biger than $\frac{12}{16}$ so $\frac{4}{5}$ is

bigger than $\frac{6}{8}$.

▲▲▲▲▲▲**Figure 14** *Lara reasoned similarly to the way Josh did. She got into a jam when she tried dividing circles into fifteenths and sixteenths. However, she was sure that she was correct, even though she couldn't find a way to explain.*

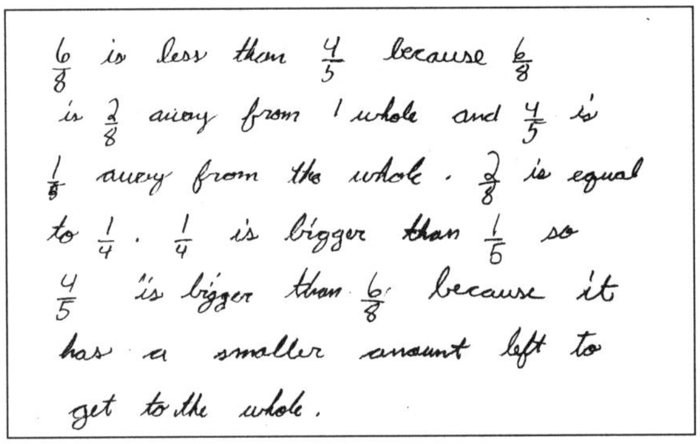

$\frac{6}{8}$ is less than $\frac{4}{5}$ because $\frac{6}{8}$ is $\frac{2}{8}$ away from 1 whole and $\frac{4}{5}$ is $\frac{1}{5}$ away from the whole. $\frac{2}{8}$ is equal to $\frac{1}{4}$. $\frac{1}{4}$ is bigger than $\frac{1}{5}$ so $\frac{4}{5}$ is bigger than $\frac{6}{8}$ because it has a smaller amount left to get to the whole.

▲▲▲▲▲▲**Figure 15** *Using a method she often relied on, Jennifer compared the fractions by investigating which was closer to 1 whole.*

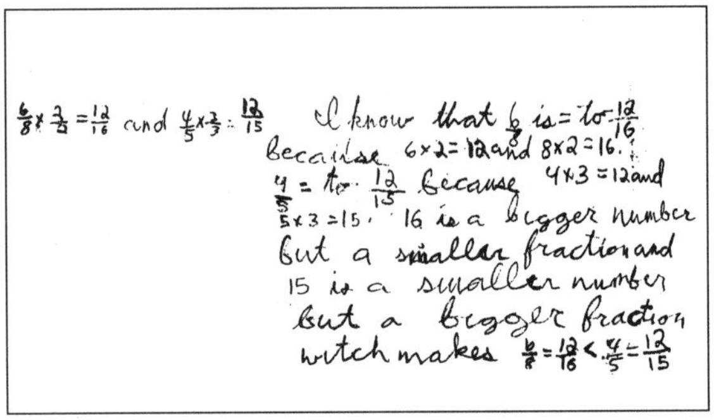

$\frac{6}{8} \times \frac{2}{2} = \frac{12}{16}$ and $\frac{4}{5} \times \frac{3}{3} = \frac{12}{15}$ I know that $\frac{6}{8}$ is = to $\frac{12}{16}$ Because 6×2=12 and 8×2=16. $\frac{4}{5}$ = to $\frac{12}{15}$ Because 4×3=12 and 5×3=15. 16 is a bigger number but a smaller fraction and 15 is a smaller number but a bigger fraction witch makes $\frac{6}{8} = \frac{12}{16} < \frac{4}{5} = \frac{12}{15}$

▲▲▲▲▲▲**Figure 16** *Josh converted the fractions so that they had common numerators and then compared them. His language is imprecise, but his thinking was confident and correct.*

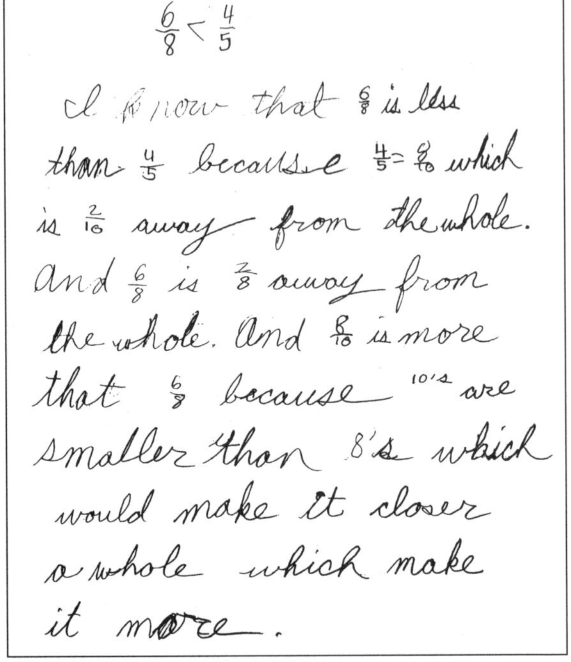

$\frac{6}{8} < \frac{4}{5}$

I know that $\frac{6}{8}$ is less than $\frac{4}{5}$ because $\frac{4}{5} = \frac{8}{10}$ which is $\frac{2}{10}$ away from the whole. And $\frac{6}{8}$ is $\frac{2}{8}$ away from the whole. And $\frac{6}{8}$ is more that $\frac{6}{8}$ because 10's are smaller than 8's which would make it closer a whole which make it more.

▲▲▲▲▲▲**Figure 17** *As Jennifer did, Dan found how far away each fraction was from 1 whole, but he also made use of common numerators to compare them.*

Who Ate More?

PROMPT

Joey and Robert each had the same size pizza. Joey cut his pizza into eight equal pieces and ate six of them. Robert cut his into five equal pieces and ate four of them. Who ate more pizza?

I gave this assessment about a month after the *Which Is Larger?* assignment. Both problems are essentially the same, requiring students to compare six eighths and four fifths. I was interested in whether students would notice this and if they would use the same approaches in each case. Only some did so and there was much less variety in the solutions for this problem. Students used one of two approaches—comparing how much pizza was left or converting the fractions so they had common denominators. Also, practically all of the students drew circles, which makes sense because of the context of pizzas, while only a few did when the problem was presented without the pizza context. When I returned the students' papers to them, I also returned the work they had done on the previous problem so that they could compare the approaches they used. I used this experience to remind them that there generally are many ways to solve a problem. (Figures 18 through 20 show three ways students solved the pizza problem.)

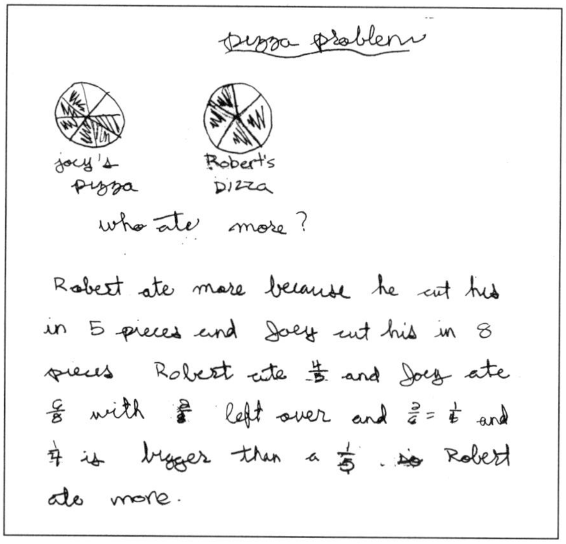

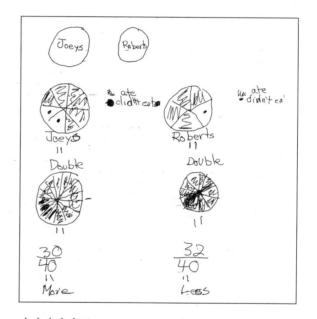

▲▲▲▲▲**Figure 19** *Grant also gave a typical solution; his drawings and explanation are clear.*

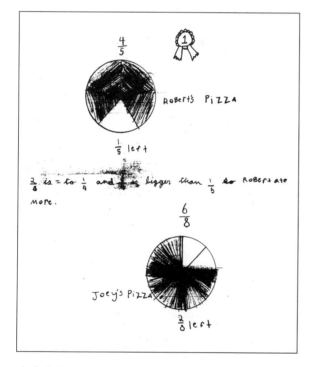

▲▲▲▲▲**Figure 18** *Sean's approach was typical of most of the students.*

▲▲▲▲▲**Figure 20** *Maggie used essentially the same approach she had used previously, but this time she included drawings.*

Write Three Statements

PROMPT

Write at least three statements about $\frac{2}{3}$. For example, $\frac{1}{3} + \frac{1}{3} = \frac{2}{3}$.

I included the example with the directions to give students a model of a mathematical statement related to two-thirds. It's a good idea to have some class discussions prior to assigning this assessment in which the class brainstorms ideas about a particular fraction. Also, an effective lesson, either before or after the assessment, is for children to work in pairs or small groups and create posters for different fractions, writing as many mathematical relationships related to them as they can think of. When groups post their work, others examine them and see if they can think about other ideas to add. (See Figures 21 through 24.)

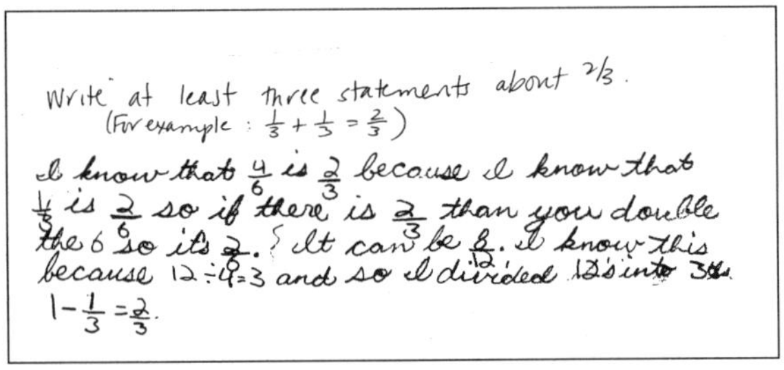

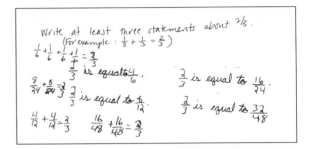

▲▲▲▲▲▲Figure 22   *Delia also talked about doubling, but used the idea correctly, stating that since $\frac{1}{3}$ was equal to $\frac{2}{6}$, then doubling both proved that $\frac{2}{3}$ is equal to $\frac{4}{6}$.*

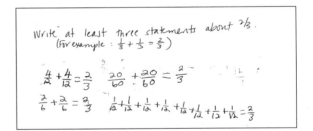

▲▲▲▲▲▲Figure 23   *Grant included eight statements in which he combined fractions and used equivalent fractions. He is comfortable and confident with fractions.*

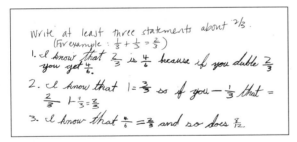

▲▲▲▲▲▲Figure 21   *In her first statement, Ruthie meant to say that if you double both the numerator and denominator of $\frac{2}{3}$, you will get the equivalent fraction of $\frac{4}{6}$. However, if you double $\frac{2}{3}$, you will get $\frac{4}{3}$. Her language error is one that students commonly make, and it's important to discuss this with the class.*

▲▲▲▲▲▲Figure 24   *Claudia was particularly proud of her last statement in which she added $\frac{1}{12}$ eight times to get $\frac{2}{3}$.*

The *Y* Problem

PROMPT

You can think about dividing a circle into thirds by drawing the letter Y with the lines meeting at the center of the circle. If you use this idea on a square, you divide the square into a triangle and two trapezoids. What fraction of the square is each part?

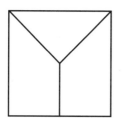

Using the letter *Y* to divide a circle into thirds is useful to help children make fairly accurate sketches. However, sometimes children erroneously use this idea when trying to divide a square into thirds. Asking children to figure out the fractional part represented by the three parts of a square—one triangle and two trapezoids—gives them a problem to solve that involves both fractions and area. The papers in Figures 25 and 26 were generated by students after a class discussion about different ways to divide a square into three equal parts. Theresa suggested the Y solution, which led naturally to asking students to tackle the problem. In classes where this doesn't occur, present the problem by explaining it was the idea of a student in another class.

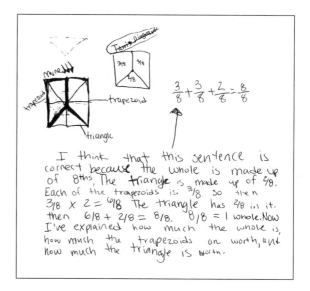

▲▲▲▲▲▲**Figure 25** *Lena assigned fractions to each of the sections in the square and then proved that the parts added up to 1 whole.*

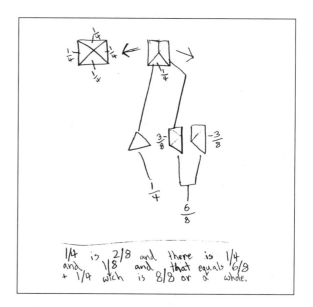

▲▲▲▲▲▲**Figure 26** *Bruce first sketched his idea and then explained his thinking.*

The Birthday Cake Problem

PROMPT

At her birthday party, Janie blew out $\frac{3}{4}$ of the candles on her cake. Draw a picture that shows the birthday cake and candles, also showing which candles were blown out. P.S. How old is Janie? Explain your reasoning.

When I reviewed the students' work, I found that students had arrived at four different answers to the question of Janie's age—four, twelve, fifteen, and sixteen. (Claire gave the answer of fifteen and said that in her family, people always had one extra candle on the cake to grow on. So if Janie had sixteen candles, she was really only fifteen years old.) I then initiated a class discussion in which students explained how they had figured their answers. A common method was to draw four candles, then draw a flame on just one of them, then draw four more, again drawing a flame on one of them. Lena noticed that you could keep going on and on that way and get many more answers. Ignoring Claire's system, the students began to skip-count by fours to figure out possible answers. I wrote on the board: *4, 8, 12, 16, 20, 24, 28* , and so on. We continued up to 160 before Josh blurted out that no one would live that long. The class decided to cut off the list at one hundred, leaving twenty-five possible answers. This was a nice reminder to the students that some problems can have more than one correct answer. (Figures 27 through 29 show how other students tackled this assignment.)

▲▲▲▲▲▲Figure 27 *Lawrence first decided that Janie was 4 years old, then drew another cake showing how she could be 12 years old, and explained why he thought her age could be as high as you'd like.*

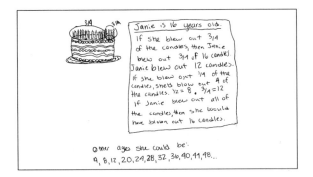

▲▲▲▲▲▲Figure 28 *Nicholas decided that Janie was 8 years old and explained why 6 was $\frac{3}{4}$ of 8.*

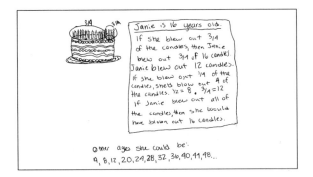

▲▲▲▲▲▲Figure 29 *Lena chose 16 for Janie's age, explained her reasoning, and then offered other ages that Janie could be.*

BLACKLINE MASTERS

Cover Up

You need:

  your fraction kit
  a fraction die with faces $\frac{1}{2}, \frac{1}{4}, \frac{1}{8}, \frac{1}{8}, \frac{1}{16}, \frac{1}{16}$
  a partner

Rules

1. Take turns rolling the fraction die.

2. On your turn, the fraction that comes up on the die tells what size piece to place on the whole strip.

3. Check with your partner to be sure he or she agrees with what you did.

4. After finishing your turn, say "Done" and pass the die to your partner.

5. The first player to cover his or her whole strip *exactly* wins. If you need only a small piece—$\frac{1}{8}$ or $\frac{1}{16}$, for example—and you roll a larger fraction—$\frac{1}{2}$ or $\frac{1}{4}$, for example—you can't play. You must roll a fraction smaller than or exactly what you need.

Uncover, Version 1

You need:

your fraction kit
a fraction die with faces marked $\frac{1}{2}$, $\frac{1}{4}$, $\frac{1}{8}$, $\frac{1}{8}$, $\frac{1}{16}$, $\frac{1}{16}$
a partner

Rules

1. Each player covers his or her whole strip with the two $\frac{1}{2}$ pieces.
2. Take turns rolling the fraction die.
3. On your turn, take one of three options:
   - remove a piece (only if you have a piece the size indicated by the fraction facing up on the die);
   - exchange any of the pieces on your whole strip for equivalent pieces;
   - do nothing.
4. Check with your partner to be sure he or she agrees with what you did.
5. After finishing your turn, say "Done" and pass the die to your partner.
6. The first player who removes all pieces from the whole strip wins.

NOTE 1: You may not remove a piece and exchange on the same turn; you can do only one or the other.

NOTE 2: You have to go out exactly. That means if you have only one piece left and roll a fraction that's larger, you may not remove the piece.

 From *Lessons for Introducing Fractions, Grades 4–5* by Marilyn Burns. © 2001 Math Solutions Publications

Uncover, Version 2

The rules are the same as for The Game of Uncover *except for the first option of rule 3.*

You need:
  your fraction kit
  a fraction die with faces marked $\frac{1}{2}$, $\frac{1}{4}$, $\frac{1}{8}$, $\frac{1}{8}$, $\frac{1}{16}$, $\frac{1}{16}$
  a partner

Rules

1. Each player covers his or her whole strip with the two $\frac{1}{2}$ pieces.

2. Take turns rolling the fraction die.

3. On your turn, take one of three options:
   - **New Rule:** remove one or more pieces from your board as long as they add up to the fraction facing up on the die;
   - exchange any of the pieces on your whole strip for equivalent pieces;
   - do nothing.

4. Check with your partner to be sure he or she agrees with what you did.

5. After finishing your turn, say "Done" and pass the die to your partner.

6. The first player who removes all pieces from the whole strip wins.

NOTE 1: You may not remove pieces and exchange on the same turn; you can do only one or the other.

NOTE 2: You have to go out exactly. That means if you have only one piece left and roll a fraction that's larger, you may not remove the piece.

Comparing Pairs

Write ">", "<", or "=" in between each pair to make
a true statement.

1. $\frac{1}{2}$ $\frac{3}{8}$

2. $\frac{3}{4}$ $\frac{5}{8}$

3. $\frac{3}{16}$ $\frac{1}{2}$

4. $\frac{1}{4}$ $\frac{2}{8}$

5. $\frac{7}{8}$ $\frac{12}{16}$

6. $\frac{1}{2}$ $\frac{2}{4}$

7. $\frac{5}{16}$ $\frac{1}{4}$

8. $\frac{8}{16}$ $\frac{2}{4}$

9. $\frac{1}{4}$ $\frac{1}{8}$

10. $\frac{3}{4}$ $\frac{11}{16}$

11.

12.

From *Lessons for Introducing Fractions, Grades 4–5* by Marilyn Burns. © 2001 Math Solutions Publications

What's Missing?

Write a number in each box to make each sentence true. For three of them, explain.

Example: $\frac{2}{4} = \frac{\boxed{4}}{8}$ because I know that $\frac{2}{8} = \frac{1}{4}$, so for $\frac{2}{4}$ you need $\frac{4}{8}$

1. $\frac{1}{2} = \frac{\square}{16}$

2. $\frac{3}{4} = \frac{\square}{8}$

3. $\frac{1}{4} = \frac{\square}{16}$

4. $\frac{3}{8} = \frac{\square}{16}$

5. $\frac{2}{4} = \frac{\square}{2}$

6. $\frac{1}{2} = \frac{4}{\square}$

7. $\frac{\square}{4} = \frac{8}{16}$

8. $\frac{2}{8} = \frac{1}{\square}$

Make up two of your own. Solve both and explain one.

9.

10.

From *Lessons for Introducing Fractions, Grades 4–5* by Marilyn Burns. © 2001 Math Solutions Publications

Fractions in Contexts

For each statement, decide if it can best be described as "exactly half," "about half," "less than half," or "more than half."

1. When pitching, Joe struck out 7 of 18 batters.

2. Sally blocked 5 field goals out of 9 attempts.

3. Of the 35 coins in Dick's bank, 14 were pennies.

     From *Lessons for Introducing Fractions, Grades 4–5* by Marilyn Burns. © 2001 Math Solutions Publications

More Fractions in Contexts

For each statement, decide if it can best be described as "exactly half," "about half," "less than half," or "more than half."

1. Maria received 13 birthday cards. Five of them arrived the day after her birthday.

2. Forty-five students signed up to work on the school paper. Twenty-seven of them were girls.

3. Twenty-five students in the class have pets. Twelve of them have dogs. Nine have cats. Six have fish.

From *Lessons for Introducing Fractions, Grades 4–5* by Marilyn Burns. © 2001 Math Solutions Publications

Raquel's Idea

Raquel thought about this statement: *When pitching, Joe struck out 7 of 18 batters.* She said that it was better to say that Joe struck out about $\frac{1}{3}$ of the batters than to say that Joe struck out about $\frac{1}{2}$ of the batters. "I think that seven-eighteenths is closer to one-third than one-half," she said. Do you agree or disagree with Raquel? Explain your reasoning.

From *Lessons for Introducing Fractions, Grades 4–5* by Marilyn Burns. © 2001 Math Solutions Publications

Wipeout

You need:

pattern blocks

a fraction die with faces marked $\frac{1}{2}$, $\frac{1}{3}$, $\frac{1}{3}$, $\frac{1}{6}$, $\frac{1}{6}$, $\frac{1}{6}$

a partner

Rules:

1. Decide if you each still start with one, two, or three hexagons.
2. Take turns rolling the fraction die.
3. On your turn, take one of three options:
   - remove a block if it's the fractional part of the hexagon indicated by the fraction die;
   - exchange any of your remaining blocks for equivalent blocks;
   - do nothing.
4. Check with your partner to be sure he or she agrees with what you did.
5. After finishing your turn, say "Done" and pass the die to your partner.
6. The first person to discard all of his or her blocks wins.

Drawing Pictures for Fractions

Draw pictures to show the following fractional parts:

1. $\frac{2}{5}$ of a set of circles are shaded

2. $\frac{4}{5}$ of the squares are red

3. $\frac{3}{4}$ of the triangles are blue

4. $\frac{1}{3}$ of the balls are footballs

5. $\frac{4}{9}$ of the fruit are apples

 From *Lessons for Introducing Fractions, Grades 4–5* by Marilyn Burns. © 2001 Math Solutions Publications

Halving Squares

Circles for Cookies

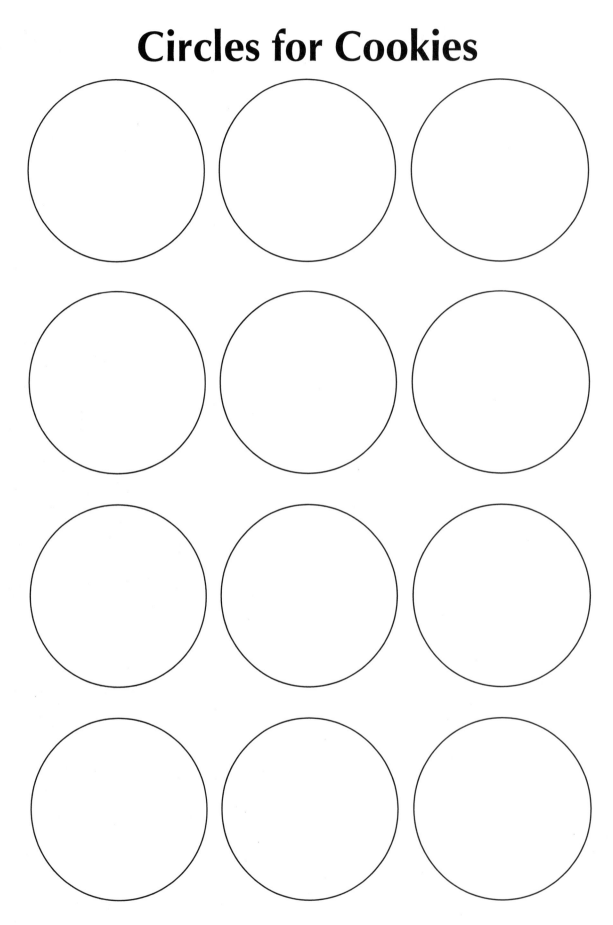

Fractions with Cookies

You need:

Fractions with Cookies worksheets

circles for "cookies"

scissors

paste or glue

a partner

1. Do five worksheets, one of each version and two others of your choice.

2. Use no more than 20 cookies for any one worksheet.

3. Cut "cookies" into equal shares and paste them in the appropriate places.

4. Record how much each person gets. Explain your reasoning.

5. For each sheet, choose a number of cookies that is not a multiple of the number of people.

From *Lessons for Introducing Fractions, Grades 4–5* by Marilyn Burns. © 2001 Math Solutions Publications

Sharing Cookies, Version 1

Share _____ cookies among 6 people.

Each person gets

Sharing Cookies, Version 2

Share _____ cookies among 4 people.

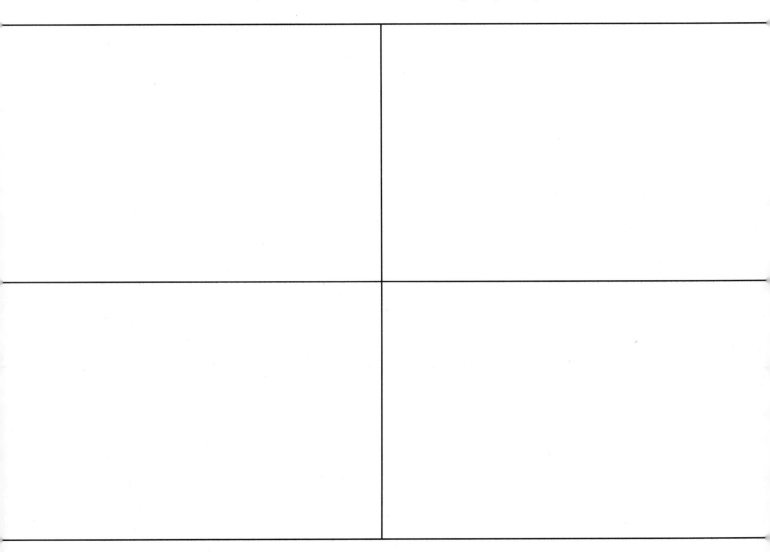

Each person gets

Sharing Cookies, Version 3

Share _____ cookies among 3 people.

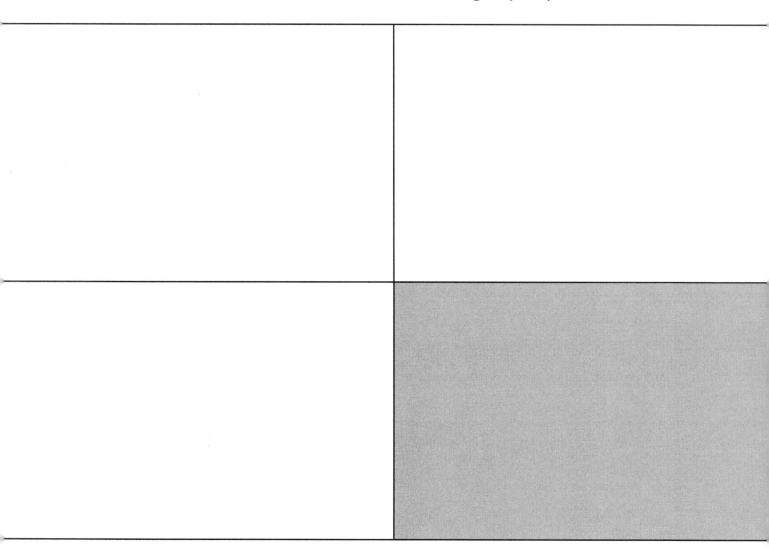

Each person gets

Pattern Block Design

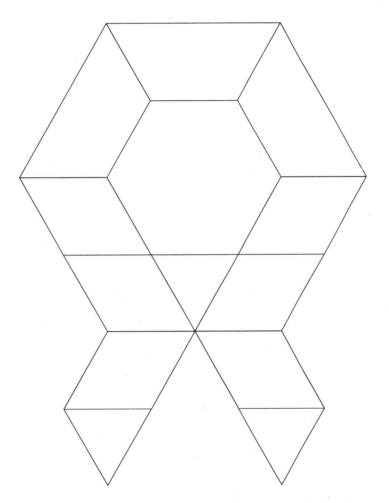

Pattern Block Triangle Paper

Nicholas's Game

1. Rule three columns and label them <, =, and >. Above the columns draw boxes for the numerator and denominator of the starting fraction.

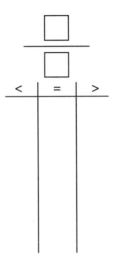

2. To find the starting fraction, roll a die twice. Use the smaller number for the numerator and the larger number for the denominator. (If both numbers you roll are the same, roll again so that the numerator and denominator of your starting fraction are different.)

3. Write at least five fractions in each column. The numerator and denominator in each fraction you write must be greater than the numerator and denominator in the starting fraction.

4. Choose one fraction from each column and explain how you know it belongs there. For example, write: *I know that $\frac{3}{4}$ is greater than $\frac{2}{3}$ because _____.*

5. You may use *only one* fraction that is equivalent to 1 whole, such as $\frac{5}{5}$ or $\frac{11}{11}$ or any fraction with the same numerator and denominator.

From *Lessons for Introducing Fractions, Grades 4–5* by Marilyn Burns. © 2001 Math Solutions Publications

Pick Two

You need:

your fraction kit

1. Make a train of two pieces on your whole strip using pieces that are *not* the same color.
2. Record.
3. Build another train the same length using pieces that are all the same color.
4. Record only one fraction.
5. Try to build other one-color trains the same length. For each, record.

Example:

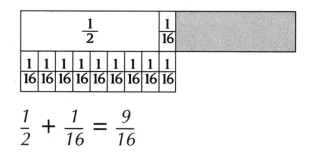

$$\frac{1}{2} + \frac{1}{16} = \frac{9}{16}$$

From *Lessons for Introducing Fractions, Grades 4–5* by Marilyn Burns. © 2001 Math Solutions Publications

Pick Three

You need:

your fraction kit

1. Make a train of three pieces on your whole strip using pieces that are *not* all the same color. (It's okay to use two of one color and one of another color.)
2. Record and also shorten, if possible.
3. Build another train the same length using pieces that are all the same color.
4. Record only one fraction.
5. Try to build other one-color trains the same length. For each, record.

Example:

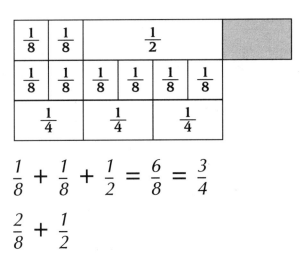

$$\frac{1}{8} + \frac{1}{8} + \frac{1}{2} = \frac{6}{8} = \frac{3}{4}$$

$$\frac{2}{8} + \frac{1}{2}$$

Roll Five

You need:

your fraction kit
fraction die

1. Roll the fraction die five times and build a train with the pieces that match the fractions that come up.
2. Record and also shorten, if possible.
3. Build another train the same length using pieces that are all the same color.
4. Record only one fraction.
5. Try to build other one-color trains the same length. For each, record.

Example:

$\frac{1}{2}$				$\frac{1}{4}$		$\frac{1}{4}$		$\frac{1}{2}$				$\frac{1}{8}$
$\frac{1}{8}$	$\frac{1}{8}$	$\frac{1}{8}$	$\frac{1}{8}$	$\frac{1}{8}$	$\frac{1}{8}$	$\frac{1}{8}$	$\frac{1}{8}$	$\frac{1}{8}$	$\frac{1}{8}$	$\frac{1}{8}$	$\frac{1}{8}$	$\frac{1}{8}$
1								$\frac{1}{8}$	$\frac{1}{8}$	$\frac{1}{8}$	$\frac{1}{8}$	$\frac{1}{8}$

$$\frac{1}{2} + \frac{1}{4} + \frac{1}{4} + \frac{1}{2} + \frac{1}{8} = \frac{13}{8} = 1\frac{5}{8}$$

$$\frac{2}{2} + \frac{2}{4} + \frac{1}{8}$$

Can you figure out two more ways to cover this train?

 From *Lessons for Introducing Fractions, Grades 4–5* by Marilyn Burns. © 2001 Math Solutions Publications

Make a Whole

You need:

your fraction kit
fraction die

1. Roll the fraction die twice and record the fractions that come up.
2. Figure out what one fraction you would add on to these two to make one whole. Use your fraction kit to help by putting on the pieces from your two rolls and then figuring out what pieces, all of the same color, you need to add to cover the whole strip exactly.
3. Record.
4. Try to find other fractions that would also work. For each, record.

Examples:

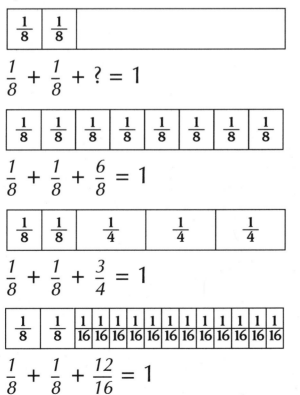

$$\frac{1}{8} + \frac{1}{8} + ? = 1$$

$$\frac{1}{8} + \frac{1}{8} + \frac{6}{8} = 1$$

$$\frac{1}{8} + \frac{1}{8} + \frac{3}{4} = 1$$

$$\frac{1}{8} + \frac{1}{8} + \frac{12}{16} = 1$$

INDEX